D1553944

Women in America

FROM COLONIAL TIMES TO THE 20TH CENTURY

Women in America

FROM COLONIAL TIMES TO THE 20TH CENTURY

Advisory Editors
LEON STEIN
ANNETTE K. BAXTER

A Note About This Volume

This is an exhaustive history of the captivity, life and death of Maconaqua, née Frances Slocum (1773-1847). Captured by Indians when she was 5 years old in what is now known as Wilkes-Barre, Frances was lost to her family for nearly 60 years. They never ceased searching for her. She was finally discovered by a fur trader in 1837 and, after word got to her family, a sister and two of her brothers visited Maconaqua, then the widow of a Miami Indian chief, near Peru, Indiana. During this encounter, they learned the story of her capture, her adoption by a Delaware family, their movement westward, her two marriages and her happy, prosperous life with her adopted people. Despite the appeals of her sister and brothers, she refused to leave her Indian life, preferring to remain on the land that the Great Spirit and Congress had granted to her daughters. She remained there even after the Miamis moved on to Kansas and she came to be known as "the White Rose of the Miamis" to the rising tide of white settlers.

BIOGRAPHY

OF

FRANCES SLOCUM,

THE

LOST SISTER OF WYOMING

JOHN F. MEGINNESS

ARNO PRESS
A New York Times Company
NEW YORK – 1974

Reprint Edition 1974 by Arno Press Inc.

Reprinted from a copy in The State
  Historical Society of Wisconsin Library

WOMEN OF AMERICA
From Colonial Times to the 20th Century
ISBN for complete set: 0-405-06070-X
See last pages of this volume for titles.

Manufactured in the United States of America

Library of Congress Cataloging in Publication Data

Meginness, John Franklin, 1827-1899.
    Biography of Frances Slocum, the lost sister of
Wyoming.

    (Women in America: from colonial times to the 20th
century)
    Reprint of the 1891 ed. printed by Heller Bros.
Printing House, Williamsport, Pa.
    Bibliography: p.
    1. Slocum, Frances, 1773-1847. 2. Indians of
North America--Captivities. I. Title. II. Series.
E87.S612 1974   970.3 [B]   74-3963
ISBN 0-405-06112-9

BIOGRAPHY

OF

FRANCES SLOCUM

FRANCES SLOCUM---MA-CON-A-QUA.

BIOGRAPHY

OF

FRANCES SLOCUM,

THE

LOST SISTER OF WYOMING.

A

Complete Narrative of her Captivity and Wanderings among the Indians.

"I am become a stranger unto my brethren,
And an alien unto my mother's children."
—*Psalms lxix.*-8.

BY JOHN F. MEGINNESS,

AUTHOR OF THE "HISTORY OF THE WEST BRANCH VALLEY OF THE SUSQUEHANNA,"
"BIOGRAPHICAL ANNALS," "THE HISTORICAL JOURNAL," ETC.

WILLIAMSPORT, PA.:
HELLER BROS.' PRINTING HOUSE,
1891.

TO THE READER.

Forty years ago, when I first read the account of the capture of Frances Slocum, and the persistent efforts of her mother, brothers and sisters to recover her, and her final discovery and death in Indiana, it made such an impression on my mind that I decided, if the opportunity ever offered, to visit her grave. After a lapse of forty years the opportunity came. In October, 1889, I was on a visit to friends at Logansport, Indiana, and remembering that it was near that place she was buried, I determined to carry out my resolution of forty years before. Accordingly, on a crisp autumn afternoon, I found my way to the Indian cemetery on the Mississinewa, and stood beside the grave of the captive. It was pointed out by a grandson, who seemed to entertain almost a holy reverence for the spot, and spoke in the most affectionate terms of his grandmother, whom he had never seen.

While standing beside her grave I resolved that if I could obtain sufficient data, I would attempt the work of compiling a consecutive narrative of her life, and put on record fuller details of her wanderings, trials and sufferings, than had yet been given to the public.

I fully realized that many newspaper and magazine articles concerning her had appeared from time to time, together with one or two little books, but nothing like an exhaustive biography had ever been printed. This, when the importance of the subject was considered, had always seemed as strange to me as the mystery of her life.

To collect the official documents relating to her Indian history, confer with her widely scattered relatives, both white and red, soon proved a laborious task, and more than a year was devoted to the work of preparation. In the progress of research, it was discovered that several grave errors regarding the story of her life had found their way into print, which quickened my interest in the work. Through the indefatigable efforts of Mr. F. C. Campbell, of Washington, her petition to Congress and the letters accompanying it, were finally found buried under the Congressional debris of forty-five years and placed in my possession.

TO THE READER.

Another visit to Indiana to confer with her Indian descendants, learn their traditions, and examine relics which once belonged to her, was found necessary. The visit was made in June, 1890, and several days were pleasantly and profitably spent among the remnants of the Great Miami tribe in the upper valley of the Wabash, when I returned with more valuable and interesting information.

Members of the Slocum family, when apprised of the undertaking, at once evinced a deep interest in the work, and promptly placed whatever information they possessed relating to Frances, at my disposal. Her Indian descendants, when informed of what was contemplated, also became enthusiastic over the enterprize, and freely imparted what they remembered of the "white woman," whose memory they seem to cherish with a warmth of affection that is remarkable.

To the following gentlemen I desire to return my acknowledgments for valuable information and assistance: Mr. George Slocum Bennett, Rev. Horace Edwin Hayden, and Dr. F. C. Johnson, Wilkes-Barre, Pa.; Dr. Charles E. Slocum, Defiance, Ohio; Mr. James Slocum, Brownsville, Pa.; Hon. Horace P. Biddle, Logansport, Indiana; J. B. Fulwiler, Esq., and W. W. Lockwood, Esq., Peru, Indiana; Rev. Peter Bondy and Mr. Gabriel Godfroy, Reserve, Indiana. A bibliography of the authorities consulted is also given at the close of the volume.

There is nothing in the annals of Indian history more pathetic and impressive than the story of the captivity, life, wanderings and death of Frances Slocum; and in her remarkable history there is much to interest the ethnologist, because of the peculiar developments which followed her association with the Indians, the loss of her mother tongue, and the tenacity with which she clung to the strange people with whom her lot was cast.

In the preparation of this book no claims are made of absolute accuracy or literary polish. It has proved a laborious task to arrange the narrative, on account of the many contradictory details, in something like consecutive order; and if I have succeeded in placing new and valuable matter within easy reach of those who are interested in the melancholy story, I will feel that my "labor of love" has not been wholly in vain.

JOHN F. MEGINNESS.

WILLIAMSPORT, PA., January, 1890.

MIAMI INDIAN BOY.

FRANCES SLOCUM,

THE

LOST SISTER OF WYOMING.

CHAPTER I.

MEANING OF THE WORD WYOMING AND DESCRIPTION OF THE
VALLEY—INDIAN INVASION AND MASSACRE—THE SLOCUM
FAMILY—CAPTURE OF FRANCES—GRIEF OF THE MOTHER.

THE scene of our story is laid in the lovely valley of
Wyoming, Pennsylvania, on the east bank of the
North Branch of the Susquehanna River, and the
thrilling incidents connected with it had their beginning late
in the autumn of 1778. But before proceeding, and in order
that the reader may have a clear understanding as to the
location of this beautiful and historic region, it is deemed
best to describe its geographical position.

Chapman, in his history of this region in 1818, says that
Wyoming is a corruption of the name given to the locality
by the Indians. They called it *Maugh-waw-wame*. The
word is compounded of *maugh-waw*, large, and *wame*, plains.
The name, then, signifies The Large Plains. The Delawares
pronounced the first syllable short, and the German missionaries, in order to come as near as possible to the Indian
pronunciation, wrote the name M'chweuwami. The early
settlers, finding it difficult to pronounce the word correctly,
spoke it Wauwaumie, then Wiawumie, then Wiomic, and,
finally, Wyoming.

The valley of Wyoming lies northeast and southwest; is twenty-one miles in length, and an average of three miles in breadth. The face of the country is considerably diversified. The bottom lands along the river overflow in time of high water. The plains are in some places perfectly level, and in others rolling. The soil is exceedingly productive, being suited to all kinds of grain and grass. The valley lies immediately over the great Wyoming anthracite coal basin, which yields thousands of tons of coal annually, and is a source of great wealth to the owners. Several railroads also pass through it.

Two ranges of mountains hem in the valley, the eastern range being of an average height of 1000 feet, and the western about 800. The eastern range is precipitous and generally barren, but is strikingly diversified with clefts, ravines and forests, and presents a most picturesque and lovely view. The western range is rapidly yielding to the process of cultivation.

There are several charming points of view which invite the attention of the lovers of the beautiful and the grand in nature: Prospect Rock, east of the city of Wilkes-Barre,* being easiest of access from the town, and the most frequently visited, is the most celebrated in the annals of travel. From this point the valley, with the slope of the west mountain, presents the appearance of a beautiful ascending plain, with the remotest border merged in the clouds, or bounded by the blue sky. A more charming landscape cannot be imagined. The view from the mountain on the west side gives you a more extensive prospect of the northern and southern extrem-

---

* The city of Wilkes-Barre is in 41 deg. 14 min. 40.4 sec. north latitude, and is the capital of the populous county of Luzerne. It derives its name from the celebrated John Wilkes and Col. Barre, who were members of the British Parliament during the Revolutionary struggle, and took a decided stand in favor of America against the measures of the British ministry.

ities of the valley. At this point you have a fair view of the northern gap through which the Susquehanna forces its way —of the Lackawanna Valley, Pittston, Wyoming, Wilkes-Barre, Kingston, Newport, and Jacob's Plains. Campbell's Ledge, at the head of the valley, has long been a favorite point of view for the romantic and athletic. The ascent is laborious, but the sublimity of the scene amply rewards the toil of the traveler.

From whatever point the valley is surveyed, the noble Susquehanna is one of the many beautiful objects that present themselves to the eye. Such are its windings, and such the variety which characterize its banks, that you have no extended view of it. It is only seen in sections, varied in size and form by the position occupied. Now it hides itself among the bowers of willow, sycamore, and maple, which fringe and beautify its borders, and now it throws open its mirror bosom to the kisses of the sunlight, reflecting the forms of beauty and grandeur of the surrounding scenery.

Such is a picture of this magnificent valley, whose grandeur and loveliness have afforded a theme for poets and historians from the earliest times. So long as the Indians occupied the country, it was one of their favorite dwelling places, and they sadly and sorrowfully bade adieu to its glories and beauties when compelled to leave it. White settlers came as early as 1762, and commenced making improvements. They were driven away; came again, and finally effected a permanent lodgement after passing through a baptism of blood.

On the 3d of July, 1778, the savages, smarting under monstrous wrongs, and goaded on to deeds of violence by the British and Tories, swooped down on the settlements in great force, and the bloody battle and massacre of that hot July afternoon followed, in which the whites suffered a disastrous defeat.* The carnage, considering the numbers engaged, was dreadful. As nearly as could be ascertained, about 200 perished in the battle and the butchery which followed during the night, while the loss of the invaders was comparatively trifling. The deeds of atrocity committed afterwards were of the most cruel and brutal character—a shame to civilization and an ineffaceable disgrace to Col. Butler, the Tory, who commanded the British troops and their red-skinned allies. The slain and the butchered prisoners were scalped, because these bloody trophies brought a stated price in British gold on being handed over to the authorities. Stockade forts and houses were reduced to ashes, the crops destroyed, stock driven off, and every effort made by the invaders to efface all traces of civilization, and leave the beautiful valley a "howling wilderness."

Such was the condition of affairs after the bloody battle of Wyoming. It was indeed a cheerless and disheartening outlook to those who had escaped the horrors of the massacre, and that a panic should ensue is not strange. Nearly all the settlers who could get away took flight, and the roads or paths leading through the wilderness in the direction of the Delaware River were crowded with fugitive women and children, and the sufferings they endured are the saddest recorded in the annals of our Indian wars. The men who escaped were

---

* A monument 62 feet in height stands on the battle ground. It is a plain obelisk in the dark gray stone of the valley. The names of 171 who perished in the battle and afterwards, are cut in a marble tablet, and a vault beneath the base contains their bones. One hundred years after—July 3, 1878—the anniversary of the battle was observed in the presence of 60,000 people. President Hayes, several cabinet officers and governors of States were present. The Delaware, Lackawanna and Western Railroad, between Scranton and Northumberland, 85 miles, runs through a portion of the grounds.

collected together to guard the rear of the fleeing column, and save what property they could from the vandal hands of the remorseless invaders.

Among the few who remained was the family of Jonathan Slocum. They had settled on the east side of the river, some miles away from the scene of the battle, and on what is now a portion of the site of the rich, populous and flourishing city of Wilkes-Barre. The battle, it must be remembered, took place on the west side of the river, and it should be borne in mind that the enemy did not cross the stream to molest the fort where many of the settlers had collected. Reinforcements, too, were expected, a knowledge of which doubtless deterred the enemy from crossing the river, and they soon hurried away in the direction of Tioga Point (now Athens) with the trophies of their victory.

Jonathan Slocum, whose ancestors came from England at an early date, was born in Kent County, Rhode Island, May 1, 1735. He married Ruth Tripp, February 23, 1757, and for several years they resided in their native State. They were both members of the Society of Friends, the "Protestants of the Puritans."*

Some time during the year 1777 Mr. Slocum, with his wife and nine children, emigrated from Rhode Island and settled on a tract of land lying near Wilkes-Barre Fort. Previous to his location here, however, he had visited the place as early as 1771, acquired land, and made preparations for the removal of his family. At that time Connecticut settlers were pouring in, and a few Rhode Islanders, attracted by reports of the fertility of the soil and the beauty of the country, joined the immigrants. The Slocum family removed to their new home in a covered wagon, and as the roads were

* See "History of the Slocums in America." p. 28.

bad and many streams had to be crossed, the journey was a long and tiresome one. Isaac Tripp, the father of Mrs. Slocum, came with them. Of the ten children comprising this remarkable and historic family, all were born in Rhode Island but one. The following epitome of their history is made up from Dr. Charles E. Slocum's great work on the genealogy and *History of the Slocums in America.* They were named as follows :

I.—Giles, b. 5 Jan., 1759; m. Sarah Ross; d. 14 Nov. 1826, in Columbia Co., N. Y. He took part in the battle of Wyoming, and was one of the few who escaped the cruel slaughter by swimming to an island in the river, rolling in the sand and hiding under a fallen tree, covered by bushes. He was a member of the Society of Friends; a farmer earlier in life; later an innkeeper (?) and merchant. Left two sons and one daughter.

II.—Judith, b. Oct. —, 1760; m. Hugh Forsman, a farmer; d. 11 Mar. 1814 in Cincinnati. Her husband was a subaltern in Capt. Hewitt's company during the Wyoming massacre, and was one of the fifteen of that corps who escaped the slaughter, and he was the only one who brought in his gun. She left several children.

III.—William, b. 6 Jan. 1762; married Sarah Sawyer; d. Oct. 20, 1810, near Pittston. He was wounded in the heel by a musket ball 16 Dec. 1778, at the time his father and grandfather Tripp were killed by Indians on the site of Wilkes-Barre. Was elected Sheriff of Luzerne County in 1695, when it included Wyoming, Susquehanna, Lackawanna and part of Bradford. He held the office until 1799, when he retired to his farm, and in 1806 was elected a Justice of the Peace. He was classed among the prominent and influential men of his county. Left four sons and five daughters.

IV.—Ebenezer, b. 10 Jan. 1766; m. Sarah Davis, d. 5 July 1810, suddenly, of apoplexy, in the street while on a visit to Wilkes-Barre. In 1798 he purchased an interest in a grist mill in Deep Hollow, now included within the limits of Scranton. Built a saw mill and a distillery. Afterwards his brother Benjamin became associated with him, and together they constructed an iron

forge in the early part of 1800, and another distillery in 1811.
They carried on an extensive business. The firm was dissolved
in 1826. Mr. Slocum was Justice of the Peace in 1821 of the
district which included the present Pittston, Providence and Ex-
eter townships. He was successful in business and accumulated
in addition to other property, 1,800 acres of land, all located
within the present limits of Scranton, and nearly all of it was
underlaid with coal. He left thirteen children, nine sons and
four daughters.

V.—Mary, b. 22 Dec. 1768; m. Joseph Towne, a farmer; resided
in Ohio near Circleville; d. 5 April, 1844. Left several children.

VI.—Benjamin, b. 7 Dec. 1770; m. Phebe La France. Resided
with his brother Ebenezer at Slocum Hollow; in 1811 was appointed Postmaster of Providence, which was the first postoffice
in Lackawanna Valley. In 1826 he settled on a farm which included the land now occupied by the borough of Tunkhannock,
and there he died July 5, 1832. He left four children, one son
and three daughters. The son, Thomas Truxton, who succeeded to the farm, gave two acres of land on which to build the
court house when Tunkhannock became the seat of justice of
Wyoming County.

VII.—Frances, b. March —, 1773; d. March 9, 1849. The Indian captive, and the subject of this narrative. She married an
Indian war chief of the Miamis, named She-pan-can-ah, (deaf
man) and left two daughters, Ke-ke-se-qua and O-zah-wah-
shing-qua.

VIII.—Isaac, b. 4 March, 1775; m. 1st Elizabeth Patrick; 2d Mrs.
Lydia Norton. First settled on a farm which included the site
of Tunkhannock, where he lived until 1823; then removed
to Sandusky County, Ohio. Died near Bellevue Aug. 26, 1858.
He was an active and prominent citizen, held several military
commissions, and served as postmaster. He took a deep interest
in his captive sister, and frequently visited her. Maj. Slocum
outlived all his father's family. He left twelve children, eight
sons and four daughters.

IX.—Joseph, b. 9 April, 1776; m. Sarah Fell; d. 27 Sept. 1855.
He was a blacksmith and farmer; was chosen the first Captain
of the "Wyoming Blues" military company in 1805, and was
commissioned Associate Judge of Luzerne County in 1840, and

filled that office three or four years very acceptably. The township of Slocum in Luzerne County, and Slocum postoffice were named in his honor. Judge Slocum was an excellent citizen and greatly respected. He left seven children, two sons and five daughters.

X.—Jonathan, b. 12 Sept., 1778; m. Martha Underwood; d. Sept. —, 1842. Was a farmer and resided late in life near Havana, Schuyler County, N. Y. He left ten children, eight sons and two daughters.

Giles Slocum, the eldest son, who was a young man of nineteen at the time of the invasion, shouldered his gun and took part in the battle. This act of hostility, it is believed, attracted the attention of the savages, and caused them to wreak vengeance on the family.

Mr. Slocum, on account of his non-combative principles and the many acts of kindness he had bestowed on the Indians, considered himself and family comparatively free from danger. His father-in-law, Mr. Isaac Tripp, also a Quaker, entertained the same opinion, as he had frequently befriended the Indians, and they had on more than one occasion, during raids, avoided molesting him. The entertainment of these opinions evidently were among the reasons why they did not fly after the battle. And possibly they would not have been molested had Giles not taken part in the bloody conflict of July 3, 1778, and escaped the carnage.* The Indians were quick to discern, and being of a savage and revengeful nature, at once concluded that deception was being practiced by the Slocums, else Giles would not have taken up arms against them; and they at once determined to seek revenge.

After the massacre straggling bands of Indians continued to visit the valley in search of scalps and plunder, until the

---

* He escaped to Monockonock Island in the river, where he concealed himself until it was safe to cross to the main land, on the east side, and finally made his way to his father's house.

conclusion of peace with England. On the 2d of November, 1778, three Delaware Indians stealthily came into the valley and, watching a favorable opportunity, approached the Slocum residence. Mr. Slocum and his father-in-law were away from home at the time. Mrs. Slocum was there, with several of her children around her, and two boys named Kingsley. Some time previously Nathan Kingsley had been made prisoner by the Indians, and his wife and two sons were taken in by Mr. Slocum and afforded the comforts of a home. The house stood just in the edge of the woods, and when the Indians approached they saw the two Kingsley boys at the door engaged in grinding a knife. Dr. Peck informs us that the elder of the boys, Nathan by name, wore a soldier's coat, which, it is presumed, was a special reason of his being marked as a victim. One of the Indians quickly drew up his gun and shot the young man dead. The discharge of the gun quickly brought Mrs. Slocum to the door, when she was horrified at seeing a stalwart savage scalping the young man with the knife which he had been grinding. Taking in the situation at a glance, Mrs. Slocum and several of the children fled into the woods,* while Mary, one of the daughters, seized her brother Joseph, aged about two years, and rushed out of the back door. The Indians shouted loudly after her and laughed to see the speed with which she ran, and the tenacity with which she held on to her infant brother. The chroniclers of the period fail to inform us what became of Mrs. Kingsley, the mother of the murdered boy, but it is inferred that she escaped from the house on the alarm being given, and saved her life, and her husband was afterwards restored to her. †

---

* Todd's Lost Sister of Wyoming, p. 91.

† Nathan Kingsley was one of the first settlers in Wyalusing. He was a native of Connecticut, and belonged to one of the most noted families in that State. He was a man of wealth and influence in that early day. He

Little Frances, according to a tradition still preserved among the Miami Indians of Indiana, endeavored to secrete herself under the stairway leading to the loft. In the meantime the Indians entered the house, which they quickly ransacked, and then prepared to depart. On descending the stairway one of the savages saw the feet of the child protruding from her hiding place, and seizing them quickly drew her forth. The surviving Kingsley boy, Ebenezer Slocum, aged about twelve years, and little Frances, were taken prisoners,* and the Indians prepared to depart before any alarm could be given. Mrs. Slocum breathlessly watched the proceedings from the thicket, and trembled with fear lest she should see the tomahawk buried in the heads of her children; but when she saw them about to leave, carrying her boy and little Frances, her motherly instincts overcame all fear and she rushed from her

occupied the old log house now standing on the lands of Mrs. Welles, a few rods east of the railroad and north of the depot. This house was built about 1768, and was for a time occupied by a brother of the celebrated missionary Heckewelder. It is, without doubt, the oldest house in the [Bradford] county. Here Kingsley, by means of great watchfulness and prudence, lived for some time unmolested by the Indians, but at length, in June, 1778, was captured by them and taken to Niagara. After a confinement of several months he was released, and returned to Wyalusing, whither his family had fled before his capture. It was during his captivity (Nov. 2, 1778,) that his son, Nathan Kingsley, Jr., was killed, and another son carried into captivity. * * * Mr. Kingsley had but one son left, Wareham, who, long after his return, married into the Turrell family, and went to Connecticut, where he died. After troubles in the valley in a measure ceased, Mr. Kingsley returned to Wyalusing, where he lived for several years. Unfortunately the old man acquired intemperate habits and became very poor, so that he became a town charge and his keeping was sold to James Armstrong, who removed west, where Kingsley died, it is said, by the falling of a tree, about the year 1800.—Craft's Hist. Wyalusing, p. 56.

Mr. Kingsley returned to his old home in 1785. He built a distillery near where Mr. Welles' stone quarry now is. He was a Justice of the Peace and Judge of the Court in 1787, and in his old age was taken west, where he died. His wife, Roccelana, died in Wyalusing, but the exact date has not been ascertained.—Hist. Bradford Co., p. 443.

*Some of the early writers assert—Miner among them—that a colored girl, seventeen years of age, was taken at the same time from the Slocum hiding place, and her countenance in unutterable language told the savages that she was the mother, and with tears streaming from her eyes she implored them to spare her children. They scorned her tears and scoffed at her supplications with fiendish glee. She frantically pointed to her son Ebenezer, who was lame, fearing that if he failed to keep up with them he would be cruelly butchered. This idea rushed with such force on her mind that she forgot all fear, and running up to the Indian who was dragging him away, pointed at the feet of the boy and exclaimed : "The child is lame; he can do thee no good!" This appeal caused the Indian to release the boy; but he instantly seized little Frances, and throwing her over his shoulder, rushed after his companions. Mrs. Slocum begged piteously for her daughter, but in vain. The child stretched out one hand imploringly towards her mother, while with the other she brushed away the luxuriant auburn ringlets which fell over her face, and as the tears streamed from her eyes she frantically called on her mother to save her. The Indian dashed into the bushes, and that was the last Mrs. Slocum ever saw of her child ! But the image of that piteous face was so indelibly impressed on the memory of the mother that she never forgot it, and to the day she descended to the grave she always recalled the sad circumstance with sorrow and deep lamentation.

---

house. But after careful inquiry among the Miami Indians of Indiana, I find that they have no tradition of such a capture, but deny it in toto. Neither did Frances refer to such a circumstance. Miner, however, says that she was afterwards seen by prisoners in the family of Col. John Butler, at Niagara, who had purchased her from the Indians. If such a person was captured it might have occurred at another time and place.

CHAPTER II.

THE SEARCH FOR THE LOST CHILD BEGINS—HER FRIENDS
GET NO CLUE—FIRST RECORD OF HER AT JOHNSTOWN—
STUPIDITY OF COL. PROCTOR—DEATH OF THE MOTHER.

THE three Indians, with Frances and the boy, Wareham Kingsley, fled rapidly into the forest, and before the terrified mother and her children could clearly comprehend what had happened, they were lost to sight. The noise and excitement of the capture had attracted attention at Wilkes-Barre Fort, situated only a few hundred rods west of the Slocum residence, and an alarm was immediately given, but the wily savages traveled so swiftly that the pursuing party could find no trace of them, and the chase was soon given up. In the meantime the grief of the mother, when she fairly came to realize the situation, was almost unbearable. The captured child was a favorite one, and the pet of the family. Her *exact* age is unknown,* as the day in March, 1773, when she was born, has been lost; but as she was carried into captivity November 2, 1778, she must have been about four years and seven months old. A tender age, indeed, to be torn away from a comfortable home and cast into the wilderness on the approach of winter in this northern latitude; but Providence, as the sequel will show, stretched forth His strong arm to shield and protect this defenceless child.

---

* See quotation giving the names and ages of the family, on p. 11.

Jonathan Slocum, the father, was away from home when the terrible calamity came upon his household. On his return he beheld the bloody corpse of the murdered young man lying at his door, and found his wife prostrated with grief at the loss of their little Frances. In a state of mind bordering on frenzy she related the story of the capture, and in piteous sobs bewailed the sad fate of her child. It is needless to add that the husband and father, on learning the situation, was almost paralyzed with horror, and he scarcely knew what to say or do. Reflecting a moment, however, he resolved, with characteristic self-control, not to allow the current of his grief to break over all its natural barriers, accepted the situation and humbly bowed to the stern decree of fate. Not so with the mother. She could not give up her child—she could not sever the maternal tie—and with deep sobs and broken sentences gave expression to the most profound and overwhelming grief. It was a sad and impressive scene around that desolate hearth as the gloom of night settled down. Sleep fled from that family. Mrs. Slocum could not banish from her sight the last look and plaintive appeal of the innocent child, as with outstretched hands, streaming eyes and disheveled locks, she disappeared from her view; and her frantic shrieks of *"mamma! mamma!"* rang in her ears and haunted her imagination like a demon of darkness. And then the question, which no human reason could solve at that terrible moment of agony, was: "What would become of the child?" Would she be cruelly murdered in the forest and her body become food for the wolves? or would she be worn out with fatigue and left to die a lingering death for want of food and comfortable clothing? Such terrible imaginations haunted her mind and she could not dispel them. The father, as he sat with his head bowed in silent grief and listened to the

sobs of his wife and children, presented a picture that is vividly drawn by the poet :

"'T was eve—a little circle sat
　　Around the cottage hearth;
Youth's voice and rose-bud lips were there,
　　But not its tones of mirth.

" But few and low were all the words
　　Of that lone fireside ring;
It seemed as though their spirits dwelt
　　Upon some fearful thing.

" Had death been in that forest home
　　To call the loved away ?
Was it for this that mother wept
　　From eve till break of day ?

" No; though they missed the baby voice
　　And little dimpled hand:
Death in his quiver hath no dart
　　Like that which pierced that band.

" They missed her when the morning came
　　To wake the voice of birds;
She was not there to mock their song
　　With her soft and simple words.

" She was not there with acorn cups
　　Beside the woodland rill,
Calling aloud to hear her voice
　　Re-echo from the hill.

" They had been there—the forest men!
　　And from her mother's breast
They tore the darling of her love—
　　The warbler from her nest.

" When evening came, the circle met
　　And wept with anguish sore;
They hoped—threw hope away, and then
　　Retired to dream it o'er.

" And in the chambers of the soul
　　One picture memory laid—

A child—one hand among her curls;
The other stretched for aid!''

Time dragged heavily in the stricken household. No
tidings of the lost child could be obtained, notwithstanding
searching parties went in the direction taken by the savages
and scoured the country carefully. They had done their work
quickly and well, and left no trace of their flight behind.

Owing to the condition of the times it was not safe for
scouting parties to venture far into the wilderness, because
the Indians lurked in the thickets ready to pounce upon them
with the agility and fierceness of beasts of prey. The settlers, too, had not fairly recovered from the terror and con-
sternation caused by the battle and massacre of July 3d, and
as so many members of families had been slain, and the western side of the valley devastated, it is not strange, perhaps,
that greater efforts were not made at the time for the rescue
of the stolen child.

A little more than a month had passed and the heart-
stricken family had not recovered from the blow, when
another more crushing was delivered, and a deeper gloom
settled on the stricken household. The relentless savages
were not yet satisfied. The distinguished historian of Wyoming, Hon. Charles Miner, says:

''The cup of vengeance was not yet full. December 16th,
Mr. Slocum and Isaac Tripp, Esq., his father-in-law, an aged
man, with William Slocum, a youth of nineteen or twenty,
were feeding cattle from a stack in the meadow, in sight of
the fort, when they were fired upon by Indians. Mr. Slocum
was shot dead; Mr. Tripp* was wounded, speared and toma-

---

* Little is known of the history of Isaac Tripp. As early as 1768 or '69,
he and Joseph Slocum, father of Jonathan, came to the valley. In 1774 he
purchased a large tract of land which embraced Capoose Meadow, now in-

hawked; both were scalped. William, wounded by a spent ball in the heel, escaped and gave the alarm, but the alert and wily foe had retreated to his hiding place in the mountain. This deed, bold as it was cruel, was perpetrated within the town plot, in the centre of which the fortress was located. Thus in little more than a month, Mrs. Slocum had lost a beloved child, carried into captivity; the doorway had been drenched in blood by the murder of an inmate of the family; two others of the household had been taken away prisoners; and now her husband and father were both stricken down to the grave, murdered* and mangled by the merciless Indians. Verily, the annals of Indian atrocities, written in blood, record few instances of desolation and woe to equal this.''

The blow was indeed an overwhelming one, and calculated to crush the widow. Her lot was a hard one. Both the slain men had often befriended the Indians, but their acts of kindness were now repaid by the most cruel ingratitude. The only explanation that can be offered for this extraordinary

---

cluded in the limits of Scranton. In 1771 Jonathan Slocum, his son-in-law, became the owner of a part of this tract, and in 1775 he purchased a lot in the second division of the town plat of Wilkes-Barre and settled in a house a few hundred yards east of the fort. Isaac Tripp was a prominent man and took an active part in the political troubles at Wyoming between the Connecticut settlers and Pennamites. In 1774 a grandson, also named Isaac Tripp, settled on a part of the Capoose farm. At the age of eighteen, and soon after the Wyoming massacre, he was captured by the Indians, and with others, marched to Canada. On the way he experienced great suffering from hunger and cruel treatment. At Niagara he met his cousin, Frances Slocum, who was also a captive. They planned their escape, but were discovered, separated, and never more met on earth. He was sold to the English and compelled to enter their service, in which he reluctantly continued to the close of the revolutionary war. He was then released, returned home and resumed the peaceful pursuits of the farm. He died April 15th, 1820, aged 60 years.—Hollister's Hist. Lackawanna Valley, p. 127 ; also Hist. of the Slocums, p. 123.

* The meadow where this tragedy occurred was located somewhere between the Slocum house and the public square, along what is now Canal street, in the heart of the city of Wilkes-Barre.

conduct was revenge for the part taken by Giles in the battle. Revenge is one of the strong points of Indian character, the feeling for which is generally caused by a suspicion of deception or inconstancy on the part of those whom they had confided in and trusted.

In moralizing upon the tragedy which had bereft this modern Ruth of both husband and father, Dr. Peck dwells upon the fact that while they were both dead, and their ashes reposed beneath the green turf, time gradually modified the poignancy of the widow's grief for the slain, but Frances, where was she? She knew that the others were at rest, and was resigned. But what was the fate of the child? The mystery grew deeper and more oppressive as time rolled on. A suspense more terrible than death hung over her fate, and lapsing years only increased the vividness of the traces of memory relating to the minutest circumstances connected with the thrilling tragedy of her capture. She called up all the little griefs and disappointments which family discipline had inflicted on her dear child. One circumstance particularly, the venerable historian informs us, which distressed her almost beyond endurance, and was constantly present in her mind, was that Frances had a pair of new shoes,* and as a matter of economy she had been required to lay them up for colder weather. She went away with bare feet, and in that condition would doubtless be obliged to travel rough roads, and perhaps through frost and snow to make long journeys. "Oh! if the poor little creature only had her shoes!" was her constant exclamation; and this thought was a source of torture to the bereaved soul of the mother for long and weary years.

Peace was finally concluded with Great Britain, and efforts

* Dr. Peck's History of Wyoming, p. 244.

C

were at once made by the infant government of the United
States to conciliate the Indian tribes of the North. Agents
were dispatched to negotiate treaties and restore confidence,
but it took a long time to appease the savage mind and bring
about a better feeling. While these negotiations were going
on, two of Mrs. Slocum's sons, who had grown into manhood, conceived the idea of making a journey north to search
for their lost sister. This was very gratifying to the mother,
who still yearned for her child, and firmly believed that she
lived and would yet be found. Accordingly, in 1784, they
started on their journey and traveled as far as Niagara. This
was an important point during the war, and prisoners were
frequently carried there when orders were issued to give them
up. Being men of means, they offered a reward of one hundred guineas for the recovery of the child, or for information
regarding her whereabouts. They thought this sum would
be sufficient to tempt Indian cupidity. But they did not consider that when an Indian undertakes to keep a secret nothing
will induce him to break the seal of his lips, nor especially
the criminality and disgrace of betraying to white men secrets
confided by Indians. As will be shown at the proper time,
the little captive lived and was widely known among the
northern Indians. For some strange and inexplicable reason
she was regarded as a treasure, and was guarded with jealous
care. Fate seemed to have woven about her a veil of obscurity which was an impenetrable mystery to her friends.
Had the disconsolate mother known the truth, how much
greater would have been her mental anguish! but this knowledge was denied her, notwithstanding some invisible power
whispered in her ear that the child was not dead.

Disheartened and discouraged the brothers finally gave up
the search and returned home, after an absence of several

weeks, almost convinced that their sister was dead. This was a sad blow to the mother, but she refused to fall in with their belief, and did not abandon hope. In some respects the mystery surrounding this case is akin to that which has so far obscured the fate of Charley Ross. But the parallel will only be complete when sixty years have rolled away and he will be discovered—if fate shall so decree it.

The first record so far discovered concerning the two captive children of November 2d, 1778, is found in a report of Cols. Fred Fisher and John Harper, of Johnstown,* N. Y., under date of March 2, 1780, relative to confiscations, and Tory families to be sent to Canada. That list contains the names of fourteen prisoners,† and among them are the following: "Hookam child; Kingsley child, Nov. 2, 1775." The fact that the last name is spelled correctly shows conclusively that "Hookam" is meant for Slocum, because both were taken at the same time. The only part of the record which does not correspond with the fact is the year, "1775," written opposite the names. But such a mistake could easily have been committed by the person making the entry. The correct day of the month being given removes all doubt as to the identity of the "Hookam child." This important record may be found in Governor Clinton's unpublished papers, Vol. IX., No. 2736.

If the brothers had had the good fortune to have found

---

* Johnstown is now the capital of Fulton County, N. Y., on Cayadutta Creek, 48 miles W. N. W. of Albany.

† The names of the other prisoners, with the dates of capture, are given for the information of the general reader, and are as follows: James Bodlack, March 21, 1779, released at Niagara, 1780; John Church (58) 1778; Jonathan Smith, 1770—1780 died; Jacob V. Gardner, — Case, Stephen Parish, July 5, 1778; Mrs. Hageman, Nov. 7, 1778; Lanorah Hageman, ditto; Bribben Jones, 1778; Zebulon Parish, Joseph Parish, 1778; Stephen Kamboll, 1778.

this record, they would have had a clue to the object of their search; but where secrecy was so strictly observed, it would, very likely, have availed them little.

As the years passed and the country became more quiet and settled, in obedience to the yearnings of the mother, the brothers, in 1788, again visited the Indian country. This time they traveled westward, and penetrated the wilderness of Ohio. They were absent for several months and enlisted the sympathy of Indian agents and traders, who aided them all they could in their researches. They offered a reward of $500 for any information with regard to their sister's whereabouts, but to no purpose, and they were forced to return home no wiser than when they went out.

Some time in 1789, according to requests of government officials, many Indians assembled at Tioga Point, (now Athens, Pa.,) with children who had been captured, to give their parents and friends an opportunity of identifying and reclaiming them. Hearing of this, Mrs. Slocum, then about 53 years of age, made a journey with great labor* to the place, and after weeks of careful search among the captives, found no one that she could recognize as her lost Frances, and she returned home in deep sorrow over the failure of her mission. But she still clung to the belief that her child was alive and would yet be found. How strange that this idea never for-

---

* To give the reader an idea of what was involved in making the journey at that time, the following extract from the journal of Joseph Ingham is given: " I traveled (1789) up the Susquehanna, following the course of the river, and found it had been very little traveled; hardly a plain path, and this very crooked and hard to follow—quite impassable for more than a man and a single horse. Along the edge of precipices, next the river and other places, I had to ascend and descend from one ledge of rocks to another, some feet perpendicular, at a great height from the water, and in some places extremely dangerous. The habitations of men were very few, and the inhabitants, instead of being glad to converse with strangers or travelers, would hardly speak to them."—Hist. of Bradford County, p. 87.

THE LOST SISTER.   25

sook her! Did some invisible spirit prompt her not to abandon hope?

Tioga, or the *Diahoga* of the aborigines, was a remarkable place. It was the open door through which their war parties passed when going south to murder, pillage and destroy, and through which prisoners were dragged on their way north to Niagara. Mrs. Perkins, in her *Early Times on the Susque-hanna*, says that the Indians, with Frances, passed up the river to Tioga in a canoe, and the "little one was allowed to amuse herself by paddling in the water, and when on land, to practice with her bow and arrow for entertainment." But the writer was mistaken, as will hereafter be shown by the statement of the captive as to how they traveled.

Late in the fall of 1790 the last great gathering of Indians took place at Tioga. Red Jacket, Cornplanter and many prominent chiefs, with hundreds of their followers, were there. They assembled to meet Timothy Pickering, who was appointed a commissioner by Gen. Washington to nego-tiate a treaty. The meeting was a memorable one, and many eloquent speeches were made, but strange to say, there is no record of the treaty on file in the Indian Office, and its terms are unknown. When the conference broke up very few In-dians were ever seen there again. To them the door was closed.

Early in 1791, General Knox, then Secretary of War, commissioned Col. Thomas Proctor to visit the several In-dian tribes inhabiting the country bordering on Lake Erie, and the Miamis of the Wabash, for the purpose of making peace and establishing friendly relations with them. Accord-ing to his journal he started from Philadelphia on the 12th of March, 1791, and on the 17th "crossed the east branch of the Susquehanna" at "Hughsburg" (now Catawissa), and spent the night at Berwick. Having served in Sullivan's Expedition of 1779 as a colonel of artillery, and while the army was ascending the river had charge of 214 vessels carrying the provisions for 6,000 men, this visit was very interesting to him, and he took pains to note in his journal the points where they had encamped twelve years before. He also speaks of owning twenty-five tracts of land* on Big Fishing Creek. Recrossing the river at Berwick he finally, with his party, reached "Wilksburg" (Wilkes-Barre) on the 19th, and met Col. Butler and Col. Pickering. The latter was then serving as prothonotary of the county. Continuing his journey up the river he arrived at Tioga Point on the 26th after a toilsome journey. On the 27th he reached Newtown (now Elmira), where he remained over night and viewed the battle ground at Horseheads, where General Sullivan defeated the Indians in 1779. On the 28th he enters in his journal :†

We proceeded to the Painted Post, or Cohocton, in the Indian language; dined and refreshed our horses, it being the last house we should meet with ere we should reach the Genessee river. * * * * Here I was joined company by a Mr. George Slocum,‡ who followed us from Wyoming, to place himself under our protection and assistance, until we should reach the Cornplanter's settlement, on the head waters of the Allegheny, to the redeeming of his sister from an unpleasing captivity of twelve years, to which end he begged our immediate interposition. *   *   *

On the 22d of April, 1791, Col. Proctor, after writing up his journal for that date, and stating the amount of money paid certain parties for services and provisions, makes this brief but remarkable reference** in connection with others:

---

* Second Series Pennsylvania Archives, Vol. IV., p. 555.

† See Pennsylvania Archives, Second Series, Vol. IV., p. 560.

‡ Pennsylvania Magazine of History, Vol. III., (1870) p. 115, Mr. James Slocum of Brownsville, Pa., shows that this name should have been written Giles. Frances had no brother named George.

** See Pennsylvania Archives, Second Series, Vol. IV., p. 579. Also In-

To cash paid Francis Slocum, a white prisoner, 7s. 6d.; do. a white prisoner at Cataraugus, 11s. 3d.; she informs me that she is a sister of Henry Kepple, in Market street, born in Germany; her husband, a Lieutenant Groves, of the Royal Americans, was killed at Venango, in the year 1761; had been prisoner ever since, but too old and enfeebled to leave them; she informed me that she was truly poor, which I had apparent reason to believe, and I mean to inform her friends of the same, which is the cause of my making this minute, as knowing her brother was under wealthy circumstances. * * * *

This is the second recorded mention that has been made of Frances Slocum since her abduction, and considering the fact of the surrounding circumstances, and the apparent indifference of the writer, is most extraordinary. After being joined by her brother at Painted Post only three weeks before, who apprised him of the object of his mission, claimed his " protection " and begged his "immediate interposition " to reclaim his captive sister, it is passing strange that Colonel Proctor should in a few brief words name the girl and the amount he paid her, and at once enter into details about another prisoner, who had a brother living in Philadelphia "under wealthy circumstances!" The simple error in the spelling of her first name amounts to nothing. She was beyond peradventure the lost child of Wyoming, for whom the family had so persistently searched for over thirteen years! And what is stranger still, she was at this time less than three hundred miles from the home of her mother—was living with the Indians congregated at Cornplanter's town on the Allegheny river—and notwithstanding a brother was either present, or near by, the commissioner of the war department treated the matter so indifferently that she was immediately lost sight of, when practically within the grasp of her friends. Was it indifference or stupidity that caused

dian State Papers, and Col. Stone's History of Wyoming, p. 256.

Col. Proctor* to treat her case so lightly? for he must have known who she was when he named her, after paying her a small sum of money.

Frances was now about 18 years old, as she was less than five when taken away, and a full grown woman. That the Indians were endeavoring to secrete her there is no doubt, for with the efforts which were being made by her brothers to find her and the large rewards that they offered, she could not have remained in obscurity if there had been any disposition to give her up. Why this desire to retain her? the reader will doubtless ask. The most plausible reason that can be offered is that she had been adopted by an Indian family that had lost a daughter about her age, and she had been carefully reared according to their custom, and had become greatly endeared to her foster parents. And above all, she had a luxuriant growth of red hair, which became almost an object of worship to the Indians. These are the reasons, it is believed, which caused them to hold on to her so tenaciously; and through care and kindness she grew up a thorough Indian and did not want to leave them.

What became of Mr. Slocum, Colonel Proctor does not tell us; but he could not have remained with him long, or he certainly would have gotten a clue to the presence of his sister. That he still remained in ignorance of her whereabouts is evident, for the early historians of Wyoming inform us that

* Rev. David Craft, of Wyalusing, Pa., in a note to his historical address, published in Sullivan's Indian Expedition, 1779, page 342, says:

Col. Thomas Proctor was born in Ireland, but in early life came to Philadelphia, where he worked at the trade of a carpenter until the beginning of the war, when he raised a company, was commissioned captain Nov. 27, 1775, and promoted colonel from major Feb. 6, 1777, resigned April 9, 1781, and died at Philadelphia March 16, 1806. He was a man of great executive ability, and was frequently serviceable to the government in other than a military capacity. In 1791 he was sent on a mission to the Western Indians, which he performed to the satisfaction of the government.

the brothers in 1797 undertook another expedition among the western Indians. This they did in obedience to the entreaties of their mother, who had never become reconciled, but firmly entertained the idea that her child lived, and must, after all, be found. Neither did the zeal of the brothers in the search decline with the lapse of years. Four of them, now mature men, and possessing ample means, entered the western wilderness and spent nearly the entire summer of 1797 in visiting the Indian settlements.

The following account of these journeys is taken from an obituary notice of Isaac Slocum,* published in *The Witness*, at Indianapolis, under date of October 27, 1858:

" As soon as the war had closed, Giles and William visited Niagara, taking with them a drove of cattle to conceal the object of their visit, well knowing that if their real business should become known she would be kept out of their way. But they could gain no intelligence of her. In 1793 another brother visited Buffalo to attend an Indian treaty, but was equally unsuccessful.

"In 1797 four of the brothers, including Isaac, started from Wyoming with a drove of cattle and a quantity of dry goods on another search. When they arrived at Seneca Lake, N. Y., three of the brothers took the goods into an open boat, while Isaac drove the cattle to Queenston, where they met and proceeded together to Chippewa, where they again parted, Isaac driving the cattle through Canada to Detroit, and the others going by water. When he arrived at Detroit he was without shoes, nearly destitute of clothing and almost famished for want of food. In order to appreciate the trials and sufferings of these brothers in search of their sister, it must be recollected that the Canadas and the northwestern portion of the United States were, in 1797, little else than an

---

* Isaac Slocum, who outlived all his brothers and sisters, died at Bellevue, Ohio, Aug. 26, 1858, in the 84th year of his age.

unbroken wilderness, inhabited by wild beasts and savage
tribes, with here and there a trading post or fort.

"On this trip through the Canadas Mr. Slocum made a
diligent search among the different tribes, and finally called
together five Indian traders and offered them a reward of $300
if they would find his sister and bring her to Detroit, but all
in vain. He wept and entreated, and they seemed to sympathize in his sorrows, but after consultation among themselves, told him they could not tell him if they knew! They
were obliged to return home without any intelligence of their
sister, after having spent the whole summer in the search.

"The following year they made another trip to the north
and west, but with no better success, and were compelled to
return disheartened and almost discouraged.

"In the meantime the object of their visits had become
known among the Indians, and Frances was kept out of the
way, and finally brought by her Indian father to Fort Wayne
and given to a chief of the Miamis who married her, she being then about twenty-five years of age."

Dr. Peck and other writers inform us that about this time
a female captive, learning of the efforts made by the Slocums
to recover their lost one, and hoping that she might be recognized as the real Frances, came to Mrs. Slocum and told her
that she was taken prisoner somewhere on the Susquehanna
when a child, and was anxious to find her friends. She knew
not the name of her father, nor her own name, but she had
come to see if Mrs. Slocum was not her real mother. Mrs.
Slocum quickly saw that she was not Frances, but she bade
her welcome. "Stay with me," she said, "as long as thee
pleases; perhaps some one else may extend the like kindness
to my dear Frances." The stranger remained a few months,
but finding that none of the attachments and sympathies of
natural relationship existed between them, took her departure, and the Slocums heard of her no more.

The eighteenth century had drawn to a close and the mystery surrounding the disappearance of the child remained as deep and impenetrable as ever to her mother, brothers and sisters. Finally the mother went down sorrowing to the grave without finding the least trace of her lost one, but left with her sons a solemn charge never to give up the search so long as the possibility remained of their recovering their sister, or of learning the circumstances of her story or fate, and the sequel will show how faithfully they carried out her dying injunction. Mrs. Slocum, borne down with grief and years, died May 6, 1807, aged 71 years, 1 month and 15 days, and was laid beside her husband in the graveyard at Wilkes-Barre, who had preceded her 28 years, 4 months and 20 days.

Some years ago all the bodies were removed from the old graveyard, but there were no remains of the Slocums to be moved. Their memory is preserved, however, by the following inscription on the Slocum monument in the Hollenback Cemetery:

JONATHAN SLOCUM,

With his family, emigrated from Rhode Island to Wyoming Valley in 1777. Was massacred at Wilkes-Barre by the Indians Dec. 16, 1778, aged 45 years.

RUTH TRIPP,

Wife of Jonathan Slocum, died at Wilkes-Barre May 6, 1807, aged 71 years.

When she died Frances had been lost to her for 29 years, 6 months and 4 days; and of her ten children, all were known by her to be living but one. And that one lived as a child of the forest, but she knew it not. How inexpressibly sad is the story of the life and death of this noble Christian woman! If it had been vouchsafed to her to know that her wandering daughter lived on the plains of the west, and was well cared for and happy, she could have departed with the consciousness, at least, of knowing that she had not suffered a cruel death at the hands of the savages. Mrs. Slocum lived and died greatly respected ; "but," says Rev. John Todd in his *Lost Sister*, "the brightest smile that ever played upon her lips was saddened by the memory of her lost child. Probably it was the deepest image which time had graven on her heart. She slept in death *almost* consoled by the belief that her child had long since ceased from among the living. But that Providence whose ways had been so mysterious and whose hand had covered the event with so thick a veil, had determined that the veil should not always remain drawn over it. His eye and His hand had guided the little captive, and she was not among the dead."

CHAPTER III.

FORTY-EIGHT years had now passed, and no light had been thrown upon the mysterious fate of the abducted child. If living she must now be over fifty years of age. The strange fate which had befallen her was the constant theme of conversation among the brothers and sisters who survived, for three of them had passed away, viz: Giles, Judith and William. The latter, it will be remembered, was present when his father and grandfather were killed, December 16, 1778, and was wounded in the heel by a spent ball from an Indian rifle.

The six survivors, viz: Ebenezer, Benjamin, Isaac, Joseph, Jonathan and Mary, had not forgotten the dying request of their mother to keep up the search until they were satisfied what had become of Frances. They were constantly on the alert. Letters of inquiry were written and information sought of persons dwelling in the west and Canada, but still no clue could be obtained.

Finally, when the mission among the Wyandot Indians* became a matter of public interest, and the chiefs Between-the-Logs and Me-nun-cu were converted, the report that the former had a white woman for his wife came to their knowledge, and the idea of the possibility of her being Frances,

---

* Dr. Peck's History of Wyoming, p. 246.

induced Mr. Joseph Slocum, attended by a nephew, to visit
the mission.   Accordingly, in 1826, they made a weary and
expensive journey to Upper Sandusky, and found the woman,
but they were soon convinced that she was not the one whom
they sought. They were received with great hospitality and
kindly treated, and came away deeply impressed with regard
to the influence of Christianity upon the moral character and
social condition of these Indians.

   For almost half a century hope had been fondly cherished
in the minds of the Slocums of some light being thrown upon
the history or fate of Frances, but all efforts to gain information with regard to her having utterly failed, they began to
despair.   No wonder.   They had spent much time and thousands of dollars; they had made many long and perilous
journeys; they had offered large rewards and enlisted Indian
agents and traders in the object of their search, but not the
slightest trace of the captive had yet been developed, notwithstanding others knew of her existence.   And had they known
when at Sandusky that they were within two hundred miles
of her cabin, how joyfully and swiftly would they have hastened thither !

   But the cup of her destiny was not yet full.   The last that
the survivors of the family knew of her was that she was
borne away on the shoulders of a stout Indian, on a bleak
November day in 1778, and as he disappeared in the thickets
of the swamp, the frantic shrieks of the child died away in
the distance and were heard no more. From that sad moment
an impenetrable cloud (to them) of darkness had enshrouded
her, which all efforts on their part failed to penetrate.* How
appropriate the lines of the poet :

> "They searched through many a forest wild,
>   And swelling rivers crossed ;

---

* Todd's lost sister p. 110.

> And yet the years brought on their wings
>   No tidings of the lost.

> "Age sprinkled on their heads its frost;
>   They cherished still that name;
> But from the forests of the west
>   No tale of Frances came."

Nearly sixty years had now passed. The lame boy who had been saved from captivity by his mother's appeal was still alive, as well as the sister who had escaped savage vengeance with her infant brother in her arms. A thousand times the family had talked over the events of that fearful day, and the probability of the removal of the veil of mystery which enshrouded the subject was now becoming exceedingly faint,* if it had not wholly passed away; the search was given over, and it almost ceased to be a matter of conversation, excepting as the capture of the child, and the great efforts which had been made for her discovery, were connected with the history of the beautiful and romantic valley in which she once lived. More than a generation had passed, and the wonderful story was only known to those who read brief sketches of it in newspapers, magazines and books.

This was the condition of affairs when suddenly startling news of the discovery of a white woman living among the Indians of a western State was received, and a new and exciting scene in this wonderful drama is about to open to our vision, apparently by accident, but really under the guiding hand of Providence; and a train of circumstances brought to light the whereabouts of the long lost Frances, and quickly revived the flickering spark of memory which had almost faded out of the minds of her brothers and sisters. How strange and yet how gratifying must this unexpected intelli-

* Dr. Peck's Hist. of Wyoming, p. 247.

gence have been! With what emotions must the news have been received! They could scarcely credit the report, because they had been so often deceived before and their hopes of success dashed to earth just at the moment they expected to solve the mystery.

Many accounts of the discovery have been published, but as they are nearly all out of print, and therefore inaccessible to the present generation, it is deemed best to be more explicit in giving the details in this narrative, so that our readers may clearly comprehend the story.

We now take the reader to Indiana, in the valley washed by the Wabash River and its tributaries. Here we find Col. George W. Ewing, an Indian trader, living at Logansport, and carrying on a large business with the Miami Indians.

Colonel Ewing having acquired the language of this and other tribes, and having business with their head men, often made journeys through the wilderness and among the Indian settlements. On one of these journeyings, when returning from Fort Wayne (Ke-ki-ong-a of the Miamis), he was benighted at what was known as "The Deaf Man's Village," situated on the Mississenewa, a few miles above its junction with the Wabash. Feeling the need of a stopping place for the night, he asked for and was kindly granted the hospitality of a respectable Indian cabin. The mistress of the dwelling was a venerable and respectable looking Indian woman, who received him with great kindness and strove to make him comfortable. She presented a marked appearance, and he noticed that great deference was paid her by the whole family circle, composed of children and grandchildren. Being weary and rather indisposed, after his journey of the day, after partaking of some refreshments provided for him, he laid himself down to rest on a bed made of deer skins and blankets in a corner of the room. The inmates soon disappeared, with the exception of the venerable head of the family, who remained to attend to some light household duties for the night. He could not sleep, and as he tossed on his bed his attention was attracted to the aged woman as she appeared before him. There was something peculiarly striking in her appearance and *hair*, and the more he observed her the more he became impressed with the idea that she might be a white woman, though she wore the costume of the tribe and was in style and manners a thorough Indian.

> " Night shrouds the western wilderness—
>   A traveler is there ;
> And worn and wearied much he begs
>   The red man's fire to share.
>
> " Within the hut sits one who seems
>   Of something fair the wreck ;
> No Indian trace was in her hair,
>   Nor olive on her neck.
>
> "The stranger asked her if her home
>   In childhood's day had been
> Within the red man's smoky hut,
>   With barbarous kith and kin.
>
> "She said the red man's cot was not
>   The home her childhood knew;
> Penn's glorious sky once o'er her hung
>   Its canopy of blue ! "

As she moved about and accidentally bared one of her arms above the elbow, he noticed that the skin was white! This discovery almost convinced him that he was right in his conjectures and he commenced a conversation with her in the Miami tongue. On gaining her confidence somewhat he pointedly asked her if she was not a *white woman !* This question seemed to startle her at first, and she evaded answering it directly. But on continuing the conversation she be-

D

came more composed and confidential, and reflecting, perhaps, that she had but a short time to live, she frankly told him that *she was not an Indian ;* she was by birth a white woman. Colonel Ewing at once became greatly interested in her, and on pressing her to relate the story of her life, she told him that when a little girl she had been captured by the Indians on the Susquehanna, carried away, adopted into an Indian family and reared by them. This was a great many years ago. She had never had any communication with the whites, and was taught to distrust them. She had to all intents and purposes become an Indian, and knew nothing about the manners and customs of the whites. She did not remember her name and could not speak her mother tongue. She thought her father's name was Slocum, and that he was a Quaker. The recital of her story greatly interested Colonel Ewing, and the more he thought over it the more he became impressed with its mystery.

In the morning Colonel Ewing mounted his horse and prepared to set out on his journey for Logansport, some twenty-five miles away. He bade the old lady and family farewell with much feeling. In accordance with Indian custom they refused to receive any compensation for their hospitality. As he rode along and thought over the strange story that had been related to him, he became more interested, and determined to make some effort to discover the friends of the white woman. Reaching home he told his mother what he had learned. At once the feelings of a mother's heart awoke, and she urged her son to write to the Indian woman's friends, telling him that the information would no doubt be a source of great joy to them. But how could he do it? She did not know where they lived—all she remembered was that she had been carried away from the banks of the Susquehanna when a child.

After much reflection he concluded to write to some one in the interior of Pennsylvania, but as he knew no one there, he was forced to abandon that idea. He then wrote a letter and addressed it to the postmaster at Lancaster, thinking that inasmuch as it was an old and important town, near the Susquehanna River, the postmaster might know if any child had been lost by the earlier settlers, and would take sufficient interest to make the Indiana discovery known. Following is a copy of the important letter written by Col. Ewing:

LOGANSPORT, IND., Jan. 20, 1835.

DEAR SIR: In the hope that some good may result from it, I have taken this means of giving to your fellow citizens—say the descendants of the early settlers of the Susquehanna—the following information; and if there be any now living whose name is Slocum, to them, I hope, the following may be communicated through the public prints of your place :

There is now living near this place, an aged white woman, who a few days ago told me, while I lodged in the camp one night, that she was taken away from her father's house, on or near the Susquehanna River, when she was very young—say from five to eight years old, as she thinks—by the Delaware Indians, who were then hostile toward the whites. She says her father's name was Slocum; that he was a Quaker, rather small in stature, and wore a large brimmed hat; was of sandy hair and light complexion and much freckled; that he lived about half a mile from a town where there was a fort; that they lived in a wooden house of two stories high, and had a spring* near the house. She says three Delawares came to the house in the daytime, when all were absent but herself, and perhaps two other children; her father and

* The lot where Jonathan Slocum's house stood, and whence Frances was taken Nov. 2, 1778, is on the corner of North Canal and North streets, Wilkes-Barre, Pa., and is now owned by Mrs. Martha Bennett Phelps and Mr. George Slocum Bennett, grandchildren of Judge Joseph Slocum. It is vacant, and not a trace of the original log house remains. The spring, on account of the march of improvement, has entirely disappeared. There are several manufactories in the vicinity, the Lehigh Valley railroad passes within one block, and an electric passenger railway is operated on Canal street.

brothers were absent working in the field. The Indians carried
her off, and she was adopted into a family of Delawares, who
raised her and treated her as their own child. They died about
forty years ago, somewhere in Ohio. She was then married to a
Miami, by whom she had four children; two of them are now living—they are both daughters—and she lives with them. Her
husband is dead; she is old and feeble, and thinks she will not
live long.

These considerations induced her to give the present history of
herself, which she would never do before, fearing that her kindred
would come and force her away. She has lived long and happy as
an Indian, and, but for her color, would not be suspected of being
anything else than such. She is very respectable and wealthy,
sober and honest. Her name is without reproach. She says her
father had a large family, say eight children in all—six older than
herself, one younger, as well as she can recollect; and she doubts
not there are yet living many of their descendants, but seems to
think that all her brothers and sisters must be dead, as she is very
old herself, not far from the age of eighty. She thinks she was
taken prisoner before the two last wars, which must mean the
Revolutionary war, as Wayne's war and the late war have been
since that one. She has entirely lost her mother tongue, and
speaks only in Indian, which I also understand, and she gave me
a full history of herself.

Her own Christian name she has forgotten, but says her
father's name was Slocum, and he was a Quaker. She also recollects that it was upon the Susquehanna River that they lived, but
don't recollect the name of the town near which they lived. I
have thought that from this letter you might cause something to
be inserted in the newspapers of your country that might possibly
catch the eye of some of the descendants of the Slocum family,
who have knowledge of a girl having been carried off by the Indians some seventy years ago. This they might know from family
tradition. If so, and they will come here, I will carry them where
they may see the object of my letter alive and happy, though old
and far advanced in life.

I can form no idea whereabout upon the Susquehanna River
this family could have lived at that early period, namely, about the
time of the Revolutionary war, but perhaps you can ascertain
more about it. If so, I hope you will interest yourself, and, if

possible, let her brothers and sisters, if any be alive—if not, their children—know where they may once more see a relative whose fate has been wrapped in mystery for seventy years, and for whom her bereaved and afflicted parents doubtless shed many a bitter tear. They have long since found their graves, though their lost child they never found. I have been much affected with the disclosure, and hope the surviving friends may obtain, through your goodness, the information I desire for them. If I can be of any service to them, they may command me. In the meantime, I hope you will excuse me for the freedom I have taken with you, a total stranger, and believe me to be, sir, with much respect,

Your obedient servant,
GEO. W. EWING.

Though the postal facilities were slow at that day, compared with what they are now, the letter reached its destination. It happened that Mrs. Mary Dickson* was the postmistress, and owner of the Lancaster *Intelligencer !* But strange as it may seem, she took no interest in the letter, and throwing it aside it laid for *two years* among a lot of old papers and letters which were deemed worthless. Here was another of those strange interpositions, as it were, to keep the knowledge of the existence of the captive from her friends. If she read the letter, her stupidity in not comprehending its importance and the value it would be to her readers as a strange Indian story, if nothing more, is only equaled by that shown by Col. Thomas Proctor forty-four years before, when he met Frances on the Allegheny River among the Seneca Indians, and wrote her name in his journal after paying her a small sum of money, but did not possess sufficient thoughtfulness, interest or sympathy, to impart the information to her brother Giles, who had met him only three weeks before, and begged his "interposition" to recover her.

---

* The records in the Department at Washington show that Mary Dickson was appointed postmaster at Lancaster, Pa., April 17, 1829, and served until Nov. 19, 1850. She was succeeded, at that date, by George W. Hammersley, who served until April 4. 1853. His successor was Henry M. Keig.

But there was a Providence in the discovery of the lost one, and would that Providence, which was concerned in the first development, allow the light to die out, and the whole matter to remain hidden from the vision of those so deeply interested in the revelation until they should pass away? We shall see.

The letter which the careless postmistress had treated so indifferently, finally fell into the hands of another person— whose name is known—who at once recognized its import-ance, and sought an opportunity to give it publicity. The *Intelligencer* had recently been sold by Mrs. Dickson, and in March, 1837, John W. Forney,* then a young man, became one of the editors and publishers, and at once entered on what proved to be a brilliant career as a journalist and politi-cian. The letter was handed to him by the lucky finder, who called his attention to the suggestion of Col. Ewing. Through his journalistic instinct Forney at once saw its im-portance and published it in his paper.

Here Providence seems to have again interposed and saved the important letter, destined to unravel a great mystery, from final oblivion. And another interesting fact in this con-nection is worthy of special mention. The letter made its appearance in a large extra edition of the paper containing some temperance documents, and these were sent to the clergymen generally through that part of the State. One of these fell into the hands of Rev. Samuel Bowman,† a distin-guished Episcopal minister, who, when a young man, had resided in Wilkes-Barre, and was acquainted with several members of the Slocum family. He had often heard from

---

* Ellis & Evans' Hist. of Lancaster Co., (1883,) p. 499.

† For a very full biographical sketch of this brilliant and eloquent di-vine, who died an Episcopal Bishop Aug. 3, 1861, near Pittsburg, see Hist. of Lancaster County, Pa., by Ellis & Evans, p. 466.

them the melancholy story of the capture of their sister, and well knew the strenuous efforts they had made for many long, dark and weary years to find her. He immediately mailed one of these papers to her brother, Joseph Slocum, who lived at Wilkes-Barre, and the wonderful developments made by the letter almost threw the community into a state of frenzied excitement. Mr. Slocum and his friends wondered and pondered over the strange but gratifying news. Many sore disappointments had been encountered before, but now Mr. Slocum felt that light was beginning to dawn, and that the veil of mystery which had concealed the fate of his sister for nearly sixty years was about to be lifted. It is true there was no mother living to say "Frances is yet alive, and I will go and see her before I die!" but there were brothers, a sister, and a large circle of nephews and nieces, whose hearts leaped for joy at the prospect of at least learning the veritable history of Frances, who had been for so many years in savage life, utterly lost to kindred, friends and civilization. Her father had died a cruel death nearly fifty-nine years before, and almost twenty-nine had passed since her sorrowing mother was laid by his side.

The relatives at once took steps to collect all possible information they could for the purpose of verifying the story, and a correspondence was at once commenced between Jonathan J. Slocum, Esq., son of Mr. Joseph Slocum, and Colonel Ewing, as follows:

WILKES-BARRE, PA., Aug. 8, 1837.

GEO. W. EWING, ESQ.,

Dear Sir : At the suggestion of my father and other relations, I have taken the liberty to write to you, although an entire stranger.

We have received, but a few days since, a letter written by you to a gentleman in Lancaster, of this State, upon a subject of deep and intense interest to our family. How the matter should have lain so long wrapped in obscurity we cannot conceive. An aunt of mine—sister of my father—was taken away when five years old, by the Indians, and since then we have only had vague and indistinct rumors upon the subject. Your letter we deem to have entirely revealed the whole matter, and set everything at rest. The description is so perfect, and the incidents (with the exception of her age) so correct, that we feel confident.

Steps will be taken immediately to investigate the matter, and we will endeavor to do all in our power to restore a lost relative who has been sixty years in Indian bondage.

Your friend and obedient servant,

Jon. J. Slocum.

What must have been the surprise as well as gratification of Col. Ewing to receive this letter? Over two years had passed since he had written to the postmaster at Lancaster, and it is reasonable to suppose that he, in the hurry and rush of business, had almost forgotten the circumstance, but he had not. He immediately, as will be perceived by the date, replied as follows:

Logansport, Ind., Aug. 26, 1837.

Jon. J. Slocum, Esq., Wilkes-Barre,

Dear Sir : I have the pleasure of acknowledging the receipt of your letter of the 8th instant, and in answer can add, that the female I spoke of in January, 1835, is still alive ; nor can I for a moment doubt but that she is the identical relative that has been so long lost to your family.

I feel much gratified to think that I have been thus instrumental in disclosing to yourself and friends such facts in relation to her as will enable you to visit her and satisfy yourselves more fully. She recovered from the temporary illness by which she was afflicted about the time I spent the night with her in January, 1835, and which was, no doubt, the cause that induced her to speak so freely of her early captivity.

Although she is now, by long habit, an Indian, and her manners and customs precisely theirs, yet she will doubtless be happy to see any of you, and I myself will take great pleasure in accompanying you to the house. Should you come out for that purpose,

I advise you to repair directly to this place ; and should it so happen that I should be absent at the time, you will find others who can take you to her. Bring with you this letter; show it to James T. Miller, of Peru, Ind., a small town not far from this place. He knows her well. He is a young man whom we have raised. He speaks the Miami tongue and will accompany you if I should not be at home. Inquire for the old white woman, mother-in-law to Brouillette, living on the Mississinewa River, about ten miles above its mouth. *There you will find the long lost sister of your father,* and, as I before stated, you will not have to blush on her account. She is highly respectable, and her name as an Indian is without reproach. Her daughter, too, and her son-in-law, Brouillette, who is also a half-blood, being part French, are both very respectable and interesting people—none in the nation are more so. As Indians they live well, and will be pleased to see you. Should you visit here this fall, I may be absent, as I purpose starting for New York in a few days, and shall not be back till some time in October. But this need not stop you; for, although I should be gratified to see you, yet it will be sufficient to learn that I have furthered your wishes in this truly interesting matter.

The very kind manner in which you have been pleased to speak of me shall be fully appreciated.

There are perhaps men who could have heard her story unmoved; but for me, I could not; and when I reflected that there was, perhaps, still lingering on this side of the grave some brother or sister of that ill-fated woman, to whom such information would be deeply interesting, I resolved on the course which I adopted, and entertained the fond hope that my letter, if ever it should go before the public, would attract the attention of some one interested. In this it seems, at last, I have not been disappointed, although I have long since supposed it had failed to effect the object for which I wrote it. Like you, I regret that it should have been delayed so long, nor can I conceive how any one should neglect to publish such a letter.

As to the age of this female, I think she herself is mistaken, and that she is not so old as she imagines herself to be. Indeed, I entertain no doubt but that she is the same person that your family have mourned after for more than half a century past.

Your obedient humble servant,

GEO. W. EWING.

The denouement had come. The kind hearted Indian
trader had made it plain what course the brothers should
pursue to meet and identify their long lost sister. That she
was the person whom they sought, there was scarcely a doubt
any longer. Col. Ewing* was justified in expressing his gratification at having performed a duty in the interest of Christian civilization which would bring happiness and joy to many
households, and cause the weary wanderer in the wilderness
to realize the true history of her origin, and what became of
her parents, brothers and sisters, whom she dimly recollected
as once dwelling on the Susquehanna. The way was now
plain, and the dramatic scenes which soon followed will be
related in another chapter.

------

* Alexander, the father of Col. Ewing, was born in Pennsylvania in 1763,
but at what place is unknown. He served in the Revolution; in 1787 he
was a trader among the Indians and established himself on what is now
the site of the city of Buffalo. A few years later he settled on a farm on
the Genessee Flats. There he married Charlotte Griffith about 1795, and
there his eldest son, Charles W. Ewing, and a daughter, were born. Meeting with reverses, Mr. Ewing removed west in 1802, and settled on the river
Raisin, in the Territory of Michigan. There three more sons, William G.,
Alexander H., and George W., the discoverer of Frances Slocum, were born.
In 1807 the family moved to Troy, near Piqua, Ohio, where they lived until
1822. The elder Ewing served under Harrison in 1812-13, and was at the
battle of the Thames. In 1822 he moved his family to Fort Wayne and
settled, and there he died in 1827. The sons became extensive Indian traders and acquired great wealth. Some time in 1830 George W. established
a trading post at Logansport, Indiana, where he carried on a large business.
In 1846 he removed to St. Louis. The firm of William G. and George W.
Ewing became very rich. The senior member left nearly a million when
he died, and the estate of the junior reached a million and a quarter. He
died May 29, 1866, at Fort Wayne, and was buried in the family tomb at
that place.

CHAPTER IV.

AS SPEEDILY as possible it was arranged that Mr.
Joseph Slocum, then residing in Wilkes-Barre,
should proceed to Ohio and join his sister, Mrs.
Mary Towne, who lived in the central part of the State, and
push on with her by private conveyance to Indiana. His
brother Isaac, who had emigrated to Ohio as early as 1823,
and located in Sandusky County, near Bellevue, in Huron
County, was to meet them somewhere near the residence of
their supposed sister in Indiana. This was in September,
1837. Isaac, who lived less than 200 miles from the village
of the Miamis, pushed on rapidly and arrived in advance of
his brother and sister. He was extremely anxious to meet
the captive, and becoming tired waiting for Joseph and Mary,
hunted up James T. Miller, the interpreter, and proceeded to
the cabin of the venerable woman so accurately described by
Col. Ewing. He found her, to all appearance, a perfect Indian. He had fixed in his mind an infallible mark of distinction. Before she was captured, one of her brothers, while
they were playing in the blacksmith shop, had struck the
fore finger of her left hand with a hammer, and so injured
the bone that the nail was permanently destroyed, and the
finger otherwise disfigured. She received him with the stoical indifference of the Indian, and did not manifest any sur-

prise at his presence. After some conversation he observed that her finger was disfigured, and taking hold of her hand led her to the light and examined it more carefully. The mark remained, with very little change naturally caused by the lapse of time and ravages of age. With his heart swelling with emotion he asked her through the interpreter:

"How came that finger injured?"

"My brother struck it with a hammer in the shop, a long time ago, before I was carried away," was the answer.

This was conclusive evidence to him of her identity, and he was satisfied beyond a doubt that the real Frances Slocum, for whom he and his brothers had so long searched in vain, had been found. How the memories of the long ago crowded on his mind and brought up fresh recollections of the golden-haired and prattling child. What a supreme moment of satisfaction, blended with grief and sorrow! She stood before him an aged Indian woman with wrinkled face and hair silvered by the frosts of nearly sixty years! She was not as his fond imagination pictured her in the days of their childhood on the banks of the Susquehanna, but there could be no doubt of her identity. She was Frances.

While these thoughts were rushing through his mind, and tears of satisfaction filled his eyes, the Indian woman said little and betrayed scarcely any emotion. She was suspicious, and evidently had no confidence in the claims of the stranger to be her brother. She had been taught that white men were deceptive and wicked, and this belief was evidently well grounded in her mind.

Sadly Mr. Slocum turned away, bade her adieu, and retraced his steps to the town of Peru, nine miles distant, where he anxiously awaited the arrival of his brother Joseph and sister, Mrs. Towne.

After several days spent in deep solicitude and weary watching they came. Their journey had been a toilsome one, as most of the way led over corduroy roads and through a country comparatively new. Houses were widely separated and of the most primitive character at that day. Few persons so far advanced in life—they were 69 and 62 years of age, Mrs. Towne being the elder—could have performed such miracles of endurance. But it was hope and anxiety that buoyed them up. After resting a short time to recover their wasted energies, they made preparations to proceed on their way to the house of the lost sister. Miller, the interpreter, and a young man named James B. Fulwiler,* who had recently settled in Peru, accompanied them. Taking the Indian path—for there were no fine roads up the river like there are to-day—they soon came to the first Indian village on the Mississinewa, a short distance above its junction with the Wabash. Here a remnant of the Miami tribe lived in small cabins scattered among the long blue grass which, without cultivation, covered the luxuriant soil, and the corn fields needed but little care and attention. During the last war these villages had been burned by United States scouting parties, but were now restored. Here the travelers found many Indians. Some were lounging about their huts, while others were at work in their corn fields, with their ponies tied near by—for an Indian will never walk if he can ride.

* James B. Fulwiler was born in Perry County, Pa., Sept. 6, 1812. He was educated at Hopewell Academy and Gettysburg Gymnasium, now Pennsylvania College. His father, William Fulwiler, was one of the early graduates of Dickinson College, Carlisle, where he was born and reared, and died in 1830, leaving a large estate. His paternal ancestry is traceable through centuries into Switzerland. The mother of James was a cousin of Hon. Jeremiah S. Black, and a daughter of the Rev. James Black, of Pennsylvania, a Scottish divine. In 1834 the subject of this notice settled in Peru, Indiana, and has resided there to the present time. He is a gentleman of culture, very intelligent, and an alderman.

In the field they dry their corn and cook their food. At night they mount their bare-back ponies and go to their wigwams to sleep.

At this point the path turned to the left from the Mississinewa and proceeded to the residence of Francis Godfroy, the *last* war chief of the Miamis. His settlement consisted of some five or six two-story log houses situated on a rising piece of ground not far from the Wabash River, and was called Mount Pleasant. Here his great store or trading post was located. His buildings stood within a square enclosure of about half an acre. A gateway admitted them to the buildings, which were quite respectable in appearance. On entering the main building the interpreter introduced them with much gravity to the chief and informed him of their errand. He received them with great dignity and politeness, and proffered them every assistance in his power to facilitate the success of their mission. Godfroy was a noble looking man, apparently over fifty years of age, majestic and solemn in countenance, and weighing over 300 pounds. He was dressed in a blue calico shirt, which came down to the knees and was profusely covered with ruffles. Indian leggins covered his lower extremities from the shirt down. He was over six feet in height, and when he arose, with his long hair gracefully tied in queue down his back, he would have made a splendid model for an artist. Nature had done much for this man. He had wealth and abundance around him, was noted for shrewdness and sagacity, and distinguished for his hospitality.

After a pleasant visit the party took their leave of the chief and hastened on a few miles to what was called the "Deaf Man's Village", so named for a deceased chief. Again they forded the Mississinewa, and entered the village in silence.

There was an expectation of the fulfillment of hopes which had been cherished for nearly sixty years. Such thoughts as these filled their minds: "Would she have any family likeness by which they might know her? Would she have any family recollections by which she might be identified? Would she be glad to see them, and if proved to be their sister would she return to the home of her birth and die where she was born? Would she be overcome at seeing them?"

"I shall know her if she is my sister," said Mrs. Towne, "by having lost the nail of her left fore-finger—you, brother, remember how you pounded it off in the blacksmith shop about a year before we lost her!"

"I do well remember it," he replied, and this was all they said until they stopped in front of a large log house, or rather two houses joined together by a shed.*

When the Slocums and party entered the dwelling they found the mistress of the house quietly sitting in her chair. She received them formally, if not coldly, and after the ceremony of introduction by the interpreter, she did not seem disposed to converse freely. In a short time, however, she relaxed somewhat in her rigidity, and gave a brief account of her family and the circumstances of her capture; but seemed utterly unmoved, and not free from suspicion that there was some plan in operation to take her away or rob her of what she possessed.

---

* Many accounts of the famous meeting have been written, but they nearly all differ, because of the lapse of time and the carelessness of the writers. The best and most reliable are those given by Rev. John Todd and Rev. Dr. Peck, because they derived their data mainly from members of the family, only a few years after the visit, and their narratives have been followed, with the addition of other details which subsequent research has developed. The former wrote nearly fifty years ago, and the latter about thirty-two, but their works have nearly all disappeared; and when found they are discovered to be lacking in that detail which the careful reader would expect them to have given.

During this time the brothers walked the floor with emotions too deep and overwhelming for utterance, while the sister (Mrs. Towne) wept copious tears. Their Indian sister, however, did not change a feature of her countenance, shed a tear or show any emotion.

Mr. Fulwiler recently informed the writer that the scene at this juncture was the saddest, most pathetic and painful he had ever witnessed during his long life of nearly seventy-eight years, and he became so deeply impressed that he was compelled to leave the room.

The brothers, in their grief, seemed to ask themselves the question : "Could it be possible that this aged and unmoved Indian woman was the dear little Frances, whose sweet smiles lingered in their memories, and which they could scarcely identify with her now? Had she been metamorphosed into this stoical, iron-hearted Indian woman—old, wrinkled, and cold as an iceberg?"

But there could be no mistake about it; the proofs were clear, convincing and overwhelming. She said her father's name was Slocum: he was a Quaker, and wore a broad-brimmed hat; he lived near a fort by a great river; she had seven brothers and two sisters; her brother hammered off her finger nail; she was taken from under the stairway; three Indians took her, with several others, a great many winters ago, when she was a little child. The question of identity was settled. Continuing she informed them that she was now a widow. Her husband was a chief. She had two daughters; the younger of the two had lost her husband; the husband of the elder was a half-breed—his father was a Frenchman—his name was Brouillette, who managed the out door affairs of the family, subject always to the views and feelings of the queen mother-in-law. The family circle scrupulously followed the lead of the venerated head of the household, making no advances, exhibiting no emotion. On this occasion one chord more tender than all the rest was touched. The long lost sister had forgotten her own name. She was asked if she could remember it if she would hear it mentioned. Her answer was: "It is a long time; I do not know." "Was it Frances?" asked one of the party. Something like emotion instantly agitated her iron-cast features, and it was evident that an idea was struggling through the dark recesses of her mind, when a smile illumined her countenance and she answered: "Yes, Franca, Franca!" The clouds of darkness which had obscured her mind so long were slowly rolled away, and she recollected the endearing name of her childhood.

> "They found her there—the one for whom
> They searched as for a gem ;
> And sore they wept, as memory brought
> The dreamlike past to them.
>
> "But she was calm and passionless,
> And as a statue still ;
> There were no chords within her breast
> At memory's touch to thrill.
>
> "They questioned her, and asked her name !
> She said she could not tell !
> They breathed that long loved name to her—
> She smiled and knew it well.
>
> "They wept, and wept with burning tears—
> That could not be repressed ;
> For she was dark—and knew not e'en
> When came the Day of Rest."

The painful situation changed a little, but very slowly. The hospitalities of the house were never denied to respectable strangers, and, of course, would be offered to the Slocums. When the conversation was concluded the Indian queen went about her business, apparently with as much indifference as

E

though nothing of interest had happened. The party surveyed the premises and were pleased to find everything in excellent order for an Indian residence. Returning from a stroll they observed the sister seated on the floor at work at a deerskin, which was nearly ready for use. She was scraping the rough places with a knife and reducing its rigidity by friction. She paid little attention to the strangers, only answering when addressed through the interpreter. The daughters evidently observed the strangers with interest, but Indian like, only cast at them side glances when they thought they were not observed.

The company proposed to the sister to accompany them, with her son-in-law and daughters, to Peru. She could not give them a positive answer until she rode over and consulted Chief Godfroy. He advised her to comply with the request, assuring her that she would be in no danger from the respectable strangers; that, being her relatives, they had certainly visited her with none other than the most friendly intentions. Her hesitancy before giving an affirmative answer showed the cautiousness as well as suspicion of the Indian. The advice of the chief assured her, however, and she gave her consent, when the party returned and took supper together at the hotel. Before separating for the night Frances promised to again visit them on the coming day, when a more particular account of her capture and succeeding history might reasonably be expected from her.

In this connection the following extract from a letter written at Peru, September 27, 1837, to their friends in Pennsylvania, and published in the *Wyoming Republican*, is given to complete the record of the visit more fully:

"We arrived here on the 21st inst. The town is new and flourishing; situated on the north side of the Wabash, a little below the mouth of the Mississinewa, which empties in from the south. The last twenty-five miles was through the Miami Reserve, without any white inhabitants. We found Isaac Slocum here awaiting our arrival. He had visited the woman in the Reserve, mentioned in the letter of Mr. Ewing, and is perfectly satisfied that she is the sister taken captive in 1778. The next day we repaired to the village with Mr. Miller, the interpreter, together with Mr. Hunt, a half-breed that was educated at Col. Johnson's school, in the state of Kentucky, and another gentleman. Fording the Wabash at this place, we passed up the river to the Mississinewa, and in about five miles came to an Indian town, surrounded with blue grass pasturage and corn fields intermixed without order. Some of the natives were about their houses; others were at tents pitched in corn fields, gathering corn, their ponies standing saddled near the tents. Whenever they have any work to do at even so short a distance from their houses, they pitch a tent, cook and live there until the work is done, a few only returning to their houses at night. We soon after came to the seat of Godfroy, the second war chief of the Miamis, consisting of five or six two-story houses, within an enclosure of perhaps half an acre, which we entered through a gate wide enough for a carriage to pass. Upon entering the house, we were all introduced to the Chief by Mr. Miller, who told him our business in the nation. He received us very courteously, and proffered us all the assistance in his power. He is probably over 50 years of age, of portly and majestic appearance, being more than six feet high, well proportioned and weighing about 320 pounds. He was dressed in leggings and a blue calico shirt that came down to the knee, profusely ornamented with ruffles of the same, his hair nearly half gray and tied in a queue hanging elegantly down his back. After taking leave of the Chief, we proceeded to Deaf Man's Village, the residence of the captive woman, a distance of about four miles further up the Mississinewa, where the natives were employed in the same way as before described. At one of which we found the husband of the youngest daughter of the captive woman. He mounted his pony and went with us to the village, where we were introduced to the captive, her two daughters, and Captain Brouillette, the husband of the elder. The girls are aged, one thirty-three and the other twenty-three. The youngest has three small children, but not by this husband. The elder had two, but both are dead.

Capt. Brouillette is a half-breed Indian, of elegant appearance, very straight and slim, and about six feet high. Uncle Joseph at once recognized his sister, and after conversing with them some time, in the course of which we endeavored, by all means in our power, to gain their confidence, it was proposed to them to accompany us upon our return to Peru. Mr. Miller had to give the old lady very strong assurances that we had no intention to take her away contrary to her inclination before she would go; but at length she consented, and accompanied by her two daughters and their husbands, she returned with us to the town, where they then joined us at the supper table and appeared to be perfectly at ease. They had now become perfectly satisfied that we were their relations, and their confidence was so much strengthened that she felt justified in proffering us their friendship. This was done by one of them placing on the stand something wrapped in a white cloth, after which they spoke with the interpreter in a solemn manner, when he rose up and said that they were our friends, and by way of acknowledging themselves as such, they presented us with a piece of fresh venison, which they wished us to receive as a token of friendship. We then rose and thanked them and received the token, Mrs. Towne taking up the ham of venison and removing the cloth, which made them satisfied. The next morning they all came to breakfast with us, and the captive gave us, in the course of the day, all the history of her life which she could recollect. Mr. Miller, to whom we are greatly indebted, and Mr. Hunt acted as interpreters. I wrote down the narration in the words of the interpreter. There are not many striking incidents in her life, but she and her family, in their native costume, their extreme simplicity of manner, the natural modesty and solemnity of their deportment, formed the most interesting group I ever beheld. They are decidedly the most respectable family in the nation, and they are also very wealthy, having upward of a hundred horses and many cattle and hogs. Capt. Brouillette is the only Indian who cultivates corn with the plow. He has a yoke of oxen, and wagon, and frequently takes beef and other articles to market.

"Mr. Miller, who has often passed the night with them, says they live well. They dress quite richly, and the old lady told me she had always had plenty and lived happily with the Indians. Her husband and two of his children were buried where she now lives, and she never can think of leaving her present abode. I cannot help thinking she is right, for the family appears to be one of the most happy I ever saw. The two daughters have returned to see us several times. They are sensible and wish to be very sociable, but labor under a great difficulty in not understanding our language. The eldest presented Isaac Slocum with a pair of moccasins for his wife, as he is to leave soon. The confidence they reposed in us seems to be complete and the more I see of these children of the wilderness, the more I respect their character. They have a natural politeness and good feeling that cannot be surpassed in the most polished circles; but this is not shown until they have every confidence in those around them; before that, in the presence of strangers, they are timorous and distant. They have just taken leave of us for home; it is four o'clock P. M., but they never hurry themselves. They frequently ride home, nine miles, most of the way through the woods, with as much *sang froid* as they would in the day time."

To some readers it may seem that more sentiment was expressed over this meeting than was warranted by the facts, but they must remember the extraordinary and deeply melancholy circumstances which surrounded the case. It stands without a parallel in American history. A sister is carried away in childhood, and after a search extending through a period of nearly sixty years, is found by her brothers and sisters changed in every respect into an Indian. She has lost the language of her people, and the memory of her parents, relatives, location, in fact everything pertaining to her early life is vague and uncertain. Her perversion from civilization is of interest to the ethnologist as well as to those who may look at it from a sentimental standpoint.

The following extract from a letter written by the late Hon. Hendrick B. Wright, under date of Dec. 31, 1877, and addressed to Mrs. Lord Butler, of Wilkes-Barre, gives another version of how Frances Slocum (her aunt) came to reveal the secret of her history to Colonel Ewing. Colonel Wright says:

"While in Congress, the XXXIII, I think, and probably in the year 1853, a gentleman of remarkably agreeable and pleasant

deportment called on me at my hotel, in Washington, and introduced himself as George W. Ewing, of Logansport, Indiana. He
said that he had been informed that I represented the Wilkes-Barre
district of Pennsylvania, and he had come to speak to me on the
subject of Frances Slocum, if agreeable to me. I told him that I
was very glad that he had called on me, and nothing could please
me more than to have a narrative from his own mouth of a matter
which I, in common with all the people of Wilkes-Barre, and
especially the Slocum family, which was numerous and highly
respected, felt so much interest.

"Colonel Ewing said that he had been on an excursion in the
vicinity of the Deaf Man's Village, the residence of the white
woman, widow of the chief whose name gave the title to the village, was belated, and darkness coming on, he concluded to remain
over night at the house. He knew her well, and could speak the
language of the people of her tribe. She provided me with a good
supper and ordered wood to be piled on the big hearth, which surprised me, as our supper was over and the Indian bed-time had
arrived. After sitting a half hour or so, and talking over ordinary
matters about her family, her crops and her cattle, and that she
was well off in the necessaries of life, I told her that I would retire
to my bed. She said ' No, I have something on my mind. I am
old and weak. I shan't live long, and I must tell it. I can't die
in peace if I don't.'

"The Colonel said that here followed a long pause, during
which she kept her eyes constantly on the fire and her body moving back and forth in her big arm chair, apparently in pain, at
least in great agitation of mind. I did not wish to break the long
silence. The family had all left us; she and I were alone.

"In this condition she remained at least a half hour. My
mind was in an excitable state, for I could not of course divine
what the secret was that she would disclose. Finally she motioned
with her hand to the stairs, and before I reached the door she said,
' Come back, I must tell it.' I came back and seated myself. A
half hour more elapsed and no sound came from the woman's lips.
I at last told her she could reveal it to me at another time. ' No,
no,' she replied, ' I may die, I may die; and then I will have no
rest in the Spirit World !'

"She said she did not wish to keep her secret for any other

person, because if she made it public her friends would come and carry her away from her home, and she wouldn't endure it—it would kill her.

"I now began to understand that her secret had reference to the subject that it finally resulted in.

"I then assured her that I would protect her in any attempt to remove her from her home or separate her from her children. Col. Ewing then stated that, with great hesitancy, she proceeded with her story, stopping often with her hand to her ear, and turning her head half round, as though some one was eavesdropping.

"When she had completed the narrative she said: 'There, now, I can die. Oh! you don't know how this has troubled me; something all the time whispered in my ear, you must do it—you must do it, and now it is done—and the great load I have carried over fifty years is off my shoulders; I am a free woman!'

"I have given as exact a statement as I remember, related to me by Col. Ewing a quarter of a century ago. I am almost certain that what I have written has never before been offered in connection with the thrilling narrative of the captivity and life of Frances Slocum. The events of it will be read with interest by the people of this valley [Wyoming] in centuries to come—and long after the Indian race has become extinct—and not one of them lives to repeat the traditions of their exploits on the war path, and their wrongs by a higher race of civilized men.

"Colonel Ewing's name will be blended with the story of Frances Slocum. When I met him he may have been forty years of age—of a tall, well built frame; very fine personal appearance—intelligent and sociable. From this acquaintance, thus commenced, I would often spend leisure hours with him with much satisfaction, and our meetings, sooner or later, would always challenge some conversation about poor Frances Slocum."

The statements of Colonel Ewing as to her hesitancy, and the extreme caution she observed before relating her sad story, differ somewhat from the version he previously gave, but instead of detracting from the interest of the narrative they increase it, and make it more pathetic. Her course also shows how she had been taught by the Indians to keep her secret, and made to believe that if her friends among the white people came to know of her existence, they would come and tear her away from her *true* friends—those who had reared, protected and defended her.   But the weight of the secret of her life increased on her mind with advancing years, and when she felt that the end was near, she could not rest happily until she had revealed it.

CHAPTER V.

IT WAS Saturday evening when the party returned to
Peru from this memorable visit, and their feelings can
be better imagined than described. They slept very
little that night. Their thoughts constantly dwelt upon the
strange scenes they had witnessed in the Indian domicile on
the banks of the Mississinewa, and they could not refrain
from talking about their sister and the life she had lived
among the Indians. They longed to learn more particulars
of her history, and the dawning of the morrow was anxiously
awaited. Would she come, as she had promised? was the
question which agitated their minds. There was only one
drawback to the circumstance of the meeting, and that was
the fact that the day fixed upon was Sunday. And was it
possible, they reasoned, that Frances had lost all idea of the
sacredness of the day, and did not know when Sunday came?
Here was an evidence to them that she had become an Indian
in everything excepting her parentage, and that she was in
fact a pagan. Nothing else could have been expected, and
yet this fact seemed as surprising as it was distressing to her
brothers and sister.

At length the day arrived, and true to her promise, Frances, accompanied by her son-in-law and two daughters, came
riding in single file, on their Indian ponies, and presented

themselves before the door of the new hotel* in Peru.   It
was a strange looking cavalcade.   They were decked in gay
barbaric apparel, as was the Indian custom when an important meeting was to take place, and attracted the attention of
the residents of the town.   It was true they were accustomed
to see parties of Indians, as hundreds lived in this section of
the State, but the movement on this occasion indicated that
something unusual was going on, and the town was all astir.

The brothers met them at the door with great cordiality,
requested them to alight, and conducted them into the
house and made arrangements for their comfort.   But, according to the custom of the Miamis—and in fact nearly all
Indians—before any intimacy could be established it was
necessary to give and receive a formal pledge of friendship;
therefore, when they were all assembled, the oldest daughter
brought in a package rolled up in a clean white cloth, which
she laid upon the table, and then, through the interpreter,
solemnly presented it as a pledge of their confidence and
friendship.   Mrs. Towne was then told to receive it, which
she did.   On removing the cloth the hind quarter of a deer
was found, which they had probably just hunted and killed
for this purpose.   Still they were not satisfied till the brothers
and sister had as solemnly received it as a token of friendship
and kindness on their part.   This being done, and the present
taken possession of by the civilized sister, they seemed at ease
and from that moment gave their new friends their entire
confidence.   The ceremony was beautiful and impressive,
and was recognized among those rude people as the seal of
faith.

The best provisions were now made for the entertainment

---

* According to the recollection of J. B. Fulwiler, Esq., this hotel stood
on what is now the site of the elegant Bearss House.

of Frances and the members of her family, and she soon became more at ease, and listened with interest to a history of the Slocum family. They told her how her father was cruelly murdered by Indians less than two months after her capture, and the deep anxiety of their mother, while she lived, to learn the fate of her lost child; how her brothers had searched for her in vain, and how they had learned of her whereabouts through the kindness of Mr. Ewing. They assured her that Mrs. Towne was the sister who ran away to the fort with her little brother in her arms, and that Joseph Slocum, now before her, was that very brother! This seemed to make a deep impression on her mind, as she listened carefully to the particulars as they were communicated to her through the interpreter. In due time preparations were made to take down in writing her Indian history. To this she seemed to have some aversion, until the reasons for it were fully explained by Mr. Miller, the interpreter, when she consented.

This was a most extraordinary meeting, and excited unusual interest in the community. Many of the residents of Peru—several of whom are yet living—knew Frances as the "old white woman," but none of them at that time knew that her history partook of such a romantic character. The people gathered in and around the hotel, gazing upon the strangers and listening with amazement and wonder. They crowded the doors and windows and so interrupted the free circulation of the air that the Indian party, so accustomed to the free atmosphere of the woods and the prairies, were almost suffocated. The food cooked by civilized methods was unpalatable to them and they did not relish it. The circumstances and the surroundings had a depressing effect upon Frances, and she sought relief in accordance with the customs of savage life. She slipped away quietly, and a few minutes afterwards was found with her blanket pulled over her head, lying on the stoop fast asleep!

After a rest the conference was resumed, when the following questions were asked and answers given : *

"Were you ever tired of living with the Indians?"

"No; I always had enough to live on, and have lived well. The Indians always used me kindly."

"Did you know that you had white relations who were seeking you for so many years?"

"No; no one told me, and I never heard of it. I never thought anything about my white relations, unless it was a little while after I was taken."

"Do you remember when you were taken away?"

"I can well remember the day when the Delaware Indians came suddenly to our house. I remember that they killed and scalped a man near the door, taking the scalp with them. They then pushed the boy through the door; he came to me and we both went and hid under the staircase. They went up stairs and rifled the house, though I cannot remember what they took, except some loaf sugar and some bundles. I remember that they took me and the boy on their backs through the bushes. I believe the rest of the family had fled, except my mother.

"They carried us a long way, as it seemed to me, to a cave, where they had left their blankets and traveling things. It was over the mountain and a long way down on the other side. Here they stopped while it was yet light, and there we staid all night. I can remember nothing about that night, except that I was very tired, and lay down on the ground and cried till I was asleep. The next day we set out and traveled many days in the woods before we came to a village of In-

---

* Dr. Peck's Wyoming, p. 261, and Todd's Lost Sister, p. 132.

dians. When we stopped at night the Indians would cut
down a few boughs of hemlock on which to sleep, and then
make up a great fire of logs at their feet, which lasted all
night. When they cooked anything they stuck a stick in it
and held it to the fire as long as they chose. They drank at
the brooks and springs, and for me they made a little cup of
white birch bark, out of which I drank. I can only remember that they staid several days at this first village, but where
it was I have no recollection.

"After they had been here some days, very early one
morning two of the same Indians took a horse and placed the
boy and me upon it, and again set out on their journey. One
went before on foot and the other behind, driving the horse.
In this way we traveled a long way till we came to a village
where these Indians belonged. I now found that one of them
was a Delaware chief by the name of Tuck Horse. This was
a great Delaware name, but I do not know its meaning. We
were kept here some days, when they came and took away
the boy* and I never saw him again, and do not know what
became of him.

"Early one morning this Tuck Horse came and took me,
and dressed my hair in the Indian way, and then painted my
face and skin. He then dressed me in beautiful wampum
beads, and made me look, as I thought, very fine. I was
much pleased with the beautiful wampum. We then lived
on a hill, and I remember he took me by the hand and led
me down to the river side to a house where lived an old man
and woman. They had once several children, but now they
were all gone—either killed in battle, or having died very
young. When the Indians thus lose all their children they

---

* This was Kingsley. It has been shown that in course of time he returned from captivity, married, and finally died in Rhode Island.

often adopt some new child as their own, and treat it in all
respects like their own. This is the reason why they so often
carry away the children of white people. I was brought to
these old people to have them adopt me, if they would. They
seemed unwilling at first, but after Tuck Horse had talked
with them awhile, they agreed to it, and this was my home.
They gave me the name of *We-let-a-wash*, which was the
name of their youngest child whom they had lately buried.
It had now got to be the fall of the year (1779), for chestnuts
had come. The Indians were very numerous here, and here
we remained all the following winter. The Indians were in
the service of the British, and were furnished by them with
provisions. They seemed to be the gathered remnants of
several nations of Indians. I remember that there was a fort*
here. In the spring I went with the parents who had adopted
me, to Sandusky, where we spent the next summer; but in
the fall we returned again to the fort—the place where I was
made an Indian child—and here we spent the second winter,
[1780]. In the next spring we went down to a large river,
which is Detroit River, where we stopped and built a great
number of bark canoes. I might have said before, that there
was war between the British and the Americans, and that the
American army had driven the Indians around the fort where
I was adopted. In their fights I remember the Indians used
to take and bring home scalps, but I do not know how many.
When our canoes were all done we went up Detroit River,
where we remained about three years. I think peace had
now been made between the British and Americans, and so
we lived by hunting, fishing, and raising corn. The reason
why we staid here so long was,, that we heard that the Amer-

---

* There can be little doubt that the place she describes was Fort Niagara
on the river of the same name, which was the concentrating point at that
time.

icans had destroyed all our villages and corn fields. After these years my family and another Delaware family removed to Ke-ki-ong-a [now Fort Wayne]. I don't know where the other Indians went. This was now our home, and I suppose we lived here as many as twenty-six or thirty years. I was there long after I was full grown, and I was there at the time of Harmar's defeat. At the time this battle was fought the women and children were all made to run north. I cannot remember whether the Indians took any prisoners, or brought home any scalps at this time. After the battle they all scattered to their various homes, as was their custom, till gathered again for some particular object. I then returned again to Ke-ki-ong-a. The Indians who returned from this battle were Delawares, Pottawatamies, Shawnese and Miamis.

"I was always treated well and kindly; and while I lived with them I was married to a Delaware.* He afterwards left me and the country, and went west of the Mississippi. The Delawares and Miamis were then all living together. I was afterwards married to a Miami, a chief, and a deaf man. His name was She-pan-can-ah. After being married to him I had four children—two boys and two girls. My boys both died while young. The girls are living and are here in this room at the present time.

"I cannot recollect much about the Indian wars with the whites, which were so common and so bloody. I well remember a battle and a defeat of the Americans at Fort Wash-

---

* The statement by some writers that her first husband was Little Turtle is incorrect. This celebrated chief was born a few miles north-east of Fort Wayne in 1747. His mother was a Mohican woman. On the death of his father he became chief of the Miamis. He died at Fort Wayne July 24, 1812, and was succeeded by Pe-che-wa, commonly called John B. Richardville. His father was a Frenchman and his mother was a sister of Little Turtle. He was born about 1761, and died at Fort Wayne in 1841, and was buried by the Catholics of that place. A monument marks his grave. He is the famous chief of whom it is said "he never took or offered a bribe!"

ington, which is now Cincinnati. I remember how Wayne, or 'Mad Anthony,' drove the Indians away and built the fort. The Indians then scattered all over the country, and lived upon game, which was very abundant. After this they en-camped all along on Eel River. After peace was made we all returned to Fort Wayne and received provisions from the Americans, and there I lived a long time.

"I had removed with my family to the Mississinewa River some time before the battle of Tippecanoe. The Indians who fought in that battle were the Kickapoos, Pottawatamies and Shawnese. The Miamis were not there. I heard of the bat-tle on the Mississinewa, but my husband was a deaf man, and never went to the wars, and I did not know much about them."

At the conclusion of this account of her capture, life and wanderings with the Indians for so many years, there was a pause for a few minutes. Every one present seemed deeply impressed with the story and the simple, artless manner in which it was related. In a short time the conversation was resumed:

"We live where our father and mother used to live, on the banks of the beautiful Susquehanna, and we want you to return with us; we will give you of our property, and you shall be one of us and share all that we have. You shall have a good house and everything you desire. Oh, do go back with us!"

"No, I cannot," was the sad but firm reply. "I have al-ways lived with the Indians; they have always used me very kindly; I am used to them. The Great Spirit has always allowed me to live with them, and I wish to live and die with them. Your wah-puh-mone [looking glass] may be longer than mine, but this is my home. I do not wish to live any better, or anywhere else, and I think the Great Spirit has permitted me to live so long because I have always lived with the Indians. I should have died sooner if I had left them. My husband and my boys are buried here, and I cannot leave them. On his dying day my husband charged me not to leave the Indians. I have a house and large lands, two daughters, a son-in-law, three grand-children, and everything to make me comfortable; why should I go and be like a fish out of water?"

Her reasons for not consenting to return were wise as well as strong, when viewed in their true light. She would have been an object of curiosity and therefore ill at ease among strangers. Too old to adapt herself to the usages of civilized life, she clearly realized that her new condition would not be a happy one, and she aptly clinched the argument by comparing herself in that event to a "fish out of water" — meaning that she would soon die. In this connection how appropriate are the beautiful lines of Mrs. E. L. Schermerhorn, entitled the "White Rose of Miami":

"Let me stay at my home, in the beautiful West,
Where I played when a child,—in my age let me rest;
Where the bright prairies bloom and the wild waters play,
In the home of my heart, dearest friends, let me stay.

"O, here let me stay, where my Chief, in the pride
Of a brave warrior-youth, wandered forth by my side!
Where he laid at my feet the young hunter's best prey,
Where I roamed a wild huntress,—O friends, let me stay!

"Let me stay where the prairies I've oft wandered through,
While my moccasins brushed from the flowers the dew:—
Where my warrior would pluck the wild blossoms and say,—
His White Rose was the fairest,—O, here let me stay!

"O, here let me stay! where bright plumes from the wing
Of the bird that his arrow had pierced, he would bring;

F

Where, in parting for battle, he softly would say,
''Tis to shield thee I fight',—O, with him let me stay!

"Let me stay, though the strength of my Chieftain is o'er,
Though his warriors he leads to the battle no more;
He loves through the woods, a wild hunter to stray,
His heart clings to home,—O, then, here let me stay!

"Let me stay where my children in childhood have played,
Where through the green forest, they often have strayed:
They never could bend to the white man's cold sway,
For their hearts are of fire,—O, here let them stay!

"You tell me of leaves of the Spirit that speak;
But the Spirit I own, in the bright stars I seek;
In the prairie, in the forest, the water's wild play,
I see Him, I hear Him,—O, then, let me stay!

When Frances had given her reasons for not leaving her
home, Capt. Brouillette, the husband of her eldest daughter,
spoke and said:

"And I know all about it. I was born at Fort Harrison,
about two miles from Terre Haute. When I was ten years
old I went to Detroit. I was married to this woman (the
eldest daughter of Frances) about thirteen years ago. The
people about here, at Logansport and at Miamisport (now
Peru) have known me ever since the country was settled by
the whites. They know me to be industrious, to manage
well, and to maintain my family respectably. My mother-in-
law's sons are dead, and I stand in their place to her. I mean
to maintain her well as long as she lives, for the truth of which
you may depend on the word of Captain Brouillette."

"What Captain Brouillette says," quickly added the old
lady, "is true. He has always treated me kindly, and I hope
my connections will not feel any uneasiness about me. The
Indians are my people. I do no work. I sit in the house with
these my two daughters, who do the work, and I sit with
them."

"But won't you at least go and make a visit to your early home, and when you have seen us, return again to your children?" asked one of the brothers.

"I cannot, I cannot. I am an old tree.* I cannot move about. I was a sapling when they took me away. It is all gone past. I am afraid I should die and never come back. I am happy here. I shall die here and lie in that graveyard, and they will raise the pole at my grave with the white flag on it, and the Great Spirit will know where to find me. I should not be happy with my white relatives. I am glad enough to see them, but I cannot go, I cannot go. I have done."

"When the whites take a squaw," said Brouillette, with much animation, as if delighted with the decision of the old lady, "they make her work like a slave. It was never so with this woman. If I had been a drunken, worthless fellow this woman could not have lived to this age. But I have always treated her well. The village is Deaf Man's Village, after her husband. I have done."

The eldest daughter, who was called *Ke-ke-se-qua*, or "Cut Finger"—probably on account of her mother's defective finger—assented to all that had been said, and added that "the deer cannot live out of the forest!"

The youngest daughter, *O-zah-wah-shing-qua*, which on being translated means "Yellow Leaf," confirmed all that was said, and thought that her mother could not go even on a visit, because, said she, "the fish dies quickly out of the water!"

This remarkable and pathetic interview now came to a

---

* She was then in her 65th year, but on account of the hardships and sufferings she had endured during her Indian bondage of sixty years, was greatly broken down, and looked much older than she really was.

close. Frances, the Indian sister, was weary and sick, and
anxious to return to her humble cabin on the banks of the
Mississinewa, so congenial with her feelings, and so endeared
to her by the tender associations which clung around it like
the tendril which entwines the sturdy oak in the forest.
There was her home by the side of the rippling river, and
there were the graves of her chieftain husband and her sons
on the beautiful grassy knoll which overlooked her habita-
tion. And there was the magnificent spring at the foot of
the hill where she had quenched her thirst for many moons,
and which is there to-day in all its purity and beauty. There
she could enjoy the wild mode of life which, by long habit,
had become her natural element, and out of which she could
not be contented and happy.

She bade them a warm adieu, and mounting her pony, followed by her daughters and Captain Brouillette, galloped
away and was soon lost in the distance. The brothers and
sister, with saddened hearts, now prepared to depart for their
homes. They had found their long lost sister Frances, but
they were unable to win her back; they had found and left
her an Indian, with almost every trace of Christian civilization erased from her soul and being, and yet there was wisdom
in her words. "She looked like an Indian," remarks Dr.
Peck, "talked like an Indian, lived like an Indian, seated
herself like an Indian, ate like an Indian, lay down to sleep
like an Indian, thought, felt and reasoned like an Indian; she
had no longings for her original home, or the society of her
kindred; she eschewed the trammels of civilized life, and
could only breathe freely in the great unfenced out-doors
which God gave to the Red Man!" And yet, after her long
captivity, what other condition could have been expected
than that in which she was found? Association, influence

and daily teaching mould the mind, warp the judgment, and if bad, destroy moral sentiment and shape the destiny of the subject for evil.

There was this, however, to comfort the Slocums: their sister was not degraded in her habits or her character, if she had been so long under Indian influence and teaching; there was a moral dignity in her manners entirely above ordinary savage life; her Anglo Saxon blood had not been tainted by savage touch, but bore itself gloriously amid the long series of trials through which it had passed. She was the widow of a deceased chief; she was rich; all that abundance and respectability could do for a woman in savage life was hers. Such was the former Frances Slocum, of Wyoming, now Ma-con-a-qua, the queen of the Miamis. This title, in the language of the tribe, means a female lion, and it was doubtless bestowed upon her on account of her strength and bravery.

The problem of discovery and identity was settled beyond peradventure—the veil of mystery which hung over the history and fate of a captive child for nearly sixty years, was now finally removed.

In due time Mr. Slocum returned from this remarkable visit to his home at Wilkes-Barre, very much gratified at what he had seen and learned. The wonderful story he had to tell was listened to with the most intense interest by his family and friends. All his acquaintances came to see him for the purpose of learning the truth from his own lips, and they plied him with innumerable questions about his sister, which he was always ready to answer—in fact he never seemed to weary of talking on the subject, and took pleasure in relating the story to all who came to see him.

CHAPTER VI.

SPECULATIONS REGARDING THE WANDERINGS OF FRANCES
WHILE IN CAPTIVITY—TWICE MARRIED AND TO WHOM—
ROMANTIC STORY OF HER LAST MARRIAGE—THE GREAT
MIAMI CONFEDERACY.

IF THE account of her wanderings while in captivity
for more than half a century, as simply related by herself through an interpreter, is intensely interesting,
how much more thrilling would it be if we could have the
story in detail? But of course this can never be.

After being carried away on that fatal November day in
1778, Frances speaks of spending the first night in a cave,
but its exact location has never been positively known, and
never will be. When the marauders left the Slocum house
with their prisoners they took an easterly course. The only
cave known to exist in that direction to-day is found in
the mountain near where a picnic ground called Mountain
Park is located, between Ashley and Laurel Run, on the Central Railroad of New Jersey. But as the Indians would have
been compelled to bear off to the right to reach it—and this
would have taken them much out of their way—it is not
likely this is the one in which they took refuge. When they
started it is believed they took the shortest and most direct
route up the river in order to reach Tioga as quickly as possible. It is reasonable to conclude, therefore, that they crossed
the Susquehanna a short distance east of the Slocum residence, and if they concealed themselves in the rocks the first

night it must have been in or about Campbell's Ledge. At this point the conditions are favorable. The escarpment of the mountain is rough and irregular, and shelving rocks abound, in which there are deep recesses, affording excellent hiding places. Here in this wild retreat they could have rested in comparative security for the first night; but as none of the early writers have ventured to locate the cave, whatever theories may be advanced regarding its location must be accepted as mere speculation.

In those perilous days all Indian raiding parties came down the Susquehanna River, and of course they returned by the same war path. The first important stopping place mentioned by Frances, was probably what is now known as Wyalusing, Bradford County, Pa., twenty-one miles below Towanda. It was a favorite place with the aborigines on account of the game which abounded, and they had a village there. The great war path followed the eastern bank of the river, and parties were passing up and down at all times. Wyalusing* being about a day's journey on this highway from Tioga, afforded to parties a convenient stopping place. Its gravelly plains made it an inviting camping ground, the abundance of game in the adjacent forests supplied them with venison, and its lower flats were well adapted to the cultivation of corn. These advantages made Wyalusing a place of note among the Indians, and their war parties generally stopped here to rest. We are therefore safe in concluding that it was the first stopping place made by the party having Frances and the Kingsley boy in charge.

After resting here a day or two she was placed on a horse, as she informs us, and carried to another village. This was undoubtedly Tioga Point, (now Athens, Pa.,) at the conflu-

---

* See Craft's Hist. of Wyalusing, p. 40.

ence of the Susquehanna and Chemung Rivers. This was
the famous Diahoga of the Indians—the great point of con-
centration—and its history dates back so far that it is lost in
the misty past.

Here the little captive was probably kept for some time;
and it was here, perhaps, that she was first decked out in
gaudy Indian costume, as a means of distracting her thoughts
as soon as possible from her home and those she had left behind.   Soon after this she was turned over to Tuck Horse
and his wife, and adopted as his daughter to supply the place
of one of similar size and age who had died.   It is much regretted that there is nothing on record to show who this Indian
was who bore such a peculiar name.   We are informed that
he was a Delaware, but it is not likely that he was an Indian
of much distinction, or we would have heard more about him.

After this we lose all trace of Frances until the early spring
of 1780, when mention is made of her at Johnstown by Col-
onels Fisher and Harper, as being among a lot of prisoners
and Tories to be forwarded to Canada for safety.   That she
was taken there is conclusive, for her cousin, Isaac Tripp,
mentions meeting her at Fort Niagara* about this time.   And
it is possible that she was not dressed in Indian attire until

* Fort Niagara stood on the east side of the mouth of Niagara River,
where it empties into Lake Ontario, at the extreme northwestern corner of
the State of New York. In 1669, during the administration of Frontenac,
a French officer named De Salle enclosed a small spot in palisades at the
mouth of the river, and in 1725 the French erected a strong fortification
there. It grew into a large fort, with bastians, ravelins, ditches, curtains,
counterscarp, drawbridge, mess house, (the latter is still standing within
the present fort,) covering eighteen acres. It was captured from the French
by Sir William Johnston in 1759, and during the war of 1812 (19 Dec. 1813)
a British force of 1,200 men crossed the river and took it by surprise. "During the American Revolution," says Devaux, "it was the headquarters of
all that was barbarous, unrelenting and cruel. There were congregated the
leaders and chiefs of those bands of murderers and miscreants who carried
death and destruction into the remote American settlements."

after her arrival at Niagara, and that her adoption by Tuck Horse took place soon afterwards. She speaks of living on a hill not far from a river, and that the "Indians were furnished with ammunition and provisions by the British." We think it is safe to conclude, therefore, that the change of dress and adoption took place at Niagara, instead of at Tioga.

After the conclusion of peace the Indians gradually moved westward; but many of them were not in a hurry to go, as they were loth to leave the country where they had lived all their lives, and where their ancestors had dwelt before them. This seems to have been the case with Tuck Horse and his family, who lingered about Niagara Falls, Buffalo Creek, on the Genessee and the head waters of the Allegheny, in the Seneca country. It was on the Allegheny that Colonel Proctor met her, soon after the interview with her brother Giles, in April, 1791, when he was making his way westward to treat with the Miamis and other tribes.

After this Tuck Horse and family slowly moved along Lake Erie to Sandusky, whence, after remaining a short time, they returned to Niagara. Whether Proctor* saw her the first or last time she was going west we have no means of knowing, as her statement is too meagre to enable us to judge. Her foster parents led a nomadic life and were constantly on the move, because of the war with the Indians of the northwest, up to the time of their crushing defeat by Wayne.

During the period of greatest disturbance she seems to have been living on the Detroit River, at Brownsville, Ontario. Here the women and children were collected in large

---

* Another circumstance in connection with the meeting of Giles and Col. Proctor at Painted Post, was overlooked in the proper place. Giles had been furnishing supplies—cattle perhaps—to the fort at Niagara, and was familiar with the roads. It is probable that he did not remain long with Proctor.

numbers for British protection, but they suffered greatly for
provisions and shelter. It was while living at Brownsville,
according to the best evidence we have, that she married a
young Delaware Indian. She states that he was named Little
Turtle. He was not the great chief of that name, as has been
shown in another place. Drake says there was another Little
Turtle, a Miami, but he could not have been her husband.
He is mentioned in the treaty of 1818. There is a tradition
still extant among the Miamis that her Delaware husband
did not treat her well, whereupon her foster parents drove
him off. She says that he went west with his people, but she
refused to accompany him, preferring to remain with the old
man and woman who had adopted and raised her. The tradition regarding his departure is believed to be founded on
fact.

About this time the Indians learned that her brothers were
seeking her at Detroit, when the family with which she lived,
accompanied by another family, came to Fort Wayne. This
was evidently for the purpose of throwing her brothers off
the track. As things were in an unsettled condition at Fort
Wayne, they found it difficult to get provisions, and were
forced to subsist on wild meat and whatever they could pick
up. She says that her adopted father could speak English,
and so could she, until he died, when she lost her mother
tongue because she never heard it spoken. They lived on
Eel River, three miles from Fort Wayne, and according to her
story they were there at the time of Harmar's defeat. This
was in 1790, one year before Proctor met her on the Allegheny. She thinks they lived about Fort Wayne for thirty
years. During this time, however, her family made frequent
journeys into different sections of the country, and the period
also included their residence at Detroit and Brownsville.

When and where her foster parents died she does not say, but it must have been near Fort Wayne, and about the time of her marriage with She-pan-can-ah, afterwards known as the Deaf Man.

The Miamis, of Indiana, have a romantic tradition as to how her last marriage came about. It is to the effect that somewhere in Central Ohio, while her parents were floating down a river in a canoe, and she was riding a horse on the shore, she discovered an Indian lying in the path and suffering from a wound which he had probably received in some skirmish with the whites. She dismounted and dressed his wounds, and when her parents came up they took him in their canoe and carried him to the point of their destination. There they cared for him until his wound was healed. He remained with them for some time and kept them well supplied with game, as he was a good hunter. At last, thinking that he had done enough to "pay for his doctor bill," as the tradition goes, he proposed to leave them and pass on. They would not hear to his departure, but insisted on his remaining with them, proposing, as an inducement, that they would give him their daughter in marriage. He did so, and became the husband of Frances. That this union proved a congenial and happy one there is no reason to doubt. This marriage, as nearly as the time can be ascertained, occurred about 1792 or '93, but it conflicts with some of the dates regarding their previous places of residence. And in what part of Ohio it took place is not known with any degree of certainty. Tradition says it was on a great prairie or plains. Possibly it might have been Piqua* on the Miami River, where there is an extensive plateau. There was a large settlement of Miami Indians here under the chieftainship of O-san-diah. He

---

*Helm's Hist. of Wabash Co., Indiana, p. 117.

was succeeded by his son, A-taw-a-taw, and he by his son, Met-a-cin-yah. While under the last chief the band returned to Indiana, making the region now composing Wabash and Grant counties their headquarters.

The cruel massacre of the Christian Indians at the Moravian town in Ohio, by white men, March 8, 1782, made a profound impression on the mind of Frances Slocum. As these converted Indians had spent some time at Sandusky and on the Detroit River, where they sought protection during the troublous times, she had become acquainted with them. The report of the butchery on their return to their home in Ohio affected her very much and caused her to distrust and hate the whites. That affair was one of the most cruel and bloody on record. Ninety-six persons, composed of men, women and children, were bound and shut up in two houses, to which the name of *slaughter houses* was given, where they were inhumanly slain by having their heads crushed by heavy wooden mallets.* It was fitly characterized by Loskiel as the most infamous act in the border war of that period. Frances, it is said, afterwards taught her children to beware of the teachings of white missionaries, reminding them of the perfidy of the whites at the Moravian town; that they would murder them. But it is gratifying to know that in the later years of her life her mind was disabused of these opinions, and she came to respect the teachings of Christian ministers.

After leaving Piqua they evidently returned to Fort Wayne, for Frances informs us that it was from the latter place they emigrated to the Osage village on the Mississinewa, located about a mile above its mouth, and her husband became its war chief.

* For a full account of this bloody affair see Allbach's Western Annals, p. 375-6-7-8-9.

She-pan-can-ah is described as a heavy set man, and was a great warrior until he lost his hearing. As a hunter, too, he is said to have been very successful, and did not cease the pursuit of game until he became too old to longer engage in the chase. It is also related of him that he would sometimes start out on his pony to look for game without removing the bell, and being unable to hear, he would ride through the forest and wonder why the game so suddenly disappeared. It was frightened away by the tinkling of the bell on his horse!

When he became too old to perform the duties of war chief, he transferred his authority to Francis Godfroy, and he served in that capacity until his death in 1840. No successor was appointed. She-pan-can-ah, after retiring from the chieftainship, removed four miles further up the river and built a log house, and the settlement that grew up around it was known as "The Deaf Man's Village." In a painting by George Winter, and now owned by Mr. George Slocum Bennett, of Wilkes-Barre, it is represented as a typical Indiana log building of the period, covered with a clapboard roof. It was one story high, with a door in the centre, and a window on each side, with a chimney at the end. The spaces between the logs were "chinked" with blocks of wood held in place with mortar. It stood on the edge of the river, and nothing now remains to mark its site but a pile of stones. Here "The Deaf Man" died about 1831 or 1832, and was buried according to Indian custom in a little cemetery on the top of a hill, only a few hundred yards away. His age, according to Peter Bondy, was very great—probably one hundred years. But in this estimate he must be mistaken. Indians rarely lived to be so old. He might have reached eighty or ninety years.

On marrying this Indian, Frances became a Miami, and was named Ma-con-a-qua. There is some difference of opinion regarding the meaning of this word. The Miamis of to-day say it means "female lion," probably suggestive of her great strength and activity. Others have asserted that it meant a young bear, because she cried so when first captured. This is probably incorrect. It might, however, have been the meaning of the first name given to her by her adopted father and mother, which she gives in her first statement.

The Great Miami* tribe was the oldest and most powerful in the Northwest, and occupied the territory now embraced in the States of Ohio, Indiana, Illinois and Michigan. There were many other tribes known by other names within this territory, yet the great centre or leading tribe was the Miami; and in later years, for the purpose of repelling the invasions of European emigrants from the territory, all the leading tribes within its limits were united into one confederacy, known as the "Great Miami Confederacy," with headquarters at Ke-Ki-ong-a, where Fort Wayne now stands. Next to the Delawares they are entitled to be recognized as the leading branch of the Algonquin group. As a tribe they have been variously designated as the "Twa-twas, Twe-twees, Twightwees, Omes, Omamees, Aumiamis," and finally the Miamis. The first treaty ever held with the Miamis was at Lancaster, Pa., on the 23d of July, 1748. Three of their noted chiefs were present from the Wabash country and met the English commissioners, when a firm treaty of alliance and friendship was then stipulated and agreed to between the parties. This treaty lasted for sixty-three years. At the end of General Harrison's campaign in 1813 the power of the Miami Confederacy was almost crushed. In 1818 the remain-

---

* See Dillon's Historical Notes, p. 294.

ing chiefs asked for a treaty to define the boundaries of their territories. It was held at St. Mary's, in Ohio. Gen. Lewis Cass was one of the U. S. Commissioners. By this treaty a reservation* for the Miamis was made of lands on the Wabash, beginning at the mouth of the Salomie, and running down to the mouth of Eel River,† at Logansport. A line on both sides of the rivers was run so as to include a territory of about 930,000 acres. The United States also agreed to build a mill at any point they might select. They chose a site on Mill Creek, four miles southwest of the city of Wabash, and there it was erected.

By the treaty of October 23, 1826, held at Paradise Springs, known as the "Old Treaty Ground," the chiefs and warriors in council with Lewis Cass, James B. Ray and John Tipton, Commissioners on the part of the United States, ceded to the latter power "all their claim to lands in the State of Indiana north and west of the Wabash and Miami Rivers, and of the cession made by the said tribe to the United States, by the treaty concluded at St. Mary's October 6, 1818." By further provisions of the same treaty‡ the State of Indiana was authorized to lay out a canal or road through any of the reservations, and for the use of a canal, six chains in width along the same, was appropriated. In payment for this land they received $31,040 53 in goods; $31,040.53 in cash. The following year, 1827, they received $61,259.47 in addition, and in 1828, $30.000. After that date they were to receive a permanent annuity of $25.000.

---

* U. S. Statutes, Vol. VII,, p, 189, Ed. 1856.

† Eel River formed a natural boundary between the Miamis and Pottawatamies. North of this stream the Pottawatamies held undisputed sway as late as 1826, and were in later years of their history superior to the Miamis in numbers, and were respected accordingly.—Helm's Hist. Wabash Co., Ind., p. 118.

‡ Helm's Hist. Wabash Co., Ind., p. 24.

Again, in 1834, the Government purchased of them 177,-
000 acres, including a strip seven miles wide off the west side
of the reserve, in what is now Cass, Howard and Clinton
counties, which was transferred to the State of Indiana to be
used for the completion of the Wabash and Erie Canal from
the mouth of the Tippecanoe River. A strip five miles wide
along the Wabash had been previously appropriated to the
construction of the canal to the mouth of the Tippecanoe.
The consideration paid for this was $335,680.

Thus the great " Thirty Mile Reservation," as it was
known in those days, kept gradually melting away. As they
saw their possessions diminishing, dissatisfaction arose among
a large portion of the tribe, because their hunting grounds
were becoming rapidly reduced and white settlers were en-
croaching upon them on all sides, and they proposed to sell
the remnant of their reservation and move further west. One
portion of the tribe wished to remain and engage in agriculture like the white people, but the majority prevailed, and
this led, after an occupancy of twenty years, to the important
treaty of 1838. As this treaty is the one which most deeply
interested Frances Slocum and her descendants, it will be
given in full in another chapter.

CHAPTER VII.

N ACCOUNT of coming too closely in contact with
the whites, the once powerful tribe of Miami Indians soon commenced to rapidly decline. All the
vices and destructive agencies of civilization had been introduced among them; the Indian trader had deceived and
cheated them in the sale of goods at enormous prices, and
whisky, the bane of mankind, was doing its work with irre-
sistible force. To the older and wiser chiefs the outlook was
discouraging. They clearly saw the defenceless condition of
the tribe, and realizing that fate was against them, they sorrowfully shook their heads and began preparations to once
more turn their faces towards the setting sun.

The proposition to hold a treaty for the purpose of disposing of the balance of their reservation having been accepted,
Abel C. Pepper was appointed a Commissioner on the part of
the United States, to meet the chiefs and head men of the
Miamis for that purpose. They met at the Forks of the
Wabash November 6, 1838.* This point, so widely known as
the famous "Treaty Ground" of the Miamis, is located at
the junction of the Wabash and Little Rivers. A meeting
here with the United States Commissioners was always a great
occasion among the Indians, and they attended in large numbers. The town of Huntington is situated a short distance
from the historic spot. It is twenty-four miles southwest of

---

*See Public Statutes at Large, Vol. VII., pp. 569—574.

G

Fort Wayne, and forty-eight east by north of Logansport, on
the line of the Wabash Railroad. Huntington is said to have
been laid out by General John Tipton, who served so long as
an Indian Agent, and afterwards as one of the first United
States Senators from Indiana.

That the reader may clearly comprehend the importance
of this noted treaty, it is herewith printed in full. Its stipu-
lations and schedule are as follows :

"ART. 1. The Miami tribe of Indians hereby cede to the
United States all that tract of land lying south of the Wabash
River and included within the following bounds, to wit: Commencing at a point on said river where the western boundary
line of the Miami line of the Miami Reserve intersects the
same, near the mouth of Pipe Creek; thence south two miles;
thence west one mile; thence south along said boundary line
three miles; thence east to the Mississinewa River; thence up
said river, with the meanders thereof, to the eastern boundary
line of the said Miami Reserve; thence north along said eastern boundary line to the Wabash River; thence down the
said last named river, with the meanders thereof, to the place
of beginning.

" The said Miami tribe of Indians do also hereby cede to
the United States the three following reservations of land,
made for the use of the Miami nation of Indians by the 2d
article of a treaty made and concluded at St. Mary's, in the
State of Ohio, on the 6th of October, 1818, to wit:

" The reservation on the Wabash River, below the forks
thereof.

" The residue of the reservation opposite the mouth of the
river Abouette.

" The reservation at the mouth of a creek called Flat
Rock, where the road to the White River crosses the same.

" Also, one other reservation of land made for the use of said tribe at Seek's Village, on Eel River, by the 2d article of a treaty made and concluded on the 23d of October, 1826.

"ART. 2. From the cession aforesaid, the Miami tribe reserve for the band of Me-to-sin-in, the following tract of land to wit: Beginning on the eastern boundary line of the Big Reserve, where the Mississinewa River crosses the same ; thence down said river with the meanders thereof to the mouth of the creek called Forked Branch; thence north two miles; thence in a direct line to a point on the eastern boundary line two miles north of the place of beginning; thence south to the place of beginning, supposed to contain ten square miles.

"ART. 3. In consideration of the cession aforesaid the United States agree to pay the Miami tribe of Indians $335,-680—$60,000 of which to be paid immediately after the ratification of this treaty and the appropriation to carry its provisions into effect; and the residue of said sum after the payment of claims hereinafter stipulated to be paid, in ten yearly instalments of $12,568 per year.

"ART. 4. It is further stipulated that the sum of $6,800 be paid John B. Richardville; and the sum of $2,612 be paid Francis Godfroy; which said sums are their respective claims against said tribe prior to Oct. 23, 1834, excluded from investigation by the late Commissioner of the United States, by reason of their being Indians of said tribe.

"ART. 5. The said Miami tribe of Indians being anxious to pay all their just debts, at their request it is stipulated, that immediately after the ratification of this treaty, the United States shall appoint a commission or commissioners, who shall be authorized to investigate all claims against said tribe which have accrued since the 23d of October, 1834, without regard to distinction of blood in the claimants; and to pay such debts as, having accrued since the said period, shall be proved to his or their satisfaction to be legal and just.

"ART. 6. It is further stipulated that the sum of $150,-000 out of the amount agreed to be paid said tribe in the 3d article of this treaty, shall be set apart for the payment of the claims under the provisions of the 4th and 5th articles of this treaty, as well as for the balance ascertained to be due from said tribe by the investigations under the provisions of the treaty of 1834; and should there be an unexpended balance in the hands of said commission or commissioners after the payment of said claims, the same shall be paid over to the said tribe at the payment of their next subsequent annuity; but should the said sum so set apart for the purpose aforesaid, be found insufficient to pay the same, then the ascertained balance due on said claims shall be paid in three equal instalments from the annuities of said tribe.

"And the said Miami tribe of Indians, through this public instrument, proclaim to all concerned that no debt or debts that any Indian or Indians of said tribe may contract with any person or persons, shall operate as a lien on the annuity or annuities, nor on the land of the said tribe, for legal enforcement; nor shall any person or persons other than the members of said Miami tribe, who may by sufferance live on the land of, or intermarry in, said tribe, have any right to the land or any interest in the annuities of said tribe, until such person or persons shall have been by general council adopted into their tribe.

"ART. 7. And it is further stipulated, that the United States will cause the buildings and improvements on the land hereby ceded, to be appraised, and have buildings and improvements of a corresponding value made at such place as the chiefs of said tribe may designate; and the Indians of said tribe are to remain in the peaceable occupation of their present improvements until the United States shall make the said corresponding improvements.

"Art. 8. It is further stipulated that the United States patent to Beaver for five sections of land, and to Chapine for one section of land, reserved to them respectively in the 2d article of the treaty made A. D. 1826, is continued between the parties to the present treaty.

"Art. 9. The United States agree to cause the boundary lines of the land of said tribe in the State of Indiana, to be surveyed and marked within the period of one year after the ratification of this treaty.

"Art. 10. The United States stipulate to possess the Miami tribe of Indians of, and guaranty to them forever, a country west of the Mississippi River, to remove to and settle on, *when the said tribe may be disposed to emigrate from their present country*, and that guaranty is hereby pledged; and the said country shall be sufficient in extent, and suited to their wants and condition, and be in a region contiguous to that in the occupation of the tribes which emigrated from the States of Ohio and Indiana. And when the said tribe shall have emigrated, the United States shall protect the said tribe and the people thereof, in their rights and possessions, against the injuries, encroachments and oppressions of any person or persons, tribe or tribes whatsoever.

"Art. 11. It is further stipulated, that the United States will defray the expenses of a deputation of six chiefs or head men, to explore the country to be assigned to said tribe west of the Mississippi River. Said deputation to be selected by said tribe in general council.

"ART. 12. The United States agree by patent to each of the Miami Indians named in the schedule hereunto annexed, the tracts of land therein respectively designated.

"And the said tribe in general council request, that the patents for the grants in said schedule contained, shall be transmitted to the principal chief of said tribe, to be by him distributed to the respective grantees.

"Art. 13. And it is further stipulated, that should this treaty not be ratified at the next session of the Congress of the United States, then it shall be null and void to all intents and purposes between the parties.

"ART. 14. And whereas, John B. Richardville, the principal chief of said tribe, is very old and infirm, and not well able to endure the fatigue of a long journey, it is agreed that the United States will pay to him and his family the proportion of the annuity of said tribe which their number shall indicate to be due to them, at Fort Wayne, whenever the said tribe shall emigrate to the country to be assigned them west, as a future residence.

"ART. 15. It is further stipulated that as long as the Congress of the United States shall in its discretion make an appropriation under the 6th article of the treaty made between the United States and said tribe in the year 1826, for the support of the infirm and the education of the youth of said tribe, one-half of the amount so appropriated shall be paid to the chiefs, to be by them applied to the support of the poor and infirm of said tribe, in such manner as shall be most beneficial.

"ART. 16. This treaty, after the same shall be ratified by the President and Senate of the United States, shall be binding on the contracting parties.

"In testimony whereof the said Abel C. Pepper, Commissioner as aforesaid, and the chiefs, head men and warriors of the Miami tribe of Indians, have hereunto set their hands at the forks of the Wabash the 6th of November, 1838.

"(Signed),   ABEL C. PEPPER, Commissioner.
J. B. RICHARDVILLE,
MINJENICKEAW,
PAW-LAWN-ZO-AW, (Godfroy)
NO-WE-LANG-GUANG-GAW, (Big
O-ZAN-DE-AH, (Poplar Tree) [Leg)
WA-PA-PIN-SHAW, (Black Raccoon)
NAC-KAW-GUAUNG-GAW,
KAH-TAH-MAUNG-GUAW,
KAH-WAH-ZAY,
TO-PE-YAW, (Francis La Fountaine)
PE-WAW-PE-YAW,
ME-SHING-GO-ME-JAW,
NAC-KON-ZAW,
NE-KON-ZAW,
WAW-PE-MAUNG-GUAW, (White
CHING-GUAW-KE-AW,   [Loon)
AW-KOO-TE-AW,
KIL-SO-AW,
TAW-WE-KE-SE-AW,
MAC-QUAW-KO-NAUNG,
MAW-YAUC-QUE-YAW. (Son of
    [Richardville)

"Signed in the presence of John T. Douglass, Sub-Agent, Allen Hamilton, Secretary to Commissioner, Daniel D. Pratt, Assistant Secretary to Commissioner, J. B. Duret, H. Lasselle, William Hurlbert, Indian Agent."

To the Indian names are subjoined marks, or totems, which
are not given here, because they would have to be engraved
to be properly represented.

The schedule of grants referred to in the foregoing treaty,
article 12th, is given for the purpose of showing the quantity
of land awarded to the principal chiefs and their friends by
the United States:

" To John B. Richardville, principal chief :

" Two sections of land, to include and command the principal falls of Pipe Creek.

" Three sections of land, commencing at the mouth of the
Salamonie River; thence running three miles down the Wabash River and one mile up the Salamonie River.

" Two sections of land, commencing at the mouth of the
Mississinewa River; thence down the Wabash River two
miles and up the Mississinewa River one mile.

" One and one-half section of land on the Wabash River
at the mouth of Flat Rock (creek), to include his mills and
the privileges thereof.

" One section of land on the Wabash River, opposite the
town of Wabash.

" All of which said tracts of land are to be surveyed as
directed by the said grantee.

" To Francis Godfroy, a chief, one section of land opposite
the town of Peru and on the Wabash.

" One section of land on little Pipe Creek, to include his
mill and the privileges thereof.

" Four sections of land where he now lives.

"All which said tracts of land are to be surveyed as directed by the said grantee.

" To Po-qua Godfroy one section of land to run one mile

on the Wabash River, and to include the improvements where he now lives.

"To Catharine Godfroy, daughter of Francis Godfroy, and her children, one section of land to run one mile on the Wabash River, and to include the improvement where she now lives.

"To Kah-tah-mong-quah, son of Susan Richardville, one-half section of land on the Wabash River below and adjoining the three sections granted to John B. Richardville.

"To Mong-go-sah, son of La Blonde, one-half section of land on the Wabash River below and adjoining the half-section granted to Kah-tah-mong-quah.

"To Peter Gouin, one section of land on the Sixth Mile Reserve, commencing where the northern line of said reserve intersects the Wabash River; thence down said river one mile and back for quantity.

"To Mais-shil-gouin-mi-zah, one section of land to include the Deer Lick, alias La Saline, on the creek that enters the Wabash River nearly opposite the town of Wabash.

"*To* O-ZAH-SHIN-QUAH, *and the wife of Brouillette, daughters of the "Deaf Man," as tenants in common, one section of land on the Mississinewa River, to include the improvements where they now live.*

"To O-san-di-ah, one section of land where he now lives on the Mississinewa River, to include his improvements.

"To Wah-pi-pin-cha, one section of land on the Mississinewa River, directly opposite the section granted to O-san-di-ah.

"To Mais-zi-quah, one section of land on the Wabash River, commencing at the lower part of the improvement of 'Old Sally,' thence up said river one mile and back for quantity.

"To Tah-ko-nong, one section of land where he now lives on the Mississinewa River.

"To Cha-pine, one section of land where he now lives on the Ten Mile Reserve.

"To White Loon, one section of land at the crossing of Langlois's Creek, on the Ten Mile Reserve, to run up said creek.

"To Francis Godfroy, one section of land, to be located where he shall direct.

"To Neh-wah-ling-quah, one section of land where he now lives on the Ten Mile Reserve.

"To La Fountain, one section of land south of the section where he now lives on and adjoining the same, on the Ten Mile Reserve.

"To Seek, one section of land south of the section of land granted to Wa-pa-se-pah by the treaty of 1834, on the Ten Mile Reserve.

"To Black Loon, one section of land on the Six Mile Reserve, commencing at a line which will divide his field on the Wabash River, thence up the river one mile and back for quantity.

"To Duck, one section of land on the Wabash River below and adjoining the section granted to Black Loon, and one mile down said river and back, for quantity.

"To Me-cha-ne-qua, a chief, alias Gros-mis, one section of land where he now lives.

"One section to include his field on the Salamonie River;

"One and one-half section commencing at the Wabash River where the road crosses the same from John B. Richardville, Jr.'s; thence down the said river to the high bank on Mill Creek; thence back so as to include a part of the prairie, to be surveyed as directed by said chief.

"To Tow-wah-keo-shee, wife of old Pish-a-wa, one section of land on the Wabash River below and adjoining the half section granted to Mon-go-sah.

"To Ko-was-see, a chief, one section of land now Seek's Reserve, to include his orchard and improvements.

"To Black Loon, one section of land on the Six Mile Reserve, and on the Salamonie River, to include his improvements.

"To the wife of Benjamin Ah-mac-kou-zee-quah, one section of land where she now lives, near the prairie, and to include her improvements, she being commonly known as Pichoux's sister.

"To Pe-she-wah, one section of land above and adjoining the section and a half granted to John B. Richardville on Flat Rock (creek) and to run one mile on the Wabash River.

"To White Raccoon, one section of land on the Ten Mile Reserve where he may wish to locate the same.

"To La Blonde, the chief's daughter, one section of land on the Wabash River below and adjoining the section of land granted to Francis Godfroy, to be surveyed as she may direct.

"To Ni-con-zah, one section of land on the Mississinewa River, a little above the section of land granted to the Deaf Man's daughters, and on the opposite side of the river, to include the pine or evergreen tree, and to be surveyed as he may direct.

"To John B. Richardville, one section of land to include the Osage village on the Mississinewa River, as well as the burying ground of his family, to be surveyed as he may direct.

"To Kee-ki-lash-e-we-ah, alias Godfroy, one-half section of land back of the section granted to the principal chief opposite the town of Wabash, to include the creek;

" One-half section of land commencing at the lower corner of the section granted to Mais-zi-quah, thence half a mile down the Wabash River.

" To Al-lo-lah, one section of land above and adjoining the section granted to Mais-she-gouin-mi-zah and on the same creek.

" To John B. Richardville, Jr., one section of land on Pipe Creek above and adjoining the two sections of land granted to the principal chief, to be surveyed as he may direct.

" To John B. Richardville, one section of land wherever he may choose to have the same located.

" It is understood that all the foregoing grants are to be located and surveyed so as to correspond with the public surveys as near as may be to include the points designated in each grant respectively."

It will be noticed that Chief Richardville, whose Indian name was Pe-che-wa, was granted a great quantity of land; but it was cheap in those days, when compared with present prices. Godfroy came next as a recipient of the bounty of the United States. Richardville lived south of Fort Wayne, while Godfroy lived on the Wabash, about one mile above where the Mississinewa empties into it. The village chiefs were Chapine, at the village east of Roanoke; White Loon, in the same vicinity; Black Loon, east of Antioch; Big Majenica, near Antioch; La Gros, near La Gro; Little Charley, north of Wabash; Al-lo-lah, south of Wabash; Cot-ti-cippin, on Treaty Creek; Joe Russiaville, Mississinewa, and Me-shin-go-me-sia, west of La Fontaine. There were other villages of minor importance, among them " The Deaf Man's Village," the home of the " white woman," or Frances Slocum. These villages extended from near the present city of Fort Wayne to La Fayette, and in a strip of territory extending south of Eel River about thirty miles. North of Eel River the Pottawatamies had their home. At that time they were the larger of the two tribes, and numbered about 2,500 warriors, the Miamis numbering about 1,100, which probably represented a membership of from 5,000 to 6,000 souls. Helm, upon whose authority this statement is made, says the Miamis were much the more intelligent and civilized people, the Pottawatamies being filthy in their habits and low in their nature.

The attention of the reader is now particularly called to another important point in the life of Frances Slocum. Historians in referring to her have always stated that *she* was granted a section of land by the government. This statement is incorrect. She never was given a foot of land. If the reader will refer to the paragraph in the schedule to the treaty of 1838, printed in italic letters, he will see that the land was granted to "O-zaw-shing-qua," the youngest daughter of Frances Slocum, and her sister, Ke-ke-se-qua, the wife of Captain Brouillette, as "tenants in common," and the title for this land was vested in the youngest daughter, who afterwards disposed of it by will among her heirs, as will be shown at the proper time. Frances, however, resided upon this tract of land during the balance of her life, was the recognized head of the family, managed the business thereof, acquired a handsome Indian competence, and when she died was buried in its soil by the side of her husband and deceased children. These facts, it is hoped, will remove a popular historical error and keep future writers within the range of truth.

The *last* treaty with the Miamis was held at the old treaty grounds Nov. 28, 1840. "Old Metosina," as he was called, having lived for four-score years at his village near the mouth of Josina Creek, requested that a reservation be made to him at that place, so that he could spend the remainder of his days in peace. His request was granted, as may be seen by referring to the VII. volume U. S. Statutes, page 569, and fourteen sections of land were given him, which made him one of the most extensive Indian land owners of his time. He was a remarkable man and possessed of many good qualities. According to tradition he lost the chieftainship of his tribe on account of prolonged absence on a hunting expedition. His people fearing that he had been killed, and having no leader, went to work and made Pe-che-wa (John Baptiste Richardville) their civil chief. When Metosina returned he found another acting in his place. He accepted the situation with good grace, evidently pleased at being relieved from the cares of office, and spent the balance of his life in ease and contentment. His descendants still reside in that section of the country, but they have greatly degenerated. This story of his early life, showing how he came to be deposed, is a very pretty one, but we have no positive evidence of its truth.

The Indians now being desirous of disposing of all their lands, so that they could emigrate, the government appointed Samuel Milroy and Allen Hamilton to meet them as commissioners. By this treaty the Miamis ceded to the United States all that tract of land on the south side of the Wabash River not heretofore ceded, and commonly known as the residue of the Big Reserve. It was also agreed that the time for removing the Indians to the West should be extended five years from that date, in order to give them time to select a location. In the meantime the old Chief Metosina having died, and his son Me-shin-go-me-sia inaugurated in his stead, it was deemed best by the commissioners to vest the title of the lands, reserved to the oldest chief at the last treaty, in his son, which was done. Me-shin-go-me-sia continued to occupy his reservation until his death, which occurred Dec. 23, 1879, at the age of 98 years, since which time the lands have been partitioned among the Indians, giving to each a legal title to the same.

It was also stipulated that the sum of $25,000 he paid to John B. Richardville, and the sum of $15,000 to the acting executor of Francis Godfroy, deceased—being the amount of their respective claims against the tribe—out of the money set apart for the payment of their debts. The fifth article reads:

AND WHEREAS, the late war chief—Francis Godfroy—bequeathed to his children a large estate, to remain unsold until the youngest of said children shall arrive at the age of twenty-one years, it is therefore stipulated that the United States shall pay to the family of said deceased chief their just proportion of the annuities of said tribe at Fort Wayne, from and after the time the tribe shall emigrate to the country assigned them west of the Mississippi.

This closed the work of treaty making with the remnant of the once powerful Miami nation on the Wabash, and the only future action on the part of congress concerning them, will be found in the passage of a couple of joint resolutions about the time of the great hegira in 1846, which relate to Frances Slocum and her descendants, and a few other Indian families, who prayed to be allowed to remain in possession of their old homes.

CHAPTER VIII.

TWO YEARS had now passed since Joseph and Isaac
Slocum, accompanied by their sister, Mrs. Towne,
had made their memorable visit to the Wabash for
the purpose of meeting and identifying their lost sister in her
Indian dwelling. The recollections of that visit were still
fresh in their minds, and they felt it their duty to look after
the welfare of their aged relative in her far western home.
Mrs. Mary Towne, who had nearly reached the age of 72, was
too old to make another journey to the Wabash. Isaac, who
lived in northwestern Ohio, had recently lost his wife and was
unable to visit his sister at this time. Joseph, however,
yearned to make another journey to the reservation for the purpose of meeting her again. Accordingly, early in September,
1839, he commenced preparations for the journey, and it was
decided that his two daughters, Hannah and Harriet, should
accompany him. The former was the oldest of his seven
children, and the latter the youngest. Hannah was the wife
of Mr. Ziba Bennett, of Wilkes-Barre, whom she had married
in 1825. She was noted for her high Christian character, and
took a deep interest in the welfare of her aunt. Harriet E.,
who was single, was about twenty years old at that time. She
soon afterwards married Charles Drake, and on his death several years afterwards married Mr. Lewis, and now resides at

Madison, New York. Mrs. Bennett, who was a methodical
woman, kept a diary in which she noted the daily incidents of
the journey. The original is now in the hands of her son,
Mr. George Slocum Bennett, of Wilkes-Barre. It is an interesting record of that toilsome journey, and as it has never
been printed in full, it is, with the permission of the owner,
given herewith without abridgment, because it forms an important part of this narrative. The start was made from
Wilkes-Barre September 10th, 1839, where the journal begins.
It is as follows:

WILKES-BARRE, September 10th, 1839.

Left home at 8 o'clock in the morning in a very poor four
horse coach, loaded with passengers and baggage. Mr. Chas.
Saylor, Mr. Courtright, Jonathan and Harriet Slocum, and
Nancy Bird, were our company to Niagara Falls. We found
the roads bad, many of the bridges down. Arrived at Tunkhannock at 5 o'clock to dine; called to see Frances Oster-
hout, who is in the last stage of consumption; she is since
dead. We reached Montrose at 11 o'clock at night tired and
weary; found father who had been waiting for some time.
He came another road in his own conveyance. We stopped
at Dr. Warner's, who keeps a temperance house. The stages
do not run daily to Owego. We here left my brother, and
father was our company. The proprietor sent us in a four
horse coach to Binghamton to accommodate us. We had a
colored man in the coach, which some of the company did not
like; we let the poor fellow ride and he was very civil. We
arrived at Binghamton at 11 o'clock to breakfast, which was
good and very refreshing, as we had not eaten since 5 o'clock
the day before. The roads were bad, our load heavy, which
kept us so late. Called to see Mr. and Mrs. Stocking, who
received me very cordially; walked around the town; found it

H

much larger than I expected. It has two banks, six churches, and is very flourishing, and is built on both sides of the river. At 3 o'clock left for Owego and arrived at 8 in the evening. After supper at Mr. Mannings, we called at Mr. Wright's; they kindly invited us to stay all night, which we did with pleasure, as I dislike tavern beds when I can avoid them. In the morning called at Mr. Ransom's and Mr. Lanning's; walked around town, which is a very thriving village. At 2 o'clock we took our seats in what ought to have been a comfortable railroad car, but proved to be an old worn out stage body, loaded with passengers and baggage, almost at the risk of our lives. I was fearful we would be crushed. The horses were lame and broken down. I thought to myself, is this proud, high-spirited New York? Such railroads, horses and cars I never saw in Pennsylvania.

The country from Owego to Ithaca is poor; in some parts low and marshy, in others broken and rough; I was disappointed. It may not be the best part where the railroad passes. As you come in sight of the lake the prospect is very fine from a high hill, where the railroad terminates. The lake and country around presents a beautiful prospect as the sun's last rays tint the horizon, as it sets in the west. We here took stage and found entertainment at Mr. Hall's, who keeps the Clinton House; it was dusk. By the time we had taken our suppers it was dark, it being cloudy. We went out but were not able to see much, and returned not much wiser for our walk, as the town was not well lighted. At 6 o'clock in the morning we went on board the steamboat DeWitt Clinton. The name is worthy of a better boat; she tows many freight boats, therefore her progress is slow. Captain Van Order was pleasant and very accommodating. They were soon to have a new boat for passengers connected with a loco-

motive on the railroad.   Cayuga Lake is a very pretty sheet
of water.   We left the steamboat about 4 o'clock at Bridge-
town; there is here a very long bridge; we went on board a
small boat which took us to Montezuma; we here passed the
outlet of Seneca Lake, entered the Great Western Canal and
went on board a line boat for Rochester, as there was no
packet there.   The boat already was well supplied with passengers before we went on board; six of us added to the crowd
did not increase our comfort.   Some parts of the country were
beautiful as we passed along, while others were broken and
uneven.   The fare on the line boat was poor; the first meals
I ate were very light, and much of the company would rank
with the fare.   We were glad when we arrived at Rochester;
it was half-past 9 on Saturday evening.   On Sabbath morning we took a short walk to see Genessee Falls, which are
grand, but much injured by the improvements.   There are
several mills and manufactories erected on the river, which
prevent more than half the water, which once formed the
river, in spending its fury in dashing over these stupendous
rocks.   So nature must give way to art.

Rochester is a large flourishing place.   There are several
fine looking churches on both sides of the river.   The Genessee Conference was sitting; it afforded us an opportunity of
both hearing and seeing the preachers.   I recognized Mr. and
Mrs. Shipman, who seemed glad to see us.   Bishop Hedding
preached in the morning from this text: Ephesians iii., 8, and
ordained fifteen deacons.   Dr. Lucky preached an hour and a
half in the afternoon, from Acts xvi., part of 17th verse, and
the bishop ordained twenty elders.   Mr. Mason was to preach
in the evening.

We thought it best to take passage in the packet for Lockport; it was to leave at seven, but did not till ten.   We were

deprived of the pleasure of hearing him, and spent the evening in the packet. The Methodist church is very large, and neatly finished, but is much in debt. Our boat was crowded, but much more pleasant than the line boats, both as to company and fare. There was an attempt in the night, by one of the passengers, to rob father; he lodged under him, and he put his hand in his pocket, which awakened father, and therefore he did not succeed. He was a poor, worthless fellow. The canal lies on very high ground; it is a ridge formed by nature, but looks as though it might have been by art. The views of the locks and excavations are splendid, as you come in sight of Lockport; we landed our trunks in the lower town, rode up to the locks and walked up them. The Capt. invited us into a small building, where there were shown us some petrified stones, excavated out of the solid rock, in the form of some small animals or bugs, which were curious. There are several mills and manufactories here.

After dining at Lockport I wrote a letter to Mr. Bennett. We left in the cars for Niagara at 5 o'clock, and arrived at 7 in the evening amid the rush and roar of mighty waters. Before the cars stopped we were assailed with a host of servants applying for passengers and baggage. The cars stop half way between the two hotels; it is difficult to make a choice; we went to the Eagle. In the morning after breakfast we crossed from the main land over to Goat Island, on a bridge not long since erected. I find that no painter's pencil, nor the pen of the most gifted, has been able to describe the grandeur of the scene that is presented before the visitor as one stands on the bridge which connects the American side with Goat Island. As far as the eye can reach the water comes tumbling and foaming over the rocks in such rapidity that before it reaches the falls it is wrought into a fury; it is in a complete foam before it dashes over the precipice, and is lost in the awfully sublime chasm below. We went to the tower, which is built of stone 150 feet high, to take a view of the British side, which is a very good one. The tower is built on the rocks some distance from the shore; we returned, went down Biddle staircase about 300 feet, went as near the falls as we could on either side; on account of the spray it is dangerous, and not a very pleasant walk. The rocks over-head are constantly dripping, which makes it rough and slippery, with the bed of the river just below. We ventured and took every possible view, clambering over rocks and down staircases. The morning was delightful and the rainbow over the falls was to be seen. I like the appearance of our falls the best, although there is not such a quantity of water pours over them; perhaps one cause is we could get nearer them than the other.

After dinner Mr. Saylor and Mr. Courtright, with Nancy, left for Erie. We staid, crossed over the river a few rods below the falls, expecting to see the Queen's troops, as they were on parade, to visit the Table Rock and the Burning Spring, but were disappointed. Before we reached the British shore it began to rain; we at first thought it was spray falling, but were soon convinced to the contrary; to our sorrow it rained incessantly. After landing on her Majesty's shores we were obliged to return wet enough, without gratifying our curiosity ; we took shelter in some miserable groceries. The Queen keeps a guard stationed at the landing. We had company—there were others that returned in the same predicament. There are a great many visitors constantly coming and going.

We left the Eagle House at half past six on Wednesday morning in the railroad cars for Buffalo; reached there just in time to eat our breakfast and take passage on board the steamboat Columbus, under the command of Capt. Dobbins. The wind was high when we left the harbor and continued to increase. After going 20 miles we were beaten back and anchored on Point Albino, on the Canada shore, where we lay for 36 hours, and we experienced all the delights of seasickness; the boat was kept in constant motion by the beating of the waves. The first dinner the captain ate by himself, although there were many passengers aboard; I suffered very little in comparison with many; father and Harriet were both worse than I. As soon as we put out again we began to get better. Thursday about 12 o'clock at night we weighed anchor and started; we touched at various ports along the lake; we lay three hours at Cleveland, having much freight on board for that place, but it being in the night we were deprived of the privilege of seeing the town. Father went out to see the great and rapid improvements of the place.

We landed at Sandusky City 9 o'clock on Saturday morning. We here found Mr. Saylor, who had preceded us, and came down to the boat to take passage to Maumee; he had concluded we had gone there without stopping at Sandusky. The cars were ready in a few minutes, and we took our passage to Bellevue without any delay. At 12 o'clock we found ourselves at Uncle Isaac's;* he lives a mile from where the cars stop. We found him in deep affliction; he buried his wife last Tuesday, 17th September. She started with one of her sons, a young man grown, to go to the weavers; he had some business by the way, and before he left the wagon he proposed tying the horses. The mother said it was not worth while, she could hold them, and to hand her the lines, as

---

* Isaac Slocum, who with his brother Joseph and sister Mrs. Towne, visited Frances in 1837.

they were old team horses, and always perfectly gentle. He had not left them five minutes before they started and ran a short distance and struck a tree. She was thrown out against the tree, striking her head, which instantly killed her. The horses were soon caught, but did not appear frightened. The call is a loud one to uncle and to us all. Be ye also ready.

We left uncle's at 2 o'clock on Sunday to take our passage in the cars for Sandusky City. It is very much against my principles to travel on Sunday; we did not like to detain our company; we might have kept the Sabbath for we were compelled to stay at Sandusky until Tuesday morning, no boat coming into the harbor, and we might have spent our time much more pleasantly with our cousins than at a public house.

The Star came into harbor on Tuesday morning, and at 4 o'clock we left Sandusky. The harbor is very large; they take a circuitous route to get in; it is five miles where they pass the point until they reach the wharf. I spent most of Monday with my eyes stretched across this bay to welcome the first appearance of a boat, but it was in vain. It was a delightful day and there was nothing to interest us much at Sandusky; we were anxious to be off. The Exchange is a very good house. The Star was the most unpleasant boat we were on board; the accommodations were miserable; I could eat but little breakfast.

It brought us safe to Maumee Bay on Tuesday afternoon; we passed Manhattan and Toledo; the latter is four miles in length; ten miles up the river we found Maumee City; it is two miles long; the buildings scattered so as to sound large abroad. We walked a mile and a half to reach the stage house, part of the way on a board walk. There is much sickness at this place; the whole country is very unhealthy, fever and ague, congestive fevers or Maumee fevers, prevail. There were several very ill in the house where we lodged. We had not been at this place very long before there were five more passengers arrived for Fort Wayne; they were moving from Maine, which made ten passengers.

In the morning it rained; our fellow travelers, Mr. Mac-Collough, wife and child, Mr. Spafford and grandson, seemed to hesitate whether to start in the rain or not. We had concluded to prosecute our journey rain or shine; they took courage from us, and we put out after borrowing a couple of umbrellas, through rain and mud, over hill and dale, almost at the risk of our lives. We arrived in safety at Fort Defiance at 8 o'clock in the evening. It was too late to see the fortifications.

We started at 2 o'clock in the morning; stopped at New Rochester for breakfast, and miserable was the fare; we could scarcely make out a breakfast; the roads were bad and it was very dangerous traveling. We dined at a house on the line between Ohio and Indiana at half past three o'clock. From this place we had a good driver and team, but came very near an upset in the canal. We reached Fort Wayne between 10 and 11, and found very good entertainment. The Court was then sitting and the house was pretty full. In the morning we walked round the town to see the fortifications, which still remain, and the block houses. Fort Wayne, on the Maumee, is pleasantly situated on rising ground; has a commanding prospect, and bids fair to be a flourishing town.

From this place to Logansport the canal is in operation; we took passage on board the packet at 10 o'clock for Peru. Capt. Mahon was very accommodating. We left Nancy Bird at her brother's; it was rainy and unpleasant. It is so

unhealthy up the Maumee that at many places where settlements were commenced, and improvements made, they are
entirely vacated.

We arrived at Peru at 3 o'clock on Saturday morning,
September 28th, 1839. We found comfortable lodgings at
Mr. Burnett's, a temperance house; this place has only been
settled four years; the country is rich but unhealthy. Mr.
Miller,* the interpreter, called to see us, and is very kind;
we passed the Sabbath here; there was a two days' meeting
held, which we attended; it was a very good one. On Monday morning father procured a two horse wagon and driver to
take us to the Deaf Man's village.

We set out about 9 o'clock in company with Mr. Miller,
Mr. Saylor and Mr. Fulwiler. Our charioteer likes a dram,
and to be sure to have a supply, he carried a bottle in his
pocket; if he had spent the money in getting his harness
mended it would have been better for us. We met Capt.
Brouillette within a short distance of their lodge† coming
down to see us; he dismounted, shook hands with us very
cordially, then mounted and rode on home like a streak
through the woods. The whole family appeared glad to see
us, and made us as welcome as they knew how. The Capt.
speaks broken English. They are much more cleanly about
their housekeeping and cookery than I expected to find them.
We stayed with them till Tuesday noon. They provided
horses and saddles for us, and in company with our aunt and
her eldest daughter, were turned to Peru; they rode astride,
all in Indian file; we passed through several Indian villages,
by Godfroy's, who lives in quite a large house and very well

---

* James T. Miller was a noted Indiàn interpreter, and was widely known.
He was raised by the Ewings and was greatly esteemed by them. He lived
to a good age and only died a few years ago.

† The residence of Frances Slocum and her daughters.

furnished, with a store, &c. It was 3 o'clock when we reached Peru;† the Capt. came afterwards, but returned in the evening. My aunt and cousin stayed till the next afternoon, when the Capt. returned and went home with them. They parted very friendly, expecting to see us again.

September 30th, 1839. This day I visited my aunt; found her living on the banks of the Mississinewa River, Indiana, in what is called a double hut. She is of small stature, not very much bent, had her hair clubbed behind in calico, tied with worsted ferret; her hair is somewhat gray; her eyes a bright chestnut, clear and sprightly for one of her age; her face is very much wrinkled and weatherbeaten. She has a scar on her left cheek received at an Indian dance; her skin is not as dark as you would expect from her age and constant exposure; her teeth are remarkably good. Her dress was a blue calico short gown, a white Mackinaw blanket, somewhat soiled by constant wear; a fold of blue broadcloth lapped around her, red cloth leggins and buckskin moccasins. The interior of her hut seemed well supplied with all the necessaries, if not with luxuries. They had six beds, principally composed of blankets and other goods folded together; one room contained the cooking utensils, the other the table and dishes; they spread a cloth on their table and gave us a very comfortable meal of fried venison, tea and short cake. Her oldest daughter is large and fleshy; I should think would weigh near 200 pounds; is smart, active and intelligent; is very observing. She is 34 years of age. The youngest is smaller, is quiet and very retiring; is 24 years of age. The mother's name is Ma-con-a-qua, a Young Bear. The eldest daughter's name, Kich-ke-ne-che-qua, or Cut Finger. The

† Peru, the capital of Miami County, a pretty little city of about 6,000 inhabitants, is situated on the Wabash River. Its main street is noted for the width and beauty of its stone sidewalks.

youngest, O-saw-she-quah, Yellow Leaf. The grandchildren's names, Kip-pe-no-quah, Corn Tassel; Wap-pa-no-se-a,
Blue Corn; Kim-on-tak-quah, Young Panther. They have a
looking glass and several splint bottom chairs. A great many
trinkets hang about the house, beads and chains of silver and
polished steel. Some of their dresses are richly embroidered
with silver broaches; seven and eight rows of broaches as
closely as they can be put together. They have many silver
earrings. My aunt had seven pairs in her ears; her daughters
perhaps a dozen apiece. They have saddles and bridles of
the most costly kind; six men saddles and one side saddle.
They have between fifty and sixty horses, one hundred hogs,
seventeen head of cattle, also geese and chickens. Their
house is enclosed with a common worm fence, with some
outhouses, principally built of logs. A never-failing spring
of excellent water is near the door, with a house over it.
They have a section of land (which is 640 acres) given to her
two daughters. The treaty was ratified by government this
spring. The land which is owned by government is now settling, which is not so pleasant for them, as intruders frequently help themselves to horses, hogs and cattle.

Captain Brouillette, her son-in-law, is now with her, pro-
viding for the family by killing game, as he is a noted hunter.
He provides the wood, which is rather unusual for an Indian,
and lays up corn and hay for the winter. The husband of
the youngest daughter and he did not agree very well, as he
was a lazy, indolent Indian; would not provide, but was ready
to spend and eat what was provided. Brouillette left, was
absent seven months, during which time the other died, in
April. In June she married a second; he was killed by a
Wea* in August. There is a dispute between the Miamis
_____
* The Weas had a common origin with the Miamis, were once a power-

and Weas respecting their annuity. The Miamis disclaim all connection with the Weas; they had a dispute, and it ended in his death. Three years ago the eldest grand-daughter died; supposed she was poisoned by Godfroys. His son wanted to marry her; her parents would not consent, as he was a drunken, worthless Indian, and as they always seek revenge, it ended in her death. Her parents mourn yet for her. At present they appear to live happy and comfortable. My aunt's husband has been dead six years. She says she was taken by an Indian chief whose name was Tuckhorse, adopted by him and his wife in the place of a daughter they had lost a short time before. If there was anything to eat she always had it. They lived one year at Niagara, where she recollects seeing a machine by which they raised goods from below the falls, and let them down; and also of Indians being afraid to cross above the falls on account of the rapidity of the current. She lived three years near Detroit. She says the old man made chairs, which he sold; he also played on the violin; he frequently went to the frontiers and played, for which they paid him. The old squaw made baskets and brooms, which they sold. The British made them presents of ammunition and food, which they had to go after under the cover of night. As to her religion, she is well apprised of a heaven and a hell, the necessity of living a quiet and peaceable life; if she is such she will be happy when she dies; this was taught her by her adopted parents. She says she is able to have a better house, but fears to do it on account of the jealousy of the Indians. She has money, some that has been saved since the

ful tribe, and lived on the lower Wabash. In 1816 the Weas and the Kickapoos entered into a treaty of peace with the United States and sold their lands on the west side of the Wabash. Two years later they disposed of all their lands in Ohio, Indiana and Illinois, except a few special reservations. In 1820 they made a final cession of all their lands and agreed to leave the Wabash, but many of them remained.

treaty of St. Mary's eighteen years ago; she has lent $300 at a time. They moved from Detroit to Fort Wayne; after the victory they lived on Eel River, three miles from Fort Wayne, where they had planted corn and made preparations in case of a defeat. They lived there about twenty years. She married a Delaware Indian by the name of Little Turtle; when the Delawares removed west she refused to go with them, and chose to stay with her adopted mother; as the Miamis had treated her kindly she would not go. She then married a Miami, She-pan-can-ah. They came to this reserve about twenty-four years since. Her adopted father could talk good English; she could speak it while she lived with him; he was very careful to publish that she was dead, and the Indians generally promised to do the same. The chief's names are Richardville and Ma-jin-i-cah.

Thursday night at 10 o'clock, Oct. 3, we left Peru on our return home; we reached Logansport* at 4 in the morning. The public house was not very neat; the females were all sick with the fever that prevails in that country. The location is pleasant and good; it has grown up rapidly; is now rather at a stand; the country is now suffering from drought; it is now eighteen months since they have had a heavy rain; we spent

* At this point the Wabash and Eel Rivers unite. The town was founded in 1828, and in 1829 the county was organized and named Cass, in honor of Gen. Lewis Cass, who was the principal commissioner in negotiating treaties with the Miamis and Pottawatamies in 1826. It was made the county seat, and the seal represents Gen. Cass and Au-bee-naub-bee, a Pottawatamie chief, shaking hands. The chief some years afterwards was killed by his son in a drunken brawl, and his skull and the knife with which he was slain, are now in the possession of Maj. S. L. McFadin, of Logansport. The name, in honor of Capt. Logan, a Shawanee chief, who lost his life while attesting his fidelity to the whites in November, 1812, in Ohio, was decided by a shooting match, and "port" was added to indicate its commercial importance. It now (1890) contains about 15,000 inhabitants.—Helm's Hist. Cass Co., p. 33.

Friday here; here we left Mr. Saylor, who has been very kind and pleasant on our journey.

On Saturday morning we left in the stage for Indianapolis. Capt. Mahon accompanied us. The road is very straight, a great part of the way through a dense forest; trees of immense size were constantly greeting us; the country is low and marshy; for the want of stones and earth, they are under the necessity of making their roads and bridges of split timber and poles, which makes traveling rough and unpleasant. The accommodations were tolerable for a new country.

We reached Indianapolis at 8 o'clock in the evening; stopped at Washington Hall, kept by E. Browning; a very good house and well kept. On Sunday morning there was a fire in the upper part of the town; one building was consumed without injuring any others. We went to the Methodist Church; heard an excellent sermon from the preacher in charge. Father left for Danville. Harriet and I went to Sabbath School, which is a very good one; in the afternoon the ordinances of Baptism and Sacrament were administered. On Monday morning we walked all round the town or city; it is the capital of Indiana. The public buildings are here; they look very well.

We left Indianapolis at 3 o'clock in the morning for Cincinnati. The tavern at which we were to dine was so much of a grog shop we concluded to fast for the present. They here changed teams for one that had run away a short time before; there were plenty of loungers to see the fun; we, however, escaped unhurt. We found a comfortable place to dine at Greensburg. We lodged at Napoleon; the dust made the traveling very unpleasant; it rose sometimes in clouds so much so as to intercept our view. We struck the Ohio River at Lawrenceburg, quite a pleasant town, and reached Cincinnati before dark; stopped at the Galt House. In the morning we, Harriet and I, walked all over the city, which is very pleasant and clean, very similar to Philadelphia, more so than any one I was ever in.

When we returned, father had engaged our passage up the Ohio on board the boat Royal; went on board not expecting the boat to start before afternoon or evening, but it started at 11 o'clock and we had not the opportunity of seeing any more of the city. We saw no more of Capt. Mahon and Mr. Bickford. We did not find any we knew at Cincinnati. The Ohio is very low; it is difficult for small boats to run. The weather very warm and dry; our boat was rather small and contracted for so many passengers; we found the company pleasant and agreeable.

October 11, we passed Maysville in the night; we passed Portsmouth at 2 o'clock; left some passengers and took some more; we ran aground several times. We reached Guyandotte on Saturday afternoon and several passengers went on shore. We laid here all night fast on a bar, from which they could not extricate us. The Captain and most of the crew and passengers engaged in playing cards and drinking, which made me quite sick, not being accustomed to anything of the kind. On Sunday morning the Forrest passed, a still lighter boat; they stopped a mile above us and sent a flat boat to take our baggage. Part of the passengers went on board, the others walked after, having landed with a good deal of difficulty. The Captain extorted from us the exorbitant price of $15.00 apiece, after having paid $7.50 to Guyandotte. So goes the world. We still met with difficulties in getting frequently on sand bars. Sometimes all the passengers except the ladies were on shore. Sometimes on the deck boat for hours together. We were much frightened. The steamboat swung against the keelboat, which struck a log; with the great weight upon it it broke in; we were afraid some of the passengers were hurt, but it proved better than our fears, although some of the deck passengers were cooking under the deck; when it fell they put out the fire, and we were soon all quiet.

When we came in sight of Wheeling the boat struck a rock and stove a hole in her bottom. The Captain turned her towards the shore, ordered her fires out, and she soon filled with water, but there was not much danger of drowning. We rode in a baggage cart up to the Virginia Hotel, where we found a house full. We had our lodging and breakfast; parted with our fellow passengers, who had become quite like old friends, being on board the boat a week together. We hired a hack, and in company with Mr. Evans, from Philadelphia, set out for Cadiz; we found the country very hilly and broken, yet rich and yielding abundant crops. We stopped to feed; I there missed my traveling bag; it was left at Wheeling; I wrote a note back and received it the next day. We reached Cadiz at 4 o'clock in the afternoon and found our friends all well and happy to see us; we stopped at Willis Bennett's. Cadiz is a flourishing town with a fine country around it; the town is on several hills, which does not make it so pleasant. I dislike the bituminous coal very much; it is so dirty; this country abounds in it; the hills are full. We talked of returning on Saturday; our friends would not consent, and we spent the Sabbath very pleasantly; we attended the Methodist Church. On Monday they sent us in a carriage to Steubenville. I was disappointed at not finding P. B. Patterson there; his health is poor and he has gone south; we passed him on the Ohio river.

On Tuesday we took stage for Pittsburg; we were here

again disappointed, as we expected to meet J. P. Dennis. They had arrived at Cincinnati after we left. Pittsburg is a rich manufacturing town, but not pleasant to live in on account of the dense smoke that is constantly settling over it. We here spent a day, and met with Mr. and Mrs. Dunlap. We were in the glass factory and museum. The sight of the museum is not worth much; I was disappointed.

October 23d, went on board the packet for Hollidaysburg; the canal passes through the Kiskiminetas salt works, which are on both sides of the river and canal; they were quite a curiosity to me. The hills, which in some places were almost perpendicular, afford coal; on the margin of the river they sink their shafts 70 or 90 feet deep and the coal is raised by steam. We reached the tunnel about 2 o'clock; it is a most stupendous piece of work; it is 907 feet through, and about one-half the distance it is arched. We reached Johnstown about 2 o'clock in the morning. We left in the cars at 5 o'clock in the morning; we came to the first inclined plane,* then through the tunnel, which is similar to the other, 901 feet through; the inclined planes are five up and five down; we breakfasted on the Allegheny mountain; we reached Hollidaysburg at 11 o'clock; went on board the Juniata packet, which started immediately for Harrisburg. In 38 miles there were 53 locks, which makes slow traveling. Capt. Voglesong was very kind and accommodating; he ran a mile to hail the Susquehanna boat that we might not be detained over Sunday, for which we shall ever hold him in grateful remembrance.

Mr. Wickes, a gentleman from Ohio, was our company.

---

* They traveled by the State Canal and crossed the Allegheny mountain on the Portage Railroad. By means of powerful stationary engines and cables the cars and boats were hauled up one plane and let down the other. The road was long since abandoned.

The boat in which we came to Northumberland went up the West Branch; we came up the North Branch; stopped a few minutes at Danville; saw Mr. and Mrs. Shoales. We reached Wilkes-Barre about 8 o'clock on Monday morning, Oct. 28th, having been absent seven weeks, with the exception of one day; traveled about 2000 miles; had uninterrupted good health; no accident befell us; the weather was unusually pleasant and we found our friends all well at home, and had been so during our absence, for which I shall ever feel grateful to Him whom the winds and seas obey. It cost us $387.69½.

HANNAH FELL BENNETT.*

Concerning this memorable visit, Harriet, now Mrs. Lewis, of Madison, N. Y., added her recollections as follows :

"On reaching the house we found our aunt seated in a chair, looking very much as represented in the water color portrait now in possession of Judge Bennett, with her two daughters standing by her."

Her father, Mr. Joseph Slocum, after the accustomed salutations, told his sister that he had brought his oldest and youngest children to see her. The coldness and reserve of the former visit were now entirely gone, and Frances expressed great joy upon the occasion of again seeing her brother, and particularly that he had brought his daughters so far to see her. The mother and daughters immediately commenced an animated conversation upon the subject of the family resemblances, which were observable. The old lady looking at her nieces earnestly, passed her hand down her cheeks, stopping the motion at the posterior point of her lower jaw. There is an unusual fullness and prominence at

---

*Mrs. Hannah Fell Bennett, author of this journal, died at Wilkes-Barre, Pa., Feb. 5, 1855, in the 53d year of her age.

that point of the Slocum face. Continuing, Mrs. Lewis said: "The preparations for dinner were soon commenced. They spread the table with a white cotton cloth, and wiped the dishes, as they took them from the cupboard, with a clean cloth. They prepared an excellent dinner of fried venison, potatoes, shortcake, and coffee. Their cups and saucers were small, and they put three or four tablespoonfuls of maple sugar in a cup. They were told our way is not to use so much sugar. They seemed very anxious to please, and would often ask, 'is that right?' The eldest daughter waited on the table, while her mother sat at the table and ate with her white relations. After dinner they washed the dishes and replaced them upon the shelves, and then swept the floor. We were surprised at these evidences of civilization, and on asking our aunt why they did these things, she made answer that her mother used to do so, and she had always done it, and taught it to her daughters. It was, therefore, a uniform rule in her house to wipe the dust from the dishes when they were put upon the table, and when the meal was concluded to wash and return them to the cupboard, and then to sweep the room.

"In the afternoon all left but Mr. Slocum, his daughters and Miller; the last remained till near night, when he returned. We strolled over the premises, and visited the burying ground. They raise a pole over the grave fifteen or twenty feet high, with a white cloth at the top, which remains until destroyed by time. The premises showed great skill and industry for savage life, and no little order and attention to comfort in its arrangements. The house was a double hut. A neighboring squaw came in to help do the work, and the Indian daughters kept close to their white cousins, and talked with them incessantly. They supposed

candles would be wanted, and to meet the emergency, the
squaw melted some tallow, twisted wicking on a stick, and
with a spoon poured the tallow down the wicks until quite a
respectable candle was produced.

"For supper they had the breast of a wild turkey stewed
with onions, quite a delicate dish. When they came to retire, the pillow, all there was in the house, was assigned to
Mr. Slocum by his Indian sister. They pay great respect to
age. They had six beds, principally composed of blankets
and other goods folded together. They were made of almost
everything. We slept sweetly, and after taking a comfortable
breakfast, commenced making preparations to return to Peru.

"After breakfast a white man came to purchase a steer,
and brought with him a colored man as an interpreter. He
could not trade for the want of the money, as he might move
away, and that would be the last of it. No business transac-
tion takes place in the family without the consent of Frances.
She usually makes the bargains herself.

"The colored man served so well in the capacity of an
interpreter that my father retained him for the purpose. My
aunt was more free in her communications through him than
she had been through Mr. Miller, and gave many circumstances in her history and recollections which she had not
previously given.

"They seemed anxious to tell their white relations as
much as possible about themselves, and to make as favorable
an impression as possible. They had made in the spring
eleven barrels of sugar."

The eldest daughter took a fancy to Miss Harriet Slocum,
dressed her in Indian costume, and said she looked like her
daughter who had been poisoned.

"Would I not make a nice squaw?" asked Harriet.

"Yes, beautiful squaw," replied her cousin, "will you be in the place of my daughter, and live with me?"

On being told that her friends could not spare her, she was satisfied. She seemed sensible that she was asking too much; but could the boon have been granted it would have been most grateful to her heart.

The brothers and sister had prevailed on Frances to have her portrait painted by George Winter, an artist then living at Logansport. It was executed in due time. Subsequently another was painted, and both are now in the possession of friends at Wilkes-Barre.

Before leaving Frances made an effort to prevail upon her brother Joseph to come and live with her; and not to be outdone by her brothers, who had made such liberal offers if she would come and live with them, she told Mr. Slocum that, if he would come to her village and live, she would give him half of her land, and this would have been no mean present. Her sincerity and earnestness in this proposition were affecting. No arrangement, however, could be made by which the brother and sister—so long separated, and to each other as dead, and now so mysteriously brought together and united in affection—could spend their remnants of life in the same neighborhood. They both bowed submissively to what was evidently the order of Providence, and tried to adjust their feelings to the separation.

The time for parting finally came, and as Frances, her daughters and Capt. Brouillette shook their relatives warmly by the hand, they gave them the most ample assurances of their high gratification with the visit, and the affection they had manifested for them in coming so far to see them. Capt. Brouillette gave Mr. Slocum the most ample assurances that he would take good care of his mother-in-law while she lived, and so far as known he sacredly carried out his promise.

This was the last time Mr. Joseph Slocum saw his sister, although he frequently heard from her down to the close of her life. His brother Isaac, however, who lived within a short distance of her home, took an active part in looking after her welfare, and visited her a number of times before she died.

The section of country where Frances lived at this time was in Miami County, which was erected March 1, 1834. It contains an area of 384 square miles, and as its soil is rich, and the land lies well, it enjoys the distinction of being one of the finest agricultural counties in Indiana. Peru, the seat of justice, was a rough, uninviting settlement at the time of the visit. At first it was known as Miamisport, and was started when the canal was being constructed. When the name was changed the place began to grow slowly, but it was a long time before it gave promise of amounting to much. It is now a prosperous little city, has a number of manufacturing industries, and contains many beautiful homes. There were no public roads at the time Judge Slocum and his daughters were there, excepting Indian paths, which in some places had been sufficiently widened to admit of the driving of wagons over them. To-day the country is noted for its fine roads and turnpikes, and the one running up the river and passing where the Indian villages stood, is especially fine, and affords a charming drive.

The Slocum homestead is now in Wabash County, being situated just across the Miami County line. Wabash County was organized in 1852, and the city of Wabash, now the seat of justice, was founded in 1849.

CHAPTER IX.

FRANCES PETITIONS CONGRESS TO BE PERMITTED TO REMAIN
AT HER OLD HOME—ELOQUENT SPEECH OF MR. BIDLACK—
CONGRESS GRANTS HER PRAYER—INDIANS DEPART.

AS IT was stipulated in the treaty of 1840 that the Miamis should abandon their homes on the Wabash in five years from the time of its ratification, there began to be much uneasiness manifested among many of the older members of the tribe as the time drew near for taking their departure. From a once powerful nation they had become weak and defenceless; they had disposed of their lands from time to time until they had nothing left; the records show that by their several treaties they had ceded an aggregate of 6,853,020 acres of land to the United States, and received in return in money and goods $1,261,707. They had been given in exchange 44,040 acres,* the aggregate value of which was $55,800, on which a few of their chiefs and head men lived. The remnant of the great tribe—the stragglers of a nation—must now prepare to move to their new reserve west of the Missouri in Kansas. They dreaded the day of departure. From time immemorial their people had dwelt in the valley of the Wabash. The graves of their ancestors were there, the endearing associations which cluster around once happy homes made it more difficult for them to sever the tie which had so long bound them to this section, and turn their faces westward. The hand of fate was against

---

* Hist. of the Upper Maumee Valley, Vol. 1, p. 42.

them, and however cruel it might seem, they must go. The
aged and infirm, unable to endure the fatigues of travel, must
die on the route and be buried by the wayside. Such reflec-
tions as these agitated their minds as the time for departure
drew near, and kept them in a constant state of excitement.
Many lingered about the graves of their fathers, mothers and
children, and wept bitter tears over their hard lot.

> " And they painted on the grave-posts
> Of the graves yet unforgotten,
> Each his own ancestral totem,
> Each the symbol of his household—
> Figures of the bear and reindeer,
> Of the turtle, crane, and beaver." *

Among those who mourned over the coming departure of
the tribe was Frances Slocum. She could not endure the
thought of making the journey, neither did she want her
children and grandchildren torn from her and hurried beyond
the great rivers. She was now over 72 years of age, and felt
that the end was near. She had been a wanderer nearly all
her life, and had endured great privations and sufferings in
the wilderness and on the plains. She prayed that this last
bitter cup might not be pressed to her lips. It was her earnest desire to be permitted to remain in her happy home on the
banks of the Mississinewa, and when she died—which must
be soon—be buried by the side of her chieftain husband and
children, on the beautiful knoll within sight of her humble
cabin. She appealed to her brothers Isaac and Joseph for
advice and assistance—all the others were dead. Her faithful sister Mary had just been laid in the tomb, and could no
longer sympathize with her in her distress. Frances was the
last one of the three sisters. Her surviving brothers were
old men, but they were not unmindful of their unhappy sister, and aided her all they could.

* Longfellow's Hiawatha.

It was finally decided to have her appeal to Congress and ask if she could not be exempted from the terms of the treaty, and, with her descendants, be allowed to remain on the reservation in Indiana which had been granted to her daughters. A petition was therefore drawn and signed by her children and grandchildren, and as it forms one of the most interesting features of this sad narrative, it is given herewith in full:

"*To the honorable the Senate and House of Representatives of the United States in Congress assembled:*

"Your memorialist, Frances Slocum, a resident of Wabash county, in the State of Indiana, would to your honorable body most respectfully represent:

"That at the age of six years, about the close of the revolutionary war, she was taken captive in the State of Pennsylvania by the Indians, and has ever since lived among them, and is now, and for the last thirty years has been, recognized as a member of the Miami tribe. That, from the time she was taken captive as aforesaid, she heard nothing of her white relatives and friends (the greater portion of whom reside at the place where she was taken, in the said State of Pennsylvania, and others in the State of Ohio, and the said State of Indiana) until about seven years since. That she has entirely lost her mother tongue, and can only enjoy the society of her adopted people, with whom she intermarried, and became the mother of a family, and with whose manners and customs she has assimilated. That she is informed that the greater portion of the Miamies will be obliged to emigrate to the home assigned them west of the Mississippi in the course of one or two years, where their annuities will thereafter be paid them. That she is too old to endure the fatigue of removing; and that, under any circumstances, she would deplore the necessity of being placed beyond the reach of her white relatives, who visit her frequently, and have extended their kindness towards her since she was discovered by them. That her children are the owners of a section of land granted to them by the treaty between the United States and said tribe of Indians of the sixth of November, A. D. 1838, who now reside upon and cultivate the same, and with whom your memorialist now lives; and that it is the wish and design of her children and their families, if it be the pleasure of the Government, to continue to reside upon and cultivate the same.

"Your memorialist further shows, that a portion of the annuities of said tribe, in pursuance of the 14th article of said treaty, is to be paid at Fort Wayne, after said tribe shall emigrate to the country assigned them west of the Mississippi; and that the payment of the annuities due your memorialist and her family at Fort Wayne or Peru, in said State, would not increase the expense or add any inconvenience to the Government of the United States.

"Your memorialist therefore prays that Congress may by law direct that the following persons, to wit:

1. Ke-ke-na-kush-wa,*	12. No-ac-co-mo-qua,
2. We-saw-she-no-qua,	13. Coch-e-no-qua,
3. Te-quoc-yaw,	14. Po-con-du-maw,
4. Ki-po-ki-na-mo-qua,	15. Tah-ki-qua,
5. Wa-pu-noc-she-no-qua,	16. Ki-ki-o-qua,
6. Ki-no-suck-qua,	17. Te-quoc-yaw, Jr.,
7. Ching-Shing-gwaw,	18. Soc-o-chu-qua,
8. Pe-tu-loc-a-te-qua,	19. Peem-y-o-ty-maw,
9, Sho-quang-gwaw,	20. So-eel-en-ji-sah, Jr.,
10. Waw-pop-e-tah,	21. Pun-ge-she-no-qua,
11. So-eel-en-ji-sah,	

children and grandchildren of your memorialist, as also your memorialist, and such children as they may hereafter have, shall hereafter receive their annuities at Fort Wayne, or at Peru, Indiana, as to your honorable body may seem most expedient and proper. And, as in duty bound, your memorialist will ever pray, &c.

FRANCES SLOCUM.

January 17, 1845."

---

* 1, Eldest daughter of Frances Slocum; 2, her youngest daughter, 3, Capt. Brouillette, husband of No. 1; 4, eldest daughter of Louis Godfroy; 5, his second daughter; 6, wife of Gabriel Godfroy; 7, one of the husbands of Frances' second daughter; 8, brother to No. 7, and afterwards the husband of his widow; 9, boy raised by Frances; 10, Peter Bondy; 11, Samuel Bondy, nephew of Peter; 12, cousin to Frances' daughter's children, and a woman; 13, daughter of No. 12; 14, daughter of No. 12; 15, daughter of No. 12; 16, daughter of No. 14; 17, son of No. 13; 18, sister to No. 17; 19, husband of No. 14; 20, son of No. 14; 21, daughter of No. 14. Very few of the foregoing signers are now living. The names are given as spelled in the petition.

"HOUSE OF REPRESENTATIVES,
January 30, 1845.

"DEAR SIR : I have just received your note in relation to the Slocum resolution. I thought of the objection mentioned by General Milroy, but the peculiarity of the application overcame with me that objection. I will not here relate what she has set forth in her petition, which you will see when you examine the case. The fact that the Government has given her children a reserve of a section of land implies a right in them to live on and enjoy it. Of this I entertain no doubt: they are by that act united with the soil, and this boon is giving them nothing more than other Miamies enjoy by the treaty. I will send you Mr. Cole's letter. Mr. Cole is known to me, and is a gentleman of high standing at Peru.

Yours, &c.,

S. C. SAMPLE.*

HON. A. S. WHITE." †

"PERU, January 16, 1845.

"DEAR SIR: I take the liberty of sending you the enclosed memorial, in the hope that you will give the matter your attention. It is a small matter, it is true, but it is one in which the subject of it feels a deep interest. You may have heard something of this Frances Slocum, whose history is briefly noticed in her memorial, as it attracted some attention at the time she was discovered by her friends; and a little volume of her life has appeared in print. She was taken, as she states, I think, by the Shawnee Indians, at the age of about six years, somewhere near Wyoming. Her friends made fruitless search for her for a great number of years, and she likewise for many years made every endeavor to return to them, but without effect. In the progress of time, she was sold to and became the wife of one of the head men of the Miamies, known as the deaf man, with whom she removed to the Mississinewa, where she has continued to reside for the last forty years. Her relatives still reside at or near the place where she was captured, and are among the most respectable families in that part of

---

* Hon. Samuel C. Sample represented the district in Congress, where the memorialists resided, from 1843 to 1845.

† Hon. Albert S. White was a member of Congress from Indiana from 1837 to 1839, and a U. S. Senator from 1839 to 1845. He filled several other high positions, and died in 1864.

the country. They discovered her through the instrumentality of Colonel Ewing, to whom she related what little she recollected of her early history. They visit her quite frequently, and it is upon this account, more than any other, that she does not wish to remove beyond the great river, where she feels confident she would never again see them. She says she has lived a life of hardships, and is now quite old, and wishes to spend the remainder of her days among her children, on their lands here; and she does not see why her great white father should not grant them the same privilege to remain here upon their lands, and receive their annuities here, as have been granted to some other families.

"I am well acquainted with the old lady, and all of her connexions which she alludes to, and feel authorized to say that they are respectable, honest, and, for Indians, uncommonly industrious people, and, in every sense of the word, good orderly citizens.

"For my own part, I can see no reason why any person should object to granting the prayer of her memorial. Certain families are required to be paid here by treaty, and it cannot increase the expense to the Government, or add any inconvenience, to pay her and her connexions at the same time and place. It is a matter of no consequence to the Government, but is everything to her. I have no doubt she would more willingly meet death, than either to be obliged to remove west of the Mississippi, beyond the reach of her white relatives, or to be left here alone by her Indian relatives. You will more readily perceive, from the memorial and what I have already written, what is required to be done, than I can tell you. We wish the bill to provide for the payment of the annuities due her, and those persons named in the memorial, and any children they may have, at this place or at Fort Wayne, forever hereafter, or at least until they or any of them see proper to emigrate to their possessions west. It is desired, in order that no misunderstanding may occur, that the bill contain all of the names.

"Please let me know what the prospect is, as soon as your convenience will permit after you receive this.

Most truly yours, &c.,

ALPHONSO A. COLE.*

Hon. S. C. Sample."

*Mr. Cole was a well known member of the Miami County Bar, and probably drew the petition at the request of the brothers of Frances.

On the 28th of January, 1845, Mr. Cave Johnson, (Tennessee) from the Committee on Indian Affairs, reported a joint resolution* for the benefit of Frances Slocum, her children and grandchildren, of the Miami tribe of Indians, and it was read a first and second time.

Hon. Benjamin A. Bidlack, of Pennsylvania, who represented the Wyoming district in Congress at that time, said he hoped "no motion or resolution would intervene to prevent the passage of this resolution. The memorialist was taken prisoner in the Valley of Wyoming at an early age, during the trials and difficulties to which the early settlers were subjected.

"Her relatives are among the most worthy and meritorious of my constituents—they are my neighbors and friends; they searched after the captive with zealous and praiseworthy efforts and diligence, from the time of her capture until within a few years, and they have found her in the condition set forth in the memorial and report. The incidents set forth and connected with her eventful history would afford a beautiful theme for elucidation and remark.

"But as debate is not now in order, I will not trespass on the indulgence and courtesy of the House. What I desire is not to make a speech, but to ask the unanimous consent of the members for the immediate passage of the resolution.

"If the resolution is sent to the committee of the whole I fear it will never be reached, and this earnest request of the memorialist will never be reached and granted.

"The proposition is intended to extend to her as the widow of an Indian chief, the same privileges in relation to the payment of annuities due her and her family, and are pro-

---

* Cong. Globe, Vol. XIV., Sec. Ses. 28th Cong., p. 208.

vided for by treaty stipulation in regard to certain of the Miami chiefs.

"Frances Slocum was taken from her white friends when a child. She is now desirous of dying among her red friends where she has lived for half a century, without being compelled to remove west of the Mississippi. Let her first and last request be granted.

"The resolution then passed."

This is the eloquent address which modern writers have been in the habit of attributing to Hon. John Quincy Adams. But the most thorough search of the records of Congress fail to show that the venerable and distinguished ex-President ever made a remark relating to the petition of Frances Slocum. He was old and feeble at that time, and three years after the introduction of the joint resolution he was stricken down and died in the House of Representatives.

It is unaccountable how the credit of making the address came to be given to Mr. Adams, when it is readily seen that the proper person to speak to the joint resolution was the representative of the district in which Frances lived when she was captured, where her parents were buried, and where many of her most deeply interested relations still lived. The remarks of Mr. Bidlack,* who also came of a historic and distinguished family, while not elaborate or diffusive, were eloquent, impressive and appropriate, and aroused such a strong feeling of sympathy for the memorialist that no one interposed an objection, and the resolution passed unanimously.

We next hear of the joint resolution in the Senate, when

---

* Hon. Benjamin A. Bidlack was born at Wilkes-Barre; was elected a representative to the 27th Congress as a Democrat, and was re-elected to the 28th Congress, receiving 5,007 votes against 2,716 votes for Willits, Whig, serving from May 31, 1841 to March 3, 1845, when he was appointed Charge d' Affaires to Columbia, May 14, 1845, and died in office at Bogota, Feb. 29, 1849.

Mr. White, Chairman of the Committee on Indian affairs, to whom it had been referred, made the following report under date of Feb. 21, 1845 :

"That the joint resolution provides for the payment in Indiana of the annuities due this family, instead of requiring them to receive payment with the nation in the emigrant territory west of the Mississippi River. The reasons assigned are that former treaties have made similar provisions in favor of other families of this nation ; that lands have been by treaty reserved to them in Indiana, to the personal enjoyment of which they have a right that cannot be embarrassed by requiring them to go west of the Mississippi for their annuities ; and, thirdly, that the petitioner is by birth a white woman, who more than forty years ago, in her infancy, was captured by the Indians, transferred to their country, lost her mother tongue, affiliated and intermarried with the Miamies, has by this marriage reared a large family of children, (who are named in the joint resolution,) but some seven years ago was for the first time discovered by her white relations, (who reside in Pennsylvania,) whom she has refused to accompany, because her whole nature has been changed by her strange destiny; and life out of the woods, and away from her husband and children, would have no charms. Yet these white relatives do frequently visit her, and minister to her wants, which they could not do if she were removed six hundred miles to the west.

"The committee cannot resist the force of these reasons, although in a conversation with General Milroy, the late intelligent agent of the Miamies, he expressed a fear that the adoption of the joint resolution might disincline other Miamies to remove to their new homes.

"This case has such a thrilling interest, that the committee beg leave to append to their report the petition itself, with the letter of Mr. Cole that accompanied it.

"They recommend that the resolution be adopted."

On the 3d of March, 1845, the joint resolution passed in the following form :

" A joint resolution* for the benefit of Frances Slocum and her children and grandchildren of the Miami tribe of Indians.

"Be it resolved, &c. That the portion or shares of the annuities

* Stat. at Large, Vol. VI., p. 942.

or other moneys, which are now or may hereafter become payable to the Miami tribe of Indians, shall be hereafter and forever payable to them and their descendants at Fort Wayne or Peru, or such other place in the State of Indiana as the Secretary of War shall direct, viz: [The name of Frances Slocum and all the others attached to her memorial of January 17, 1845, are then recited.]

"And further resolved. That if any of the aforesaid Indians shall hereafter remove to the reservation of the Miamis west of the Mississippi, no portion or share of such annuities shall be paid to such person so removing."

The prompt action of Congress in granting the prayer of Frances Slocum pleased her greatly, and removed a load of anxiety from her mind, which was weighing her down in her old age. She and her descendants were now free to remain at their Indiana homes, whilst those not exempted were compelled to depart. The great flight commenced in 1846, and the sad scenes and incidents of the removal are vividly recalled by many witnesses yet living in that part of Indiana. Under guides and a military escort the long Indian train moved across the country, over the plains of Illinois and Iowa to the new reservation provided for them in Kansas. As they left their cabins and favorite places of resort on the Wabash and Mississinewa, they cast long, lingering looks behind, and sorrowfully bade adieu to the scenes of their childhood forever.

Their deserted cabins stood for many years as relics of a race now in rapid decline, and finally tumbled into ruin. On departing they left hundreds of dogs behind, because they were unable to care for them, and they remained about the deserted cabins until starvation drove them forth, and for a long time the white settlers were greatly pestered by the hordes of hungry curs which overran the country like ravenous wolves. In course of time the surviving Miamis drifted down to the Indian Territory, and there a remnant still lives. They have preserved the traditions of their ancestors, and occasionally those who are able, make pilgrimages to the Wabash to visit the graves of their fathers and relatives, and linger for a short time among their friends who were permitted to remain behind, when they return and try to forget the sad days of the past.

Residents of Peru and Logansport, who occasionally visit the Indian Territory, say that they often meet descendants of the Miamis, and they always anxiously inquire after their friends on the Wabash. It is a marked trait of the Indian character for them to hanker after the scenes of their childhood, and whenever they can do so, they return and visit those places. And in this respect they do not differ from their white brethren, for where is the man or woman, in the language of the poet, "with soul so dead," who does not love the land of his or her birth.

One thing that caused such a bitter feeling among the Miamis who were compelled by the terms of the treaty to depart, was that certain favored members of the tribe were permitted to remain. The ignorant never could understand why this was so, and they looked upon them with feelings of envy.

The descendants of Frances Slocum and the other favored families probably do not number two hundred souls to-day; and through intermarriages and admixture with the whites they are rapidly disappearing. It is noticed, however, that where the French blood predominates there are evidences of more stamina and thrift in the race; but outside of this the tendency is downward. In a few years it will be impossible to find a Miami of pure blood on the Wabash. Among the Indians nothing seems to cause their degeneration quicker than contact with civilization, and from this cause they are rapidly disappearing. Extinction seems to be their destiny.

J

CHAPTER X.

DEATH OF FRANCES—THE CLOSING SCENE—CHRISTIAN RITES
AT THE GRAVE—PLACE OF BURIAL—DEATH OF DAUGHTER
—A CURIOUS INDIAN CUSTOM—MORE ABOUT HER CAPTURE.

WHEN FRANCES was fully convinced that she would be permitted to remain at her old home, where she had lived so long, and where she wished to die, her mind became more tranquil. The sorrowful scenes incident to the departure of many of her Indian friends and acquaintances, however, had a depressing effect on her mind, and it was some time before she fully recovered her equanimity. She was now about seventy-three years of age, but on account of the hardships and exposures of nearly sixty years, she had the appearance of being over eighty. Her constitution, originally rugged and strong, was so badly shattered that when she began to decline, she lost her vitality rapidly and became quite feeble.

During the thirty or more years she had lived on the Mississinewa, she had, through good management, economy and frugality, accumulated much personal property, and was reputed rich by those who knew her circumstances. Her son-in-law, Peter Bondy, says that at one time she owned 300 Indian ponies, and had cattle, hogs and chickens in large numbers. The desire to accumulate was inherited from her parents. It was an Anglo Saxon trait which did not belong to the Indians, though she had through training and association acquired their manners and customs.

After the departure of the Miamis, there was a rush of speculators to acquire their lands, and new settlers soon began to arrive and make improvements all around the Slocum reservation of 686 acres. And as the country rapidly filled up, extra vigilance was required to guard her stock and prevent encroachments on her premises. Many of her ponies were stolen from time to time, as horse thieves abounded in those days, and there were plenty of adventurers who did not consider it a crime to appropriate the property of the "white woman," whom they regarded as possessing such an abundance of ponies that she did not need all of them, and therefore would not miss a few head.

The presence of this class of neighbors was not calculated to promote the comfort and quiet of her latter days. Peck informs us that she was, in fact, still suspicious that she and her family might at last be robbed of the home which the government had just granted them by the terms of the treaty, as the patent for the land had not yet been issued. With these fears on her mind she communicated with her brothers and begged Joseph to come and protect her from the frauds which she apprehended were likely to be practiced upon her. Owing to his age he could not leave his home at Wilkes-Barre and take up his residence in a new country. She then sent for her brother Isaac, who resided at Bellevue, Ohio, to come to her. He promptly obeyed the summons, when she informed him that she wanted his son George to come and live with her. The arrangements were made, and he came at her request and looked after her affairs.

With the departure of the majority of her associates a new order of things was established; and despairing of the return of the scenes of the past, she sighed for release from the associations and vices of civilization which she witnessed around her. Contrasting the freedom and the romance of savage life with the thirst for gain and the overreaching policy of a white frontier settlement, she thought she had truly fallen upon evil times, and was really weary of life. The prestige of her character and her name had departed with her tribe, and she was looked upon simply as a favored old Indian woman, whose claims to equal rights with her white neighbors were entitled to very little respect.

In her younger days, says Mr. Bondy, Frances was extremely active and strong. She could handle the lariat with great expertness, and it was no trouble for her to lasso a pony and bring him to bay. She was also fleet of foot, and to use his own words, "could run as swiftly as a man." Her physical strength and powers of endurance were great, which were largely acquired by her long and active outdoor life. Her health was generally good, and it was only the weight of years that bore her down.

Soon after the last visits of her eastern friends she had a new log house built on the hill a few hundred yards in rear of the old residence, which stood on the brink of the river. The former, according to a painting by George Winter, was a low log building with clapboard roof. The door was cut in the centre, and there was a window on each side of it. The half story contained a loft, which was used for the storage of goods, and probably for sleeping purposes. A short distance to the right, and near where the great spring of pure water bubbles from underneath the hill, stood another log building. These, with a few outhouses, and several cabins on the other side of the river, constituted the "Deaf Man's Village." On the opposite side of the river from the house is a high rocky bluff which shuts off the wind and storms. It is still covered with timber. At the time of the visits of her brothers the Indian path leading from Godfroy's trading post came up to the river just below the bluff, where there was a ford. It is not in use now, but it is easily pointed out. A fine modern road now runs along the hillside near where her last residence stood, and is much traveled. Nothing now remains to mark the site of the original log cabin but a small pile of stones, which belonged to the chimney. When the author visited the place last, in June, 1890, the ground was covered with a luxuriant growth of weeds.

The new residence stood in a commanding position on the hill, and afforded a lovely view up and down the river. Frances had only moved into this house, and was fairly settled when she was taken with her last illness. In her declining years she was blessed with the presence of both her daughters, their husbands, and her devoted nephew, Rev. George Remington Slocum, all of whom looked after her kindly and administered to her wants. Her last illness was not of long duration, but she declined rapidly and became very feeble. She realized that the end was near, was resigned and happy, and welcomed the approach of death. She refused all medical aid, declaring that as her people were gone she wished to live no longer. The end finally came on the 9th of March, 1847, and the spirit of the weary wanderer was at rest. In describing the last moments of her life, Peter Bondy informed the author that she died peacefully and calmly with her head resting on his arm, in the presence of her daughters and friends. Such was the closing scene in the life of this remarkable woman; the sweet murmur of the waves of the river gently blended with the music of the angelic choir which waited to bear her weary spirit to the Happy Land.

> " Now bloom the hedge and prairie flow'rs,
> And sunlight falls in golden show'rs,

Where Ma-con-a-qua's sandl'd feet,
In autumn chill and summer's heat,
Trod lithsome through the forest glades.
And while Miami's hordes reside
Beyond the Mississippi's tide ;
Her line, with nobler blood alli'd
In onward tread of Time's decades,
By mystic enterweaving strains
Will know no more distinctive's grades,
But kinsmen all with kindred veins,
As under Eden's blissful shades,
The patriarch of Israel's flock
Asenath's Nile-born sons caress'd ;
He grafted them on Judah's stock,
And with adopting blessing bless'd,
And He, exalted pow'r Supreme,
Who mingled in one common stream
The blood of Jordan and the Nile,
Shall in His providence erewhile
With Saxon warp and woof entwine
The threads of Ma-con-a-qua's line.

" Down where the meadow lark sings,
And the climbing jasmine clings ;
Where the daisies grow,
And hyacinths blow,
And the air is perfume
With the red clover's bloom,
Hid by the prairie's soft mantle of green
Peacefully sleeps the Miami queen.
Above her are sweet symphonies—
The bird song and hum of the bees,
The sheen of the sun on the plain,
And zephyr's enchanting refrain,
A murmuring hymn in the trees.

" Long, long may the dew of the morn,
(Bright pearls of the beautiful Giver),
The green mound with spangles adorn
Above the lost one by the river,
And *she*, of the grief-burden'd breast

Whose blossom was blown from the stem,
  In the home of the blest,
  The glad haven of rest,
  At last shall regain
  And forever retain
Her Frances, her darling, a beautiful gem."*

The tenacity with which she clung to the spot where she died, and her obstinate refusal to leave it for the associations of civil society, is one of the prominent facts in her wonderful story, and shows how deeply the Indian character had been grounded in her mind. Her ancesters for a hundred years before her birth had been reared in the Quaker faith, and her father was taught the same doctrine and belief, but through long years of captivity with a savage tribe, all trace of the faith of her people was effectully eradicated, and she acquired all the tastes, habits and desires of the Indian, and died reverencing the name of her adopted people.

Her age, as nearly as can be ascertained, was 74 years. It might have been a few days less or a few days more. This cannot be accurately determined, because the day in March, 1773, when she was born in Rhode Island, has been lost. And as she was carried away when about four years and seven months old, she had been a captive and dwelt with the savages for a little more than sixty-nine years! But as she had been discovered ten years before her death, she had enjoyed the civilizing influences of Christianity for a short time. Through the ministrations of her nephew, Rev. George R. Slocum, who had lived near her for several months, much of the darkness of barbarism, which had clouded her mind so long, was dispelled, and she came to partly realize and experience the beneficent influences of Christianity.

She received a Christian burial, a prayer being made at

*Caleb Earl Wright's Frances Slocum.

the house and her remains conducted to the grave by a Baptist clergyman and her nephew.   The name of the clergyman has not been positively ascertained, but it is believed Rev. James Babcock was the man.   According to Helm's History of Wabash County, he was the first minister of that denomination to begin preaching in that section of the country.   A Baptist Society was organized several years before 1859, when the first church* was built.   Mr. Slocum may have been instrumental in founding the society, as he came there in 1846.

The remains of Frances Slocum were laid at rest in the Indian burial ground a few yards from the house where she died, by the side of her husband and two infant boys.   At the request of her brother Isaac, her funeral sermon was preached in the Baptist Church at Bellevue, Ohio, by Elder Eaton, from the text found in Psalms lxix., 8: "I am become a stranger unto my brethren, and an alien unto my mother's children."   No more appropriate words could have been selected for the occasion, and the lesson was as beautiful and impressive as the sermon was able and pathetic.

The cemetery where her ashes repose is located on the crowning summit of a beautiful knoll, at the edge of a clump of heavy timber, and commands a fine view.   It contains half an acre of ground, and there the ashes of a large number of Indians now mingle with the soil.   A substantial fence encloses the sacred premises, and by the terms of the will of O-zah-wah-shing-qua, the youngest daughter, it must be kept forever as a burial place for the descendants of the family. There are a number of marble headstones erected to mark the burial places of those who have since died, but the ma-

---

* Among the first members of the Antioch Missionary Church were: George R. Slocum, Capt. Brouillette, Peter Bondy and wife and William Godfroy. Peter Bondy appears as a trustee.—Helm's Hist. Wabash County, pp. 476-7.

jority of the graves are unmarked by stick or stone. When the writer first visited the place in the autumn of 1889, a grandson (Judson C. Bondy) pointed out the spot where the remains of Frances were laid. After searching for a few minutes, and carefully noting the headstone of his mother's grave, he selected a depressed spot, and brushing away the tangled mass of grass and brambles, sorrowfully said: "Here is grandmother's grave!" Although she had been dead for more than forty years, and her history conceded to stand alone in strangeness of circumstance and detail, not a memorial stone, however plain or humble, has been reared to mark her quiet resting place! *

Frances Slocum was a remarkable woman. The strongly marked features of her face, as shown in her portraits, indicate firmness. Her intellectual faculties were well developed, and had it been her fortune to have been permitted to remain among her kindred and receive an education, she would have risen above mediocrity and made her mark in civilized society. That she possessed a logical mind is shown by the reasons she advanced why she could not return to civilized life, when her brothers insisted on her doing so. She was noted for firmness and decision of character, and she always commanded the respect and admiration of the rude people among whom her lot was cast. They not only deferred to her in matters of business, but honored her as a superior person. According to her testimony they always treated her well, which had so won her love and esteem that she was contented and happy in her Indian life, and had no desire to leave them. Her fine growth of chestnut brown hair was a novelty among the Indians, and

---

* It was recently decided by the descendants, children and grandchildren, of Hon. Joseph Slocum, brother of Frances, to erect a suitable monument over her grave. This will be done in the spring of 1891, and the long delayed tribute to her memory will be an accomplished fact.

they admired it almost to the point of worship. Peter Bondy
says there was a peculiar spot on the side of her head in
which the hair was redder than at any other part, and it was
the first to turn gray. She was affectionate and took a deep
interest in her children and grandchildren, and prayed that
they might never be called on to endure the trials and hardships she had undergone. Her long captivity caused her to
lose her mother tongue, and she died without fully recovering the language of her childhood.

The eldest daughter, Ke-ke-se-qua,* wife of Capt. Brouillette, who was ill at the time of the death of her mother, was
so prostrated by the sad occurrence, that she died March 13,
1847, four days later, and joined her in the Spirit Land.
She was forty-seven years old, having been born about 1800.
These two deaths occurring so closely together, caused much
sorrow among the relatives of the deceased, and they mourned
deeply over their loss.

Ke-ke-se-qua, or Cut Finger, was married twice, but the
name of her first husband is unknown. He was a Miami Indian, and probably died soon after marriage. He left one
daughter, who lived to the age of seventeen or eighteen years,
when, it is alleged, she was poisoned by the friends of a
lover, because her mother would not consent to her marrying
him, on account of his being a lazy, worthless fellow. And
it was for this daughter that the mother and grandmother
were mourning when their eastern friends first visited them.
How long she remained a widow is not known, but it must
have been for several years.

---

* There is a great dissimilarity among writers in spelling Indian names,
the difficulty being in expressing the proper sound. By some her name is
spelled Ke-ke-na-kush-wa, by others kick-e-se-qua. It can readily be seen
how easily it is to express the same meaning by the word Ke-ke-se-qua, and
the latter method has been followed in this work.

KE-KE-SE-QUA---NANCY BROUILLETTE.

She next married Captain Jean Baptiste Brouillette, a half-breed Frenchman. This union, which was without issue, seems to have been a happy one. The Captain was attentive and devoted to his wife, and looked carefully after the wants of his mother-in-law, for whom he appears to have had great respect. When Ke-ke-se-qua died she had been married to Brouillette about thirteen years. Little is known of her history and character. She was either born at Fort Wayne, or in the Osage village, of which her father, the Deaf Man, was war chief. That she was warmly attached to her mother there seems to be no doubt, for we find her in her company all the time. She was present at the interviews which took place with her eastern friends, and was foremost in interposing objections to her mother's going to Wilkes-Barre to visit her brother. It is believed that she inherited much of the ability and sagacity of her mother, and died a thorough Indian. Born and raised among the Miamis, and taught their language, manners and customs, she could not have been anything else. She did not live long enough to become sufficiently acquainted with her white relatives to entirely change her views regarding the white people, or to embrace their religious beliefs and habits of life. She only spoke the Miami language, and had little opportunity of learning much about the country and the customs of the people, as she appears to have been so closely attached to her home on the Mississinewa that she traveled little. She was buried by the side of her chieftain father and beloved mother, and like them her grave is unmarked by stone or tablet.

Soon after the death of Frances Slocum and her daughter, a number of prominent members of the Miami tribe, who still lingered in the valley of the Wabash, petitioned Congress for authority to remain on the lands which had been granted them at the treaty of 1838. Their petition was favorably entertained, for on the 1st of May, 1850, Congress passed the following resolution: *

"A resolution to extend the provisions of a joint resolution for the benefit of Frances Slocum and her children and grandchildren of the Miami tribe of Indians, approved March 3, 1845.

" *Resolved,* by the Senate and House of Representatives of the United States of America in Congress assembled, That the provisions of the above mentioned joint resolution be and the same are hereby extended to the following persons and their families and descendants, to wit:

Me-zo-quah,	Ko-as-see,
Pe-che-wah, (John B. Rich-	Ah-mac-con-ze-quah,
O-san-diah, [ardville.)	Wah-kit-e-mung-quah,
Al-lo-lah, (Black Raccoon,)	Young Revoir, alias Shap-pe-
Waw-pe-mun-waw, (Joe	Peter Langlois, [ne-maw,
Seek, [Richardville,)	Elizabeth Langlois.

who are residents of the State of Indiana."

After the death of Frances and her daughter, Captain Brouillette continued to reside at the old homestead, as he inherited a share in the estate of his wife, who was a tenant in common with her sister, in whom the title for the land was vested. He was active, industrious and kind-hearted, and so far as known, was free from bad habits in the latter part of his life. He still gave some attention to agriculture, and tilled his fields of corn in an advanced method to that usually followed by Indians. Laying some claim to the practice of the healing art, he did much towards alleviating the distress of the sick, and made himself useful in the settlement.

The history of the nephew, Rev. George Remington Slocum, who came to live with his aunt, at her request, and did such good missionary work among her people, is best told in

---

* Stat. at Large, Vol. IX., p. 806.

an obituary notice which appeared in *The Witness*, a Baptist paper published at Indianapolis, under date of February 21, 1861. It says:

"George was the youngest son of Isaac Slocum, and was only two years old when his father settled at Bellevue, Ohio. While the father strove with many difficulties common to a new country, the mother, who was a Christian woman belonging to the Baptist denomination, sought the spiritual interests of her children. Her Godly conversation and spiritual hymns were not forgotten. George always remembered his mother's teaching. Her voice seemed the sweetest to him of any he ever heard. At the age of sixteen he lost his mother.* This made a deep impression on his mind, and her teachings resulted in his joining the Baptist church. Anterior to this his aunt, Frances Slocum, was found living on the Indian Reserve near Peru.

"In 1845, as George, in pursuit of his business, was to pass through Peru, he decided to stop and visit his aunt. She received him very kindly, and requested him to come again; but he found her and her Indian associates in perfect heathenism. They knew not that there was a Sabbath, or God of the Sabbath. His religious feelings were interested for their spiritual welfare, and he resolved to visit them again. In the autumn of the same year he spent a week with them, during which he tried to teach them the importance of industry and frugality. The red men laughed at the idea of an 'Indian working. The business of Indians was to hunt.'

---

* She died September 16, 1839, from injuries received by being thrown from the wagon against a stump by frightened horses. Her name was Elizabeth, and she was a daughter of Abel and Elizabeth (Hurlbut) Patrick, of Kingston, Luzerne County, Pa., and formerly of Norwalk, Connecticut, where she was born April 26, 1780. She left twelve children—eight sons and four daughters—and George Remington was the youngest of the family. —Slocums in America, p. 224.

'Oh but you must work,' said he. 'Do you not see that your hunting ground is being settled by the white men? Soon there will be no game. Come, I will go with you to-day and we will see how much corn we can gather.' Thus, by example as well as precept, he won them along from their indolence and moral darkness, to habits of industry and a knowledge of Christianity.

" Early in the spring of 1846 his aunt sent for her brother Isaac to come and see her, as she had important business with him. On his arrival at her house, he found her business with him was to have him give George to her, to be her son, as she termed it. She said: 'Many of my white relatives have visited me, but I like George best!' Her brother said: "My other sons have left me; George is the youngest and last; I need him with me on my farm; but this my most cherished plan I give up. George may come if he is willing!'

"With much joy beaming from her features she said, 'Thank you, my brother; you shall have my best horse, saddle and bridle. Go tell him to come, for I need him so much.'

"Isaac went home and told the story. The result was that in November, 1846, George took his wife and two young daughters and removed to the Miami Indian reserve, then a wilderness. George and his wife had been baptized one month, and to leave their pastor, church and relatives was no small trial. Having been used to refined society, too, they often looked back to their loved home with longing. But here was work. Great things were to be achieved. A remnant of a once powerful nation of people was to be brought into the ranks of civilization—to be taught agriculture, and to learn the ways of life. The aunt died March 9, 1847, leaving them only her blessing.

"Mr. Slocum seemed not to let an opportunity slip of improving the minds of the Indians. Six years passed away before he saw any practical impression that his labors for their spiritual improvement had made. Then Brouillette, a son-in-law of his aunt, came to him asking to sign the temperance pledge for one year. One year elapsed and he had been faithful to the pledge; but at the end of the time he was induced to drink, and got very drunk! He came home in the night from Peru, crossed the river three times, banks full and ice floating down; lost his riding whip and cap, got home at length, but almost perished with cold. In the morning, after having slept off the effects of the liquor, he went to see his counsellor and friend, and addressed him as follows: 'George, my friend, I want you to write another pledge. Make it strong for ten years. I think I shall not live longer than that, considering my present age!' He wrote a pledge, and as Brouillette signed it, standing up, he raised his hand and said: 'Now call God to witness that I no more get drunk!' George administered the oath, and the once drunken Indian warrior ever kept his pledge. It was two years after this before he joined the church, but he always dated his conviction back to that time, when George read to him from the Bible and portrayed to him the dangers he had passed through, and the goodness of the Lord towards him in not suffering him to be drowned in the raging stream. It made a lasting impression on his mind. Peter Bondy, also another son-in-law of Frances, dates his conviction of sin to a reproof in a conversation with George. Thus he led them along from year to year. He was greatly rejoiced when he saw the work of grace in their hearts, and thanked the Lord for what he had accomplished.

"During his last illness in 1859, Brouillette went to see him. The stamp of death was already upon his brow. He went to his bedside, took George's hand in both of his own and said, while tears fell fast, 'O my brother! my brother! must we part? must we part?' George turned his eyes calmly upon him and said: 'My dear brother Brouillette, it is the Lord's will; it must be so. His will be done!' Then he began to talk to him in Miami, and told him above all things to be faithful in his ministry. 'O,' said he, 'my brother in the Lord, be not again shaken, but be firm and strong in the doctrines of your Divine Master. Follow the teachings of the Holy Spirit and strive to meet me in heaven.' Then his strength failed him, and he could say no more for a time. Brouillette sat down, and after a little while kneeled down and prayed most earnestly for the Lord to restore his dear friend and helper in the Lord. But the time seemed to have come and the decree to have gone forth that he must be gathered to his fathers, and prayer could not prevail. The most earnest petition of his wife was only answered by a calm, resigned feeling to God's holy will. A short time before his spirit's departure, as he was reclining his head on his wife's shoulder, she said: 'My dear husband, it is very hard to part with you; I would that I could go with you!' He turned his face towards her, and impressing a kiss upon her cheek, said: 'It cannot be; the Lord has willed it otherwise.' His lips were then cold as the marble that now stands over his grave. Soon after he turned to a friend who stood near and whispered: 'You understand my business better than any other man; help my wife to settle my business, and treat her as a sister.' They then laid him down and with a sweet smile on his features, the impress of heavenly peace, the spirit immediately took its flight. He died January 28, 1860. This friend of the red man is gone, but his name and his work still live.''

> '' His epitaph is graven well on stone,
> But better, the savage hearts he won.''

Dr. Charles E. Slocum, the genealogist, in a letter to the author, says:

"He must have been a strong man in his religious character, and persevering withal. He resided in Rochester, N. Y., for a time after marriage, and there he and his wife joined the Washingtonian Temperance Society; and probably it was largely through his successful efforts to check the intemperate tendencies of the Indians, that he won their confidence. They soon recognized his honesty of purpose and looked upon him as a strong tower of refuge in time of trouble. It was so with Frances. When the Indians returned from the trading post intoxicated and boisterous, she would pass the night at his house.

"George arrived at Reserve with his family November 20, 1846, and at first occupied a cabin near the river. Continued rains raised the river about the cabin, and Frances took the family to her house, and would not permit them to return until everything was well dried and renovated.

"There was practical missionary work. He taught by example as well as by precept. He was self-sustaining. He cleared land and cultivated it, and induced some of the Indians to do likewise."

Mary Cordelia Slocum, a daughter of the deceased missionary—now Mrs. L. G. Murphy, of Xenia, Indiana—thus writes concerning herself and her curious experience with Frances Slocum and her descendants:

"I was born at Bellevue, Huron County, Ohio, February 7, 1846, and was married January 1, 1872, at our farm at Seaton Ford, Waltz* Township, Wabash County, Indiana. My husband built a house at the little village of Peoria, near where Frances lived, and there we resided for some time.

---

* So named in memory of Lieut. Frederick Waltz, who was killed at the battle of the Mississinewa December 12, 1812. Hist. Wabash Co., p. 465.

"There is one peculiarity about my hair—it is like that of my great grandfather, a dark auburn. Frances Slocum's hair was the same shade. Like her I have a light brown spot on the back of my head. This was one of the peculiar marks by which her brothers and sister identified her. She thought I resembled her very much, and just before she died she gave me her name, 'Mah-cones-quah.' And after her death her children and grandchildren, sons-in-law, and all of the relatives, looked on me the same as if I was her. Indians never allow their relatives to die. They will have some one to take the place of the deceased, who they think looks like them. I was only nine months old when her daughter (Mrs. Bondy) commenced calling me mother, or Mingiah, (Miami for mother,) and Ma-co-mah, grandmother, as long as I can remember. Gray-haired sons-in-law of Mrs. Bondy call me Ma-co-mah. They always held her memory in such reverence. There was a captive woman married to White Wolf, adopted in Frances' place. She was near her age, and lived a number of years afterwards. They called her Mingiah, because they wanted some one to be her, so that she would never die. That was why I was chosen. My parents never liked it, and tried to discourage them, but they were unmovable, and now call me Mingiah."

In this statement we have further evidence of one of the reasons why the Indians were so anxious to retain Frances Slocum, and therefore guarded her with such vigilance and care. It was on account of her peculiar and luxuriant hair. And that this peculiarity should have already run through three generations is a question for the consideration of ethnologists. The superstitious custom of having the dead represented by some living person who bears the strongest resemblance to the deceased, is one of the strange beliefs of these people; but as it is of pagan origin, it will have little weight with the enlightened of to-day. The information conveyed by Mrs. Murphy, however, is of very great importance and adds materially to the interest of the narrative, by describing a strange custom still so religiously adhered to by a race now nearly extinct.

Mrs. Eliza O. Slocum, mother of Mrs. Murphy, who now resides at Magnolia, Iowa, in a letter received too late to be incorporated in the chapter on speculations concerning the wanderings of Frances after her capture—and who, from association with her, had ample opportunities of learning much of her history from her own lips—gives several facts which are of such great value that they cannot be omitted. They are, therefore, condensed and inserted here:

Mrs. Slocum says that the three Delaware Indians who invaded Wyoming Valley in November, 1778, "came for the purpose of stealing a child for their chief (?) who had lost by death a loved daughter. Then, as now, the Indians recognized the superiority of the white race, therefore they sought a white girl for their captive." When the attack was made on the Kingsley boys, and Mrs. Slocum was attracted to the door by the sound of the gun, and began interceding for her son, whom an Indian was in the act of dragging away, "little Frances came and stood by her mother in the door, and when the Indian saw her he pushed the boy toward his mother, caught up Frances and fled to a cave." From this place of concealment Frances informed her that some time during the day she "saw her father and eight soldiers hunting them." That the pursuing party were close upon the Indians and their prisoners is evident, for, continues Frances, "a big Indian stood over me with drawn knife and said, 'me kill, me kill!'" This terrible threat was made to prevent her from giving any alarm. Think of the situation! Her father in sight, and yet she was deterred from crying out to him by fear of death, which would no doubt have been her fate at the hands of the savage if she had uttered a cry. How the terrified child restrained herself under the circumstances is a question hard to decide.

"When it was dark," she continues, "they started, wading in the water [possibly this was when they crossed the river] until they came to a thicket of woods where their horses were tied, and mounting them they rode all night and came to an Indian village, [Wyalusing]. They left all there but the three Indians, who continued with Frances."

She was rapidly carried north, and in course of time reached Canada. According to the statement of Frances, "the old Indian trail crossed under the sheet of water close by the high rocky wall of the great Niagara Falls. She remembered the boom and roar of the Falls. When they got to their home they dressed her in fine, showy clothes, and took her to their chief (?) who adopted her as his own child."

"In after years," she continues, "when she was twenty-two years old, and her brothers were seeking her, they offered the French traders $500 to tell them where to find her; but they said the Indians would kill them if they did." This was probably when the Indians were congregated in large numbers at Detroit and Brownsville, Canada.

"When the chief (?) heard," continues the narrative, "that her brothers were searching for her, he took her and his wife and went to the north part of Indiana to the Miami tribe, and gave her to be the wife of a chief of that tribe, and after a number of years they moved to Miami county and the tribe centered at Osage village, three miles from Peru. She did not like to be with so many Indians, so, one day, she started to find a pleasanter home. She found the beautiful spring and good land surrounding it. She returned and told her husband what she had found, and the next day he went with her to the place. They built a house and moved there, and it was there that her brothers and sister found her.''

"When near the closing years of her life," continues Mrs. Slocum, "she told James T. Miller, the interpreter, to write to her brother, Isaac Slocum, in Huron County, Ohio, to come and see her immediately, as she had important business with him. He came, according to her request, when she told him to give her his son George to be her son, for she had no son living to take care of her property, and if he would give him to her to be her son she would make him an equal heir with her two daughters. It was a hard request to grant, as her brother had chosen that particular son to live with him, he being the youngest of his family. By a special act of Congress, through the influence of her white relatives, one section* of land had been set off for her. She had a hundred ponies, some of which were very beautiful, and the whites were stealing them and other personal property. She plead her long captivity with the Indians and the great need of her white relatives to help her. At the end of her appeal she said, 'now give me George!' The brother arose in great agitation, while the tears coursed down his furrowed cheek, and said, 'I will, if he is willing to come.' ''

That he consented and came to the assistance of his aunt has already been stated. Mrs. Slocum then continued:

"She then," when he came, "went through the form of adoption according to the tribal laws, as she understood no other, and she kept her contract of adoption as long as she lived. George moved in November, 1846, and she died the

*The title to this land, it will be remembered, was vested in the youngest daughter, and she and her sister occupied it as "tenants in common."

6th* of March, 1847. Her estate has never yet been settled according to law. Her oldest daughter died four days after her mother. She took after her in principle and ability for business; the youngest after her Indian father in treachery, and in thwarting her mother's will and wishes.''

A tinge of sadness runs all through this narrative which the reader will not fail to notice. The statements of Frances seem to convey the impression that she was not always satisfied with her captivity, notwithstanding her declarations to the contrary. But being kept in ignorance of the efforts that were being made to recover her, and having grown up and acquired the manners and customs of the Indians, she gradually lost all desire to return to her friends, and became reconciled to her condition. And when she married and had children she apparently banished all thoughts of ever changing her life, and resolved to stay with those among whom she had fallen. It is likely that if she could have escaped while yet a young woman, she soon would have returned to the habits of her own people; but after passing the meridian of life, her tastes, feelings and ideas were so firmly fixed that she could not have comfortably adapted herself to a new condition, however hard she might have tried.

---

* All other accounts agree in fixing the time of her death on the 9th of March. Mrs. Slocum is probably mistaken in the date.

CHAPTER XI.

MANY RELICS and mementos of Frances have been preserved by her relatives and descendants, and they are all highly prized; not so much on account of their intrinsic value, but on account of the associations which cluster around them. The most precious as well as cherished, perhaps, may be found in the possession of Rev. Peter Bondy and Mr. Gabriel Godfroy, residents of Miami and Wabash Counties, Indiana. The former, it will be remembered, was the last husband of O-zah-wah-shing-qua, the youngest daughter, resided with the family, and was present when his mother-in-law died. He still survives at the age of nearly 74, and informed the writer in June, 1890, that among the keepsakes in his possession is a set of silver hair pins which were used by Frances for many years in dressing her hair, which was always such an object of admiration by her adopted people. He also has many little trinkets which he prizes highly. When her house was destroyed by fire in 1882 many Indian relics of curious and exquisite workmanship, besides numerous ornaments used on ceremonial occasions, perished. Their loss is deeply regretted, and when speaking of them he heaved a deep sigh of sorrow over their loss, for there is nothing that an Indian prizes more highly than keepsakes of a venerated friend who has departed.

But the finest collection known to be in existence is found in the hands of Mr. Gabriel Godfroy, who married her favorite granddaughter. She was made the custodian of her aunt's most valued costumes, silver ornaments, rings and keepsakes, which she had accumulated during her long residence among the Miamis. And as she was so highly esteemed and respected by her Indian friends, many of these articles were presents from them, which, on account of their associations made them doubly valuable to them.

In Mr. Godfroy's collection is a brown cloth mantle or blanket ornamented with embroidery, two shawls, a French calico waist, profusely ornamented with silver broaches set in rows across the breast; a pair of scarlet flannel leggins of exquisite workmanship, and a fine pair of buckskin moccasins, neatly ornamented with bead work. The fold of fine Mackinaw cloth was worn wrapped around the body and held in place by a sash. The bottom is handsomely adorned with bead and lace work, showing great skill on the part of the maker. The needle work on these garments is extremely neat and artistic, the stitches being as fine and regular as if they had been executed on one of our best modern sewing machines. These articles, which once belonged to the wardrobe of the Indian queen, are greatly admired by all ladies who examine them, on account of the fine stitching and taste displayed in the workmanship.

While these articles of dress undoubtedly once belonged to Frances, it is not positively known whether she manufactured them with her own hands, although we are assured that she did. But as she was known to be an excellent wigwam keeper, on account of having inherited much of the tastes and ideas of her ancestors, we readily conclude that she also possessed taste and genius in the execution of needle work, and considering her opportunities, certainly excelled in its production. We doubt not, therefore, that these articles are genuine specimens of her handiwork; and although the deft fingers that fashioned them have long since mouldered to dust, we accept them as evidences of what she did in her humble capacity and with her limited means in the smoky wigwam of the red man, and admire the love and veneration shown by those who treasure them as sacred souvenirs of a dearly beloved and departed friend.

In the same collection is a magnificent silver cross, evidently of French manufacture, which measures 10¼ inches

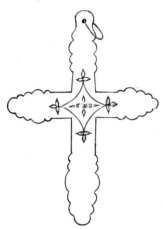

Frances Slocum's Cross.

in height by 7⅝ in width. The cut is an exact counterpart, only that it is reduced in size from the original. There is little ornamental work on it, the design having been, no doubt, to make it simple and plain. It is of sufficient thickness to give it necessary strength. It was evidently fashioned after the style of those worn by the Jesuit Fathers of the last, and the beginning of the present, century, and was very likely obtained from them when the Indians resided in and about Detroit, or in Canada. Catholicism was the only religion taught the Indians at that time, and that many of them should become converts is natural. The French traders, too, might have introduced these emblems for ornamental purposes, knowing the tastes and inclinations of the Indians for such things. But it is believed they were only used in religious ceremonies, or on stated occasions. At the upper end of the cross is a ring, by which it was attached to a string or ribbon, which encircled the neck, and the emblem was worn by being suspended on the back between the shoulders, after the style of the monks of old. Mr. Bondy, on being asked regarding it, said that Frances wore it on stated occasions, and she had it on her body at the time of her death. But there is no evidence to show that she ever became a devout Catholic, although it is probable she was under the influence and teachings of the Fathers, who labored so earnestly and zealously among the Indians during the earlier years of her captivity. That they had great control over them during the French occupancy of the Mississippi Valley and the lake region, is well authenticated by history; and once the French won the confidence of the Indians they never lost it, and to this day they are respected by them.

But it is not strange that the captive should have possessed this emblem and revered it. French and Indian blood had become intermingled, and close relationships established through the ties of consanguinity, which will not be severed for generations to come. Francis Godfroy, the last war chief of the Miami tribe, was a half breed Frenchman; both Brouillette and Bondy, her last two sons-in-law, were of the same origin, and the blood of the two races courses through the veins of her descendants down to the present time. J. B. Richardville, the last *great* civil chief of the tribe, was also half French, and when he died was buried with Catholic rites in the cemetery of that church at Fort Wayne. Through such associations and ties of relationship it is natural that Frances should have come under the teachings and influence of the Jesuits—whether she became a convert to their doctrines or not—and adopted some of the emblems used in their pious devotions.

Her brothers and sister when they first visited her obtained many relics which have been carefully preserved by their descendants. The portraits painted by George Winter are still in excellent condition. The first, a full length painting in oil, is owned by Mr. George Slocum Bennett,* of Wilkes-Barre, and bears this inscription on the back: "Frances Slocum, the Lost Sister, Mon-o-con-a-qua, wife of She-buck-o-nah, the Deaf Chief. The original sketch made A. D. 1839, at the Deaf Man's Village, by George Winter." In a post-script Mr. Winter added: "This is the first full length portrait in oil of the Lost Sister." A copy of this painting forms the frontispiece of this work. A copy was also made from it for Dr. Peck's *History of Wyoming.*

Mr. Bennett also owns a painting of the Deaf Man's Village, by the same artist, bearing this inscription on the back: "The Deaf Man's Village on the river Mississinewa, Indiana, the home of the Lost Sister. Sketched A. D. 1839, and painted by George Winter." The log cabin where they lived is shown conspicuously in the foreground. The surrounding scenery is also given, with one or two other cabins to the right and rear. Mr. Bennett purchased these paintings from Mr. Winter during a visit to his home at La Fayette, Indiana, in 1871, only four years before he died.

---

* Mr. Bennett gives his recollections of the artist as follows: "I met George Winter, the artist, in October, 1871, at La Fayette, Indiana, where he resided. He was an Englishman, of medium height, of full habit and of a ruddy complexion. He was about 65 or 70 years old, and appeared to be a man of culture and of artistic tastes. I understand he came to the United States at an early day, went out on the then western frontier and Indian country, and became interested in the study of the Indian character. He painted portraits of many of their chiefs, and made sketches of their villages. He made several paintings of Frances Slocum and the different members of her family, and also of her home at the Deaf Man's Village. He kept records of his early experience among the Indians, and I believe they are still unpublished."

In addition to the foregoing, Mr. Bennett owns a pair of buckskin moccasins which were once worn by Frances, and a small piece of calico taken from a garment used by her. This garment was splendidly ornamented with circular buckles made out of a white metal resembling silver, and a number of them are attached to this remnant.

He also possesses the original copy of the journal kept by his mother, Mrs. Hannah Fell Bennett, when she visited her aunt in the autumn of 1839, in company with her father, Judge Joseph Slocum, and sister Harriet, now the wife of Hon. Henry Lewis of Madison, N. Y. This record of the journey is printed in full in this work for the first time, and the original is sacredly preserved as a precious souvenir of his departed mother.

Mrs. Martha Bennett Phelps, of Wilkes-Barre, is the owner of a small water color picture of Frances, painted by George Winter from his large oil painting; also a full length painting in oil, by Mr. Winter, of Ke-ke-se-qua, (Cut Finger,) daughter of Frances, from a sketch made of her in 1839. She is represented in full Indian costume. Mrs. Phelps also owns a full length painting in oil of Captain Brouillette, husband of Ke-ke-se-qua, painted from a sketch made by Winter in 1837. It represents him clad in a semi-civilized costume of gaudy colors.

And last of all, Mrs. Phelps owns a pair of silver earrings, once worn by Frances. These relics, though small, are highly prized, not on account of their intrinsic value, but for their associations, and the memories they recall of her great aunt.

Mrs. Mary Slocum Butler Ayres, of Audenried, Pa., owns a large oil painting of Frances,* made for Hon. Joseph Slo-

---

* Benson J. Lossing made a copy of this portrait, which was used in his Field Book of the Revolution.

cum, by George Winter. It hangs in the parlor of Mrs. Ruth Ross Butler Hilliard, of Wilkes-Barre, and has been examined by many persons interested in the wonderful history of the subject. Mrs. Hilliard also possesses two pairs of moccasins and one pair of earrings, which once belonged to and were worn by the captive.

No painting was ever made of O-zah-wah-shing-qua, the younger daughter, but as she lived until 1877 she had photographs taken, and her likeness is preserved. She adopted an English dress, and made a very good appearance, although she retained to the last many of the customs of the Indians.

There are doubtless other trinkets owned by relatives, the whereabouts of which have not transpired, and therefore they are not enumerated. Mrs. Harriet E. Lewis, of Madison, New York, who accompanied her father on a visit to her aunt in 1837, was also the possessor of a few mementos, but gave them to her relatives.

The widow and children of Rev. George R. Slocum, on account of their long residence near where Frances lived and died, were enabled to acquire many trinkets and other things which once belonged to, or were associated with, their famous relative.

Among the extremely rare mementos of Frances, is one now in the possession of the author, which he values highly on account of its remarkable historical associations, which are far greater than its intrinsic worth. It is a Belgian coin of the mintage of 1794, and was once the property of the captive. The history of this silver dollar is as follows: During the Revolution of 1794 there was no coinage in France. Europe was convulsed and business deranged. At that time the Austrian monarch, Francis II., who ruled what is now the Empire of Austria, was the titular Emperor of Germany, and his dominions comprised the Archduchy of Austria and its dependent provinces, the Kingdom of Hungary, the Duchy of Milan or Lombardy, and the Low Countries, now known as Belgium. For each of these four regions there was a distinct coinage. The Brabantine, or Belgian, was designated by an X shaped cross, profusely ornamented, and bearing three crowns.*

These coins found their way across the ocean in the hands of French adventurers, and through the English, who occupied Canada, and were largely in use along the lakes in the early part of this century. French traders, who abounded among the northwestern Indians, also gave circulation to this money, and it soon found a lodgment in the hands of the Indians. Frances Slocum, who undoubtedly possessed a large amount of Anglo Saxon acquisitiveness, secured many of these dollars and carefully hoarded them. When Gabriel Godfroy married Kin-o-zach-wa, (Elizabeth,) her favorite niece, the old lady presented her with about thirty of these Belgian dollars. Mr. Godfroy says he was not aware that his wife had this money until some time after their marriage. One day he was going to Peru, when she handed him two of these dollars, and requested him to make some small purchases for her. Noticing the peculiarity of the money, he asked her where she had obtained it. She immediately replied: "Grandmother gave it to me; she had about thirty of these dollars." Mr. Godfroy states that he saved the coins and used other money in their place. On the occasion of the author's last visit to his house in June, 1890, and when he was just ready to step into a carriage to proceed to the railroad station, Mr. Godfroy approached him and said: "I wish to present you with something that once belonged to Frances

---

* See Memorial of Gold and Silver Coins, Ed. 1851, p. 21.

Slocum. Here is a silver dollar that was given to my deceased wife by her grandmother, which I think you will prize as something rare and valuable. There is no doubt of it once having belonged to the old lady. And out of the number that belonged to my wife, the whereabouts of only two are now known. I have one and you have the other. Keep it as a memorial of her in whose history you are interested."

The recipient of the old coin was as greatly surprised as he was gratified at receiving such a testimonial, and felt that he was highly honored by having such confidence reposed in him by one whom he had only met for the second or third time. The coin is prized as more valuable than something that might have cost hundreds of dollars, on account of its peculiar history and the thrilling events with which it was identified nearly a hundred years ago.

CHAPTER XII.

DEATH again invaded this Indian household. The next member of the family to pass away was Captain Brouillette, who, after a short illness, died at the old home on the 17th of June, 1867, aged 71 years. He had exceeded the time assigned by the Psalmist for man to live by one year. His wife* had preceded him by just twenty years. During the greater portion of the time he outlived her he had been engaged in the work of a missionary among the remnant of his tribe, having been converted as early as 1854. This change in his life was owing to the faithful labors of Rev. George R. Slocum, his newphew by marriage, and who had attended the funerals of both his mother-in-law and wife. He became very devout in his new calling, and threw all the energies of his life into the work he had taken up, and there is reason for believing that he accomplished much good and died in the full belief of a new life beyond the grave. It is unknown what minister officiated at his burial, for his faithful nephew had died nearly eight years

---

* According to accounts he married as his second wife, Eliza Godfroy, who was a daughter of his sister-in-law, O-zah-wah-shing-qua, by her first husband, and therefore his niece-in-law. By her he had one daughter, named Frances, and she married William Pe-cong-a. Little is said about this marriage. Brouillette claimed that he entered into this relation "while he was in the dark"—after "he became a Christian he was in the light."

Capt. JEAN BAPTISTE BROUILLETTE.

before. His remains were laid at rest by the side of his wife, and a marble headstone bears this inscription:

REV. J. B. BROUILLETTE,
Converted to the Christian Religion, June, 1854;
Died
June 17, 1867, Aged 71 Years.

He was born in the dark and stormy days of 1796 on the Wea Plains, of French and Indian parentage, was brought up a Miami Indian and died a minister of the Christian Church. He came into this world amidst the storms of war and the clangor of arms on the western frontier, and went out of it soon after the close of the mighty rebellion which shook the republic to its foundations. During the course of his long life he witnessed the gradual change of many of his people from barbarism to civilization, and died in the belief that they would all come into the fold of the Redeemer. With his death the name of Brouillette perished, for he left no son to perpetuate it.

George Winter, the English artist, who at one time lived at Logansport, and died at La Fayette, knew him well, and in the La Fayette *Courier* of July, 1867, paid a glowing tribute to his life and character:

"Jean Baptiste Brouillette," says Mr. Winter, "needs not the flattering touch of the artist's pencil or the poet's fanciful recitals to make him attractive to the public attention separately from his innate qualities as a man. I remember distinctly when I first saw Brouillette. He was on a visit to Logansport in the fall of the year of payment. The Pottawatomie Indians were at that time very commonly seen in Logansport. Ewing's establishment was a means of attracting the Indians to that point. It was headquarters, too, for the receiving of peltries, brought in large quantities. There

L

they were properly packed and shipped to the east. It was
not unfrequently that some of the Indians came to Logansport to buy goods at Ewing's trading post, which stood diago-
nally to Washington Hall, then kept by our old friend Capt. C.
Vigus. The Miamis were frequent visitors to the vicinity of
Logansport for the purpose of paying a reverential tribute to
the memory of the dead, as there was, but a few rods distant
from the south section of the bridge which immediately led to
the National Reservation, an extensive Indian burial ground,
which was an attraction to the curious traveler as he was passing through this new and undeveloped country.

"Captain Brouillette was a French half breed, of elegant
appearance, very straight and slim. In personal appearance
he had a decidedly commanding mien. In height he stood
six feet two inches. His *tout ensemble* was unique,* as his
aboriginal costume was expensive and showy. He wore round
his head a rich figured crimson shawl a la turban, with long
and flowing ends gracefully falling over the shoulders; silver
ornaments, or clusters of earbobs, testified their weight by a
partial elongation of the ears. His hair was jetty black and
ornamental to a face by no means handsome; forehead not
expansive, and his visage as a whole was meagre, but withal
his face was certainly thoughtful, and expressive of great
power. He wore a fine frock coat of the latest fashion.
When the Indian assumes the white man's garb, he always
chooses a frock coat. It is an object of beauty to his eye.
His 'pesmoker,' or shirt, was white, spotted with small red
figures, overhanging very handsome blue leggings, 'winged'
with very rich silk ribbons of prismatic hues, exhibiting the

---

* Mrs. Bennett thus describes him in her journal: "His head was covered
with a handkerchief something like a turban, with nearly a yard of red calico hanging down behind. As he ran his horse through the woods with his
red streamer flying after him, he made a grotesque appearance!"

squaw's skillful needle work. A handsome red silk sash was thrown gracefully over his left shoulder, and passing over his breast and under the right arm, with clusters of knots, and fringed masses, gave point and style to Brouillette's tall and majestic figure. Intellectually, the Miami soared far above mediocrity. His mind was clear and strong. He had great comprehension and scope of thought. Brouillette had a fine reputation as an orator, possessing great volubility of language. He was a very peaceable man, and a great friend of the whites, among whom he claimed many friendships. He was a great 'Medicine Man,' (though not a juggler,) professing a knowledge of the healing art. I well remember some time in the summer of 1842, when in Berthelot's trading establishment at Peru, word was brought that Pee-waw-pe-o had stabbed his squaw in revenge for some family grievance, and that she had been taken up to 'Deaf Man's Village,' on the Mississinewa, where Brouillette resided with his mother-in-law, Frances Slocum, known as the 'Lost Sister.' Under Brouillette's care the Indian woman recovered from her wounds.

"Captain Brouillette, for he was proverbially known among the whites by that sobriquet, was the first Miami Indian that cultivated corn with the plow.

"He often visited La Fayette. In the year 1851 I met him. He was then on his way to the Wea Plains,* a spot identified with his early childhood. The purpose of his visit there was to obtain certain roots possessing medicinal properties. At that time the noble looking Indian, though still retaining his erect bearing, yet the unmistakable marks of increasing years were shown in the deepening lines of the face,

---

* The famous old Wea town—the Ouiatenon (Wah-wee-a-tenon) of the French—stood on a tract six miles square on the Ouabache (Wabash) River, near what is now La Fayette. See Dillon's Indiana, p. 396.

and the former jet black hair being impinged with Time's
frosty touch.

"More recently, perhaps in 1863, Brouillette, with some
other Miamis, were on a visit to Peter Langlois', in the
vicinity of La Fayette. These red men were attracted to the
artesian well, and were observed testing the qualities of the
water, when I approached the group and found among them
'Jim' Godfroy, son of the old war chief, Francis Godfroy.
Captain Brouillette and 'Jim' gave a friendly recognition,
and a little pow-wow followed relating to the time when I had
made sketches of them 'long years ago.'

"Brouillette's birthplace was on the Wea Plains. The
period of his birth [1796] was a time of fearful strife, and
when 'grim visaged war' disturbed the peace of this remote
region. The famous village of Ouiatenon was a stronghold
of the Miami Indians, and to destroy this ancient village was
regarded of such importance by the United States Government that an expedition, in the year 1791, was sent out from
Kentucky, 800 strong, commanded by Brigadier General
Scott. Dillon, in his historical notes, in reference to this
valley, states that many of the inhabitants of Ouiatenon were
French, and lived in a state of civilization. By the books,
letters, and other documents found there, it is evident that
that place was in connection with and dependent on Detroit.
A large quantity of corn, a variety of household goods, peltry,
and other articles, were burned with the village which consisted of seventy houses, and many of them were well furnished.

"The citizens of to-day can hardly realize that but a few
miles distant from La Fayette there existed such an extensive
community of mixed, civilized and savage people at so early
a period as 1790, yet an earlier period of historic existence

precedes it. An Indian once very beautifully and touchingly expressed himself in reference to the strife that grew out of the pale face's invasion of their country. "Know ye, that the village of Ouiatenon is the sepulchre of our ancestors!"

"Brouillette was a half breed. His father* was a French-man, and was made a captive when a youth. By a remarka-ble coincidence, Captain Brouillette's wife's mother was also a captive, whose discovery in her old age, after a captivity of sixty years, (in the year 1837) on the Mississinewa River, awakened an intense interest.   *   *   *   *   *

"H. T. Sample has known this locality over forty-five years and was acquainted with the Deaf Man, Brouillette and the captive. I visited the village in the fall of 1839 and made a sketch of the captive, a valuable subject for the pencil. She died some sixteen years since. Captain Brouillette died at the village on the 7th ult. There are but few of his tribe remaining in the old forest home to hold him in remembrance. But while a Miami lives Brouillette will ever have a place in the mind and heart. He became a convert to Christianity through the missionary labors of Rev. George R. Slocum, a nephew of the captive, who settled among the Miamis after the discovery of his aunt. Brouillette attached himself to the Baptist denomination. He entered into his religious pro-fession with an earnest zeal, so much so that he became a missionary among the few of the tribe that yet remained in the State of Indiana, along the Mississinewa River, Pipe Creek, and other old cherished localities of the Miami peo-ple."

That Brouillette was a strange character, in which the

---

*In a petition to the American commander of the post, regarding the cultivation of land, signed by a number of French settlers, in May, 1789, ap-pears the name of Francois Brouillette. He afterwards became the father of the subject of this notice.—Dillon's Indiana, p. 407.

traits of the Indian and French were peculiarly blended, we have abundant testimony. And although wayward in his youth, his strength of mind was sufficient, when brought under proper influence, to overcome what was evil, and he died a pious, honored and respected teacher of the rude people with whom he claimed allegiance, and with whom he had always been associated.

The deep sorrow he expressed at the deathbed of his pious friend, Rev. George R. Slocum—spoken of in a previous chapter—shows the sympathetic nature and character of the man, and the grateful feelings he entertained for his dying friend. His earnest and solemn prayer on that occasion is further evidence of the high respect he entertained for his benefactor.

It will be remembered how Brouillette, after a night of dissipation, and his mind racked with remorse over his bad conduct, went to Mr. Slocum and desired him to draw up another pledge, make it binding and strong, and of a sufficient period to cover the balance of his life, which he took with uplifted hand, calling God to witness that he would not indulge in drink again. And it was this affair to which the dying man referred when he besought him to always remain firm and not give way to temptation again. That deathbed scene was a memorable one, and it is believed that Brouillette never violated his pledge, but remained firm in the faith to the close of his life.

CHAPTER XIII.

A WOMAN WITH FIVE HUSBANDS—DEATH AND BURIAL OF
O-ZAH-WAH-SHING-QUA—THE FULL TEXT OF HER WILL
—NAMES OF THE DESCENDANTS OF FRANCES SLOCUM—
YOUNGEST GREAT GRANDCHILD.

STRANGE, indeed, were the marital relations of O-zah-
wah-shing-qua, the second daughter of Frances Slocum. She was born about 1816, on the Mississinewa,
lived much longer, and had a more eventful life than her
elder sister. According to the best information that can be
gathered from the remnant of the Miamis now living in Indiana, she was married five times. Her husbands may be enumerated as follows:

I. Louis Godfroy, a nephew of Francis Godfroy, the last
war chief of the Miamis. The date of this marriage is unknown, but she must have been quite young when it took
place. This marriage did not prove a congenial one, although
she bore her husband two daughters. He maltreated and
abused her greatly, and often threatened to kill her. This
caused her mother much trouble, and finally, when his treatment became unbearable, and the daughter was in daily dread
of her life, her mother appealed to Gen. Tipton, who was
then Indian agent at Fort Wayne. In her distress she revealed to him the secret of her life, and declared that if
matters grew worse she would appeal to the government for
protection, as she was a *white woman!* This, it is claimed
by her people now living in Indiana, was the *first* time she
spoke of her origin and captivity to a white man, and that

Colonel Ewing was *not* the first man who knew her secret, although he acted promptly in her behalf, and as his sympathies were aroused to the point of action, he succeeded in imparting the information he had gained to her friends on the Susquehanna, and she was discovered and identified. Tipton, it appears, took little notice of the complaint, and nothing came of it. Perhaps he considered it a trifling matter among Indians, and was not sufficiently interested or moved by sympathy, to exert himself. Money getting and land speculations were paramount to all other considerations at that time, and may have had something to do with his lack of interest in the case of the "white woman's" daughter. However, it seems that her husband was either killed or left her, and she became a free woman again.

II. Wap-shing-qua, in course of time, became her second husband, and by him she had one daughter. He suddenly died a violent death. This daughter, who was born Sept. 25, 1836, was named Kin-o-zach-wa, or Elizabeth in English. She grew to womanhood and married Gabriel Godfroy, a son of the famous chief of that name. She was a lady of rare accomplishments, considering the time in which she lived, and the union was a happy one. She died October 28, 1879, aged 43, and a handsome marble stone marks her grave in the Godfroy cemetery. She left four sons, Peter, Joseph, Frank and Judson, and one daughter, Sarah Joanna. All are deceased but Peter and Frank. Kin-o-zack-wa was the favorite granddaughter of Frances Slocum, and she left her several of her finest dresses and many trinkets and keepsakes when she died. These are now in the possession of Gabriel Godfroy, and he preserves them with scrupulous care as tender mementos of "grandmother," as he reverently terms her.

III. Tac-co-nah was her third husband. By him she had

one son, but he died in infancy. Her husband was killed by a quarrelsome Indian, and she was a widow again.

IV. She then married a brother of Tac-co-nah, named Ma-ma-mundra. By this union there was one daughter. She was named Chan-shing-qua, or Lavinia, and is still living. Her father did not live long.

V. Her fifth and last husband was Wah-pah-pe-tah, or Peter Bondy, who is still living. They had seven children, four sons and three daughters, but only two sons and two daughters are living. One of these sons, Judson C. Bondy, married Sarah Joanna, the only daughter of Gabriel Godfroy, by his second wife, Kin-o-zack-wah, whose mother was the youngest daughter of Frances Slocum, and married for her second husband, Wap-shing-qua. This is a curious comminggling of French-Indian-American blood through the Godfroys and Slocums, and the question of relationship is a tough one for genealogists to solve.

Judson C. Bondy's wife died a few years ago, leaving two sons, Peter and Joseph, and two daughters, Josephine and Mabel Ray. The latter, now (1890) about three years old, is the youngest female descendant of Frances Slocum, and like her great grandmother, she has a luxuriant head of chestnut brown hair.

The children of Judson Bondy, as well as those of Gabriel Godfroy, by his wife Kin-o-zack-wa, are all great grandchildren of Frances Slocum. A more complicated relationship, through intermarriages, is rarely met with, and the problem of establishing the true relationship which one family bears to the other will afford a study for those who take delight in unraveling such knotty questions.

O-zah-wah-shing-qua died January 25, 1877, aged 67 years, just thirty years after her sister, Mrs. Brouillette. Her ill-

ness was not long, and her death took place in the house
built by her mother on the hill near the Indian graveyard.
Burial services were conducted according to the usages of the
Baptist church, and her remains were laid by the side of her
kindred in the family cemetery.   Her grave, unlike those of
her mother and sister, is marked by a plain marble tomb-
stone, which bears this inscription:

O-SAW-SHE-QUAH,

Wife of

PETER BONDY,

Died January 25, 1877,

Aged 67 years.

The marble cutter evidently spelled the name to suit
himself, as it differs from the way it is usually expressed by
Miamis and spelled by modern writers.   Her English name
was Jane Bondy, and she was better known by this title towards the close of her life than by the one given her by her
parents.

According to the account already given, she was married
five times and was the mother of twelve children, four sons
and eight daughters.   But of this number only two sons and
three daughters are living.   As a woman she was much more
rugged and strong than her sister, else she could not have
endured the hardships and troubles she did and lived to the
mature age of 67.   She lived long enough to see great changes
wrought among her people through civilizing influences, and
witnessed the land of her birth changed into a populous,
happy and prosperous country.   Indian habits and superstitious notions were largely banished from her mind, and under
the pious teachings of her nephew, and husband,* she expe-

---

* In a letter to the author, Mr. George Slocum Bennett, who visited the
Mississinewa nineteen years ago, relates his recollections of the family as

rienced the blessings which flow from a more clear understanding of the duties of life, and the happiness in store for
those who turn away from darkness.

In her habits and manners she was a thorough Indian, and
never learned to speak the English language. Mrs. Lewis,
when she visited the family in 1839, with her father and sister, Mrs. Bennett, speaks of her as being reserved and of a
retiring disposition. But, like her mother, she was industrious and desirous of accumulating property. Mrs. Lewis
says that "they had clothes and calicoes enough to fill a
country store." The daughters were anxious to learn from
their cousins how to make garments, and the art of knitting
was especially curious to them, and they took lessons until
they had learned "the stitch." It was hard at first to adapt
themselves to the usages of civilized life. When they spent
a night with their friends at the hotel in Peru, they could not
be induced to occupy a bed, but wrapping their blankets
around them, reposed on the floor and slept soundly. The
industrious and methodical habits of O-zah-wah-shing-qua
were shown in the business-like manner in which she disposed of her real and personal property before she died.

---

follows : "Mrs. Bondy appeared to be about seventy years old when I saw
her at her home near Peru, Indiana, in October, 1871. I was accompanied
on the visit by Mrs. Miller, wife of James T. Miller, who was the interpreter
for my grandfather, Joseph Slocum, my aunt and my mother, on the occasion of their visit to Frances Slocum in 1839. Mrs. Miller knew the family
well and introduced us—my wife and myself—to Mr. and Mrs. Bondy and
their children. Mrs. Bondy was rather tall, her hair was somewhat gray,
and she seemed shy of strangers. At first she was reserved. She did not
speak in English, and I could hold no conversation with her. The children
and Mr. Bondy were the interpreters. I read to the family from my mother's journal the account of her visit in 1839. When Mrs. Bondy learned
who I was, and of the relationship existing between us, and heard me read
the Indian names of all of the family, her reserve passed away and she
became very friendly. She seemed to be a woman of character, and possessed deep religious convictions."

As she owned a large body of land, and there were a number of heirs, she very wisely made a will apportioning it among them.   And in order to fully complete the record of her life, the patent from the government, and the will, are given in full, so that the reader may have easy access to these documents.   Following is the patent:

"THE UNITED STATES OF AMERICA.—To whom these presents shall come, greeting: Whereas, by the twelfth article of the Treaty, between the United States of America and the Miami Tribe of Indians, made and concluded at the Forks of the Wabash, in the State of Indiana, on the sixth day of November, one thousand eight hundred and thirty-eight, as ratified on the eighth day of February, one thousand eight hundred and thirty-nine, the United States agreed to grant to O-zah-shin-qua, and the wife of Brouillette, daughter of the Deaf Man, as tenants in common, one section of land on the Mississinewa River, to include the improvements where they now live, which Reserve has been surveyed and designated as number twenty-five, containing six hundred and forty acres, in township twenty-six, north of range five, east of the Second Meridian, Indiana, and according to a return of survey, with diagram, as certified on the fourth day of September, one thousand eight hundred and forty-nine, by the Surveyor General at Detroit, Michigan, is bounded and described as follows, to wit:

"Beginning at the northwest corner at a post, (marked A) on diagram, from which a Burr Oak, fifteen inches in diameter, bears south sixty-two degrees east, distant thirty-nine links, and a Hickory, ten inches in diameter, bears south twenty-one degrees west, distant forty-three links; thence along the left bank of the Mississinewa River up stream, north eighty degrees east two chains and twenty links, north seventy-seven degrees east six chains, south eighty-seven degrees, east nine chains and fifty links, north eighty-seven degrees east nine chains, south eighty-six degrees, thirty minutes, east nine chains and fifty links, north eighty-eight degrees east six chains and fifty links, north eighty-one degrees east, nine chains and fifty links, south eighty-nine degrees east five chains, south fifty degrees east six chains, south thirty-three degrees east eight chains, south twenty-one degrees thirty minutes east ten chains, south fourteen degrees thirty minutes east

thirteen chains and fifty links, south seventeen degrees east five
chains, south twenty-seven degrees east three chains and fifty
links, south forty-three degrees east eight chains and fifty links,
south twelve degrees thirty minutes east four chains, south three
degrees east three chains and fifty links, south seventeen degrees
west ten chains and fifty links, south six degrees east three chains
to a post at the northeast corner, (marked B,) from which a Hickory twelve inches in diameter, bears north two degrees east, distant twenty-two links, and a Hickory ten inches in diameter, bears
north sixty-eight degrees east, distant three links; thence south
along the east boundary nineteen chains and fifty links and a half
to a post at the southeast corner, (marked C,) from which a Beech,
twelve inches in diameter, bears north thirty-nine degrees west,
distant fifty-three links, and a Buckeye twenty inches in diameter,
bears south eighty degrees west, distant twenty-one links; thence
west along the south boundary eighty chains and fifteen links to
the southwest corner, (marked D,) from which a Sugar, twenty-
four inches in diameter, bears north thirty-five degrees west, distant twenty-seven links, and a Sugar, fourteen inches in diameter,
bears south thirty-five degrees east, distant fifteen links; thence
north along the west boundary eighty-four chains, twenty-three
links and a half link to the place of beginning.

" Now know ye, That there is therefore granted by the United
States unto the said O-zah-shin-qua and the wife of Brouillette,
daughter of the Deaf Man, as tenants in common, and to their
heirs, the tract of land above described.

" To have and to hold, the said tract with the appurtenances
unto the said O-zah-shin-qua and the wife of Brouillette, daughter of the Deaf Man, as tenants in common and to their heirs and
assigns forever.

" In testimony whereof, I, Zachary Taylor, President of the
United States, have caused these letters to be made patent and the
seal of the General Land Office to be hereunto affixed. Given
under my hand, at the City of Washington, the twenty-sixth day
of September, in the year of our Lord one thousand eight hundred
and forty-nine, and of the Independence of the United States, the
seventy-fourth.

" By the President.

"[Seal.]   Z. TAYLOR.

" THOMAS EWING, JR., Sec'y.

"Jos. S. WILSON, Acting Recorder of the General Land Office, ad interim.

"General Land Office.—I, John Wilson, Commissioner of the General Land Office, do hereby certify that the foregoing of pages 1 and 2 is a true copy from the record, Vol. II., pages 19, 20 and 21, of this office.

"In testimony whereof, I have hereunto subscribed my name and caused the seal of this office to be affixed, at the City of Washington, this seventh day of August, 1854.

"JOHN WILSON, Commissioner.

"Wabash County Recorder's office,—Received and recorded Nov. 29th, 1854, in Book P, pages 567, 568 and 569, at 2 o'clock P. M.   W. STEELE, R. W. C.

By J. R. POLK, Deputy.

"Re-recorded this 6th day of December, 1877, at 2 o'clock P. M., pages 127, 128, 129 of Vol. No. 25 of Deeds Records of Wabash County, Ind.   JOHN H. DICKEN, R. W. C.

[By quit claim deed, and in consideration of one hundred dollars, Nancy Brouillette (Ke-ke-se-qua) had conveyed her interest in the estate "as a tenant in common," to the testatrix, and it was recorded at Wabash March 1, 1872.]

"I, O-zah-shin-quah, or Jane Bondy, of Wabash County, and State of Indiana, do make and publish this my last will and testament:

"Item 1.—I direct that all my just debts be paid, and should I not leave sufficient money or money demands to pay the same, I direct that such indebtedness shall be made a charge on the respective lands as herein devised, in equal portions on the lands of my children and grandchild. If the proportional amount of such indebtedness and expense of administration is paid to my executor by any legatee, such share shall be released from such charge, but in case the same is not so paid within three months from my death, my executor shall take possession of such share and lease the same for such time as the rents thereof will pay the same, and additional expenses of leasing, and interest and charges accruing by such failure to pay.

"Item 2.—For the purpose of making a division of my real estate and designating the respective shares devised, I include in one body Reserve number twenty-five, in township twenty-six, north of range five east, situate in Miami and Wabash Counties, in the State of Indiana, granted to me and my sister Ke-ke-na-ke-shua by the United States, also lot number four (4) in section number fifteen, in Miami County, and lots numbered six (6) and seven (7) in section number fourteen, in Wabash County, in the township and range aforesaid. Said lots lying immediately south of said Reserve, and with it making a total of six hundred and eighty-six acres, more or less. This body of land to be divided by an east and west line parallel to the southern boundary, and twenty-nine chains and seventy-five and (1-2) links north of the southern boundary of said Reserve, for the purpose of making the subdivision granted to the several legatees as hereinafter specified. A plat or map of which body of land, with such subdivisions indicated thereon, being hereto attached for the purpose of readily showing the same. [Plat omitted].

"Item 3.—I will and devise to my daughter Pe-me-sack-quah, or Rose Ann Bondy, in fee simple, one hundred and six (106) acres in the southwest corner of said body of land as specified in item 2, and shown on the plat, being a part of said Reserve number twenty-five and lot No. 7 in section No. 14, in Miami and Wabash Counties, described as follows: Bounded on the south by the south line of said lot No. 4 and part of lot No. 7; on the west by the west line of said Reserve No. 25, and the west line of lot No. 4; on the north by said division line running east and west, and 35.68 chains north of the south boundary of said lots, and on the east by a line parallel with the western boundary and 29.70 chains east therefrom.

"Item 4.—I will and devise to my daughter Sack-cat-queah, or Hannah Mon-o-sah, in fee simple, sixty acres of said body of land in Wabash County, Indiana, as specified in Item 2, and shown on the plat, described as follows: Bounded on the south by the south line of said lot No. 7, in section 14; on the west by the lands of Pe-me-sack-quah as specified in Item 3; on the north by said east and west line 35.68 chains north of the south boundary of lot No. 7, and on the east by a line parallel with the western boundary and 16.81 and 1-2 chains east therefrom.

"Item 5.—I will and devise to my daughter Wah-pah-nock-shin-quah, or Frances Wilson, in fee simple, sixty acres of said body of land as specified in Item 2, and shown on the plat, being part of said Reserve No. 25, and part of said lot No. 7, in Wabash County, Indiana, and described as follows: Bounded on the south by the south line of said lot No. 7; on the west by the east line of the lands herein described, to Sack-cot-quah-tah as specified in Item 4; on the north by said east and west division line 35.68 chains north of the south boundary of lot No. 7; on the east by a line running parallel with the western boundary thereof, and 16.81 and 1-2 chains east therefrom.

"Item 6.—I will and devise to my granddaughter O-zah-nock-ke-sun-quah, or Nancy Mon-go-sah, in fee simple, sixty acres of said body of land as specified in Item 2, and shown on the plat, being a part of said Reserve No. 25, part of lot No. 7 and said lot No. 6, in Wabash County, Indiana, described as follows: Bounded on the south by the south line of said lots 6 and 7; on the west by the east line of the lands described herein to Wa-pah-nock-shin-quah, as specified in Item 5; on the north by said east and west line, 35.68 chains north of the south boundary of lots 6 and 7; on the east by the Mississinewa River; the east line of said Reserve No. 25 and the east line of said lot No. 6 being 16.81 and 1-2 chains wide on the southern boundary. This devise to said O-zah-nock-ke-sun-quah is made subject to a life estate or charge of one-half of the proceeds or rents thereof for the use and benefit of Ke-pa-ke-min-quah, or Eliza Brouillette,* during her life.

Item 7.—I will and devise to my daughter Ke-no-zah-quah, or Elizabeth Godfroy,† in fee simple, sixty acres of land in the northwest part of said Reserve No. 25, in Miami County, Indiana, as specified in Item 2, and shown on the plat, bounded as follows: on the south by the east and west division line, 29.75 and 1-2 chains north of the south boundary of said Reserve, on the west by the west line of said Reserve, on the north by the Mississinewa River, and on the east by a line parallel with the western boundary, and 10.70 chains east therefrom.

"Item 8.—I will and devise to my son Ke-pah-ke-cop-wah, or Judson C. Bondy, in fee simple, one hundred and forty acres of

---

* Her daughter by first marriage, who became the second wife of Capt. Brouillette, referred to in the note on page 164.

† She married Gabriel Godfroy and died Oct. 28, 1879, in her forty-third year. She was a great favorite with her grandmother, Frances Slocum.

land in said Reserve No. 25, in Miami and Wabash Counties, Indiana, as specified in Item 2, and shown on the plat, and bounded as follows: on the south by said east and west division line, 29.755 chains north of the south boundary of said Reserve; on the west by the east line of the lands herein devised to Ke-no-zah-quah as specified in Item 7; on the north by the Mississinewa River; on the east by a line running parallel to the western boundary of the same, and 24.98 chains distant therefrom: provided said east line includes the barn on the east side of the same near the river, but in case such east line would strike said barn or run west of the same, then said east line shall' start at the river and run south so as to run one chain east of said barn, and to a point one chain south; thence west to such point that a line running south and parallel with the west boundary shall cut off from such tract and amount of land equal to the extra amount included by moving such line east so as to include said barn. The tract of land hereby devised includes a private burial ground;* for which one-half acre is reserved for burial purposes for the use of members of my family.

"I also will and devise, in fee simple, to my said son a part of the Ta-ko-nong Reserve, in township No. 26, north of range No. 5 east, in Miami County, Indiana, and described as follows: The south half of that part of said Reserve lying between a tract of forty acres conveyed by me and my husband to Ke-no-zah-quah, or Elizabeth Godfroy, on the west, and the part of said Reserve now in possession of James T. Miller on the east, the south boundary line of the south boundary of said Reserve; and bounded on the north by the Mississinewa River and the road known as the river road from Peru to Peoria. Said tract hereby devised containing forty-two acres, more or less.

"I also will and devise to my said son one-half of all the personal property of which I may die possessed.

"Item 9.—I will and devise to my husband, Wah-pah-pe-tah, or Peter Bondy, in fee simple, in lieu of his interest in my lands, sixty acres of said Reserve No. 25, in Wabash County, Indiana, bounded and described as follows: On the south by said east and west division line 29.755 chains north of the south boundary of

---

* This is the ground in which Frances Slocum and her children are buried.

M

said Reserve; on the west by the east line of the lands devised to
Ke-pah-ke-cop-wah, as specified in Item 8, and shown on the plat;
on the north by the Mississinewa River, and on the east by a line
parallel with the western boundary; such western line being subject to changes specified in said Item 8. If no changes are made
in said west line, the eastern boundary to be 10.70 chains distant
therefrom.

"Item 10.—I will and devise to my son Tak-quah-ke-uh, or
Camillus Bondy, in fee simple, one hundred and forty acres of
land in the northeast part of said Reserve No. 25, in Wabash
County, Indiana, as specified in Item 2, and shown on the plat,
and bounded as follows: On the south by said east and west line
29.755 chains north of the south line of said Reserve; on the west
by the east line of the tract of land devised to Wa-pah-pe-tah in
Item 9, and the north and east by the Mississinewa River.

"I also will and devise to my said son, in fee simple, the south
half of said portion of the Ta-ke-nong Reserve in Miami County,
Indiana, as described in Item 8, of which my son Judson C. Bondy
was the other half. Said tract hereby devised containing forty-
two acres, more or less.

"I also will and devise to my said son Camillus Bondy the one-
half of all the personal property of which I may die seized.

"Item 11.—I will and devise, in fee simple, to my daughter
Chan-shin-gan, wife of Nelson Taw-a-taw, all that part of the Ta-
ko-nong Reserve, in township No. 26, north of range 5 east, in
Miami County, Indiana, which is bounded as follows: On the
north and west by Mississinewa River; on the east by the part of
said Reserve in possession of James T. Miller, and on the south
by the road leading from Peru to Peoria, known as the river road.
Said tract of land hereby devised containing thirty-five acres, more
or less.

"Item 12.—I hereby nominate and appoint my husband, Peter
Bondy, executor of this my last will and testament, and I do
hereby direct that he shall not be required to give bond as such
executor.

"Item 13.—I hereby revoke all former wills by me made. In
testimony hereof, I have hereunto set my hand and seal this tenth
day of July, in the year 1873.

          "O-ZAH-SHIN- (HER X MARK) QUAH.   [Seal.]
"Attest, J. M. Brown.
"T. F. Richardville.

"Signed and acknowledged by said O-zah-shin-quah, or Jane Bondy, as her last will and testament in our presence, and signed by us in her presence.

"JAS. M. BROWN.
"T. F. RICHARDVILLE.

" (See Will Record 'B,' page 220).

" Plat of Reserve No. twenty-five, in township 26 N. range 5 east, and lot N. 4 in section 15, and lots 6 and 7 in section 14, with subdivisions as made by will of O-zah-shin-quah, wife of Peter Bondy, omitted.

"State of Indiana, Wabash County:

"I, James P. Ross, Clerk of the Circuit Court of Wabash County, Indiana, do hereby certify that the within annexed last will and testament of O-zah-shin-quah, or Jane Bondy, has been duly admitted to probate and duly proved by the testimony of Jas. M. Brown, one of the subscribing witnesses thereto; that a complete record of said will and the testimony of said O-zah-shin-quah, or Jane Bondy, in proof thereof has been by me duly made and recorded in Book 'B,' at page 220 of the Record of Wills of said County.

"In testimony whereof, I have hereunto subscribed my name and affixed the seal of said Court, at Wabash, this 15th day of February, 1877.

"JAMES P. ROSS,
" Clerk of the Circuit Court.

" Recorded April 13, 1878, in Deed Record No. 23, at pages 566 to 570, of the Deed Records of Wabash County, Indiana."

Much of the land embraced in this tract, and which she took such pains to apportion among her heirs, is hilly and broken, and the soil is thin. That portion lying along the Mississinewa River, however, is very good, and produces fine crops of corn. Several of the heirs have sold their shares, and others still live there. There are houses and outbuildings on several of the divisions, and they are occupied by the descendants of the devisor, or tenants.

Near the great spring where the "white woman" first settled, a good, modern two story frame dwelling house was erected a few years ago. It belongs to Judson C. Bondy, who inherited the ground upon which it stands from his mother, and it was occupied by him until the death of his wife by consumption a few years ago.

The house on the hill which Frances Slocum occupied when she died, was destroyed by fire in 1882, and a large number of Indian relics and antiquities that belonged to her perished. The loss, which was irreparable, was greatly deplored. Many things were saved, but some of the most valuable and curious trinkets, the accumulations of a long life among the people with whom her destiny was cast, were lost forever. The site of this dwelling, like the one where she first lived, is now marked by a pile of stones, and the vegetation around the spot in summer time is rank and luxuriant. How appropriate it would be, on account of her strange and eventful life, to erect a tablet on the spot to tell visitors who come and go every spring, summer and autumn, that here is where she breathed her last, and in yonder cemetery her ashes repose!

That the reader may have a better understanding of the line and the number of descendants of Frances Slocum, and their names, the following table is inserted. It was prepared by a member of the family of Rev. George R. Slocum, who, from long residence in the Miami settlement, had ample opportunities to become well acquainted with the descendants, and therefore give their names and line of descent correctly. It is as follows:

KIN-O-ZACH-QUA.
(Mrs. Gabriel Godfroy.)

WAH-PAH-NACH-SHING-QUA.
(Half Sister to Kin-o-zach-qua.)

REV. PETER BONDY.
(Wah-pah-pe-tah.)

MABEL RAY BONDY.
(Youngest Descendant.)

PARENTS.	CHILDREN.	GRANDCHILDREN.	GREAT GRANDCHILDREN.
She-pan-can-ah, Frances Slocum.	Two sons who died before she was found. Ke-ke-se-qua, (Nancy Brouillette) O-zah-wah-shing-qua, (Jane Bondy)	Eliza Godfroy, Frances Godfroy, Elizabeth ———, Melvina Bondy, Mary Bondy, Hannah Bondy, Rosanna Bondy, Camillus Bondy, Judson Cary Bondy.	Nancy Brouillette, Peter Godfroy, Joseph Godfroy, Franklin Godfroy, Joanna Godfroy, Judson Godfroy, Emma Tawetaw, Frances Tawetaw, Ellen Tawetaw, Camillus Tawetaw, Rosanna Tawetaw, Josephine Bondy, Peter Bondy, Joseph Bondy, *Mabel Ray Bondy.*

Mabel Ray Bondy, now about three years old, is claimed by her grandfather, Gabriel Godfroy, to be the youngest female descendant of Frances Slocum. And like her, he says, "she is red headed!" Mabel is a very pretty child, and greatly beloved by her grandfather. Her hair, like that of her great grandmother, is luxuriant in growth and falls in graceful ringlets over her shoulders. It is difficult to discover a trace of Indian blood in her countenance—the French and American predominating.

Nancy Brouillette, who married James Mongosa, is reported to be the mother of a son named Julius, and it is possible that there are others who may have had children in this line since the foregoing information was obtained. Julius Mongosa is the only known great great grandchild. But that Mabel Ray Bondy is the youngest descendant in the female line there seems to be no doubt, and her relatives attach great importance to this fact.

Judson C. Bondy, who inherited 140 acres of land from his mother, lives at the old homestead in accordance with her expressed wish before she died. These people have a superstitious veneration for their deceased relatives, and they cherish the memory of their great grandmother (Frances) as something sacred, and are governed by the expression of the Great Spirit in Job v., 23: "For thou shalt be in league with the stones of the field; and the beasts of the field shall be at peace with thee."

The great Miami Confederacy, once so powerful, has long since ceased to exist, and its wide domain, now cut up into four or five of our most thrifty and populous Western States, over which great chieftains ruled with regal sway, is now controlled by another race—the race which seems to have been selected by the hand of destiny to drive the red man from his home and possessions in the Western World.

When the remnant of the tribe left the Wabash and emigrated to their reservation in Kansas, in 1846, they only remained there about eight years, when they were called upon to meet in treaty again. This was in 1854, when they ceded 500,000 acres, which had been set off to them by act of Congress, February 25, 1841, on condition that they were to each take 200 acres, and near their reserves to have 70,000 acres in a body in common, and a section for school purposes. There are accounts of lengthy settlements of previous transactions; the $25,000 annuity ceased in 1855, and an annuity of $7,500 was to be paid for twenty years, and $50,000 invested for the tribe.

Finally, in 1868,* the unfortunate Miamis, in spite of all the "forevers" and "pledges" theretofore made, were required to make a treaty by which they were removed to the Indian Territory, and confederated with the Peorias, Kaskaskias, Weas and Piankeshaws, and from this last refuge, if any of them remain, no one can say how soon they will be called on to depart. But, in that event, whither will they go?

We have now traced the history of Frances Slocum from her birth in Rhode Island, in March, 1773, down to her death in Indiana, in 1847, and noted everything relating to her wonderful career that could be obtained through persistent and careful research and by interviews with her Indian friends. If an exhaustive record of her life and wanderings, from capture to discovery, could be given, it would form one of the most interesting, as well as startling and pathetic, chapters in American annals. And looking at it in this light, we cannot refrain from regretting that greater efforts were not made when she was alive to gather from her lips a fuller account of her life with the savages. What strange scenes

---

*See History of the Valley of the Upper Maumee, p. 198.

and ceremonies she must have witnessed in the days of war along the lakes and in Canada; what acts of cruelty, torture and death must have come under her observation when living at Detroit, Ke-ki-ong-a, the interior of Ohio, and other points, until the shattered remnants of her powerful tribe drifted down the Wabash, and she finally settled on the banks of the little river where she died! The sorrows, hopes and fears of a life of captivity for nearly sixty years—from prattling childhood to mature old age—came within the scope of her mental vision and rose up like a spectre to haunt her mind whether in the forest, on the plain or the river. What if everything occurring in her long and sad career could be written in a book!

One hundred and twelve years—over eleven decades—have rolled away and disappeared in the misty past since that unlucky day when she was rudely snatched from her mother's arms by a stalwart savage and borne into the forest, to be lost to parents, relatives, friends and civilization for over half a century. And now, although we are in the decimal of the nineteenth century, and the country has grown rich and prosperous, and great wars have come and gone, the pathetic story of her captivity and recovery has not been forgotten, but possesses as deep an interest, excites as much sympathy in the minds of those familiar with it, and causes as many tears to be shed as if it had occurred but yesterday. The story of Frances Slocum will never be forgotten as long as we have a language and a history, and in the distant future it will be as eagerly read and wept over as it is to-day by young and old.

The Slocum family is an illustrious one. It has prospered, multiplied, and spread all over the land; it has produced many men of eminence—men who have attained to high distinction in the civil and military professions—men who have brought great honor to their country, and transmitted unsullied names to their posterity. The ancestry of this family is traced back more than two hundred and fifty years, and to-day its membership will reach nearly two thousand in America. What a line of descent. The family name, so far as known, has been free from tarnish. And among all the distinguished men and women who have borne the surname, it is believed there is not one, notwithstanding the opportunities of education, enlightenment, culture, and the refining influences of society which they have enjoyed, who has shown a higher degree of native intellect, a greater breadth of inborn genius, and executive ability, than the Lost Sister, whose lot, by a strange decree of fate, was cast among barbarians, and for the period of a long life denied every opportunity which we consider essential to intellectual development and moral power. And there are few among the great number bearing this name who have passed away, who were more respected, than she whose ashes commingle with the soil of one of our great Western States, or whose memories are more fondly cherished by their descendants. Deprived of the comforts of civilized life, of education and general knowledge, the child of sorrow and suffering; yet her untutored mind towered above all and commanded the love, respect and admiration of her tribe. Verily, as in this case, truth is stranger than fiction; and in the ways of Providence there are many mysterious things, and in this affair we have one of the most mysterious of all.

APPENDIX.

BY HORACE P. BIDDLE.*

In May, 1836, George Peters, Retrom Harrison Peters, and myself, left the State of Ohio, on our horses, for a journey through the West, without any particular objective point. We passed through Dayton and Greenville, into the State of Indiana at Winchester, thence to Muncie, thence northward to the Mississinewa River, at the point where Jonesborough, in Grant County, now stands. The road to this point, in

---

* From a very full biographical sketch, by Mrs. Eva Peters Reynolds, it is learned that Hon. Horace P. Biddle, the eminent retired jurist, was born in Fairfield County, Ohio, March 24, 1811; studied law under the direction of H. H. Hunter, of Lancaster, Ohio, upon the recommendation of Hon. Thomas H. Ewing, and was admitted by the Supreme Court at Cincinnati in 1839. In the fall of that year he located at Logansport, Ind., and opened an office. He soon had a lucrative practice, rose to the first rank in the profession, and received the highest judicial honors of the State. He served as president judge from 1846 to 1852, and again from 1860 to 1872. In 1874 he was chosen to the Supreme bench. In 1881, at the age of seventy, he retired from active life and devotes his time to the study of literature and music. He lives in a plain brick house, on an island in the Wabash River, at Logansport. His library, the largest private collection in Indiana, comprises over 7,000 volumes. He is the author of seven or eight books, principally poetry, and a valuable work entitled the "Musical Scale." Judge Biddle has invented two musical instruments—one a viol, which he has named "Tetrachord," the other a harp, which he calls "Eureka." He is well read in law, literature, science and art, is a delightful companion, a charming conversationalist, and his company is much sought after.—The Author.

the State of Indiana, was one gore of deep black mud. From Jonesborough down the river to Marion, the county seat, the road was good. At Marion, finding Oliver Goldthwait, an old friend of mine from Ohio, who was our landlord at the hotel, we tarried several days. Court was in session at the time. I was then a law student; the proceedings were very interesting and instructive to me, as I then had an eye to a location in the West. We then started for Peru, Indiana, through the Miami Indian Reserve—a distance of thirty miles—without any laid out road, but plenty of Indian trails, and blazed lines, along, about, across, and around which we wandered as in a maze, and in something of an amazement, too. We occasionally questioned the Indians as we met them or passed them, about the road to Peru, but they would neither look at us nor talk; but after a solemn pause they would wave a hand slowly in the general direction toward Peru, when there would be two or three forks in the trails in sight, which did not much relieve our perplexity. Thus we wandered until in the afternoon James T. Miller overtook us, and informed us that he was going directly to Peru, and re- quested us to follow him. Mr. Miller understood and spoke the Miami language, also the Pottawatamie. On the way he told us the story of the finding of Frances Slocum by George W. Ewing—that she had been stolen by the Indians soon after the Wyoming massacre in Pennsylvania. She had been discovered the summer before. We passed near her wigwam, but did not see her. We also passed the residence of Chief Godfroy—a very comfortable house. We saw the chief who— half his blood being French—politely recognized Mr. Miller, spoke a few words with him in the Miami language, as Mr. Miller informed us, and we passed on. In a short time we came to the Wabash River, opposite Peru, ferried it over— man and horse, and soon found ourselves in comfortable quarters in a long barracky hotel, kept, if I remember right, by James B. Fulwiler, whom I have favorably known ever since.

It may be said, though not directly in the line of our subject, that we continued our journey down the Wabash River to Logansport, where we found friends and acquaintances, and tarried several days. This place was then the residence of Col. Ewing. After our enjoyment we continued our way to La Fayette—pausing at the then celebrated battle-ground of Tippecanoe, where General William Henry Harrison won his fame. He was then a candidate for the presidency. From La Fayette we took a northwestern direction over the prairies, crossing the Illinois River at Peoria, and reaching the Mississippi at New Boston, opposite the mouth of the Iowa River. There we crossed the Mississippi and went up the Iowa near where Iowa City now stands, and saw the celebrated Indian chief Black Hawk—called in Indian Me-she-ki-ah-ka-guah— in his tent. This was soon after the Black Hawk war, which gave peace to the territory out of which Iowa, and other States west of the Mississippi, have been formed. The old chief had been deposed, and seemed much humiliated. He would not look towards us, but turned his head away, and would not answer any questions. We then wandered northward, turning eastward till we returned to the Mississippi River at Rock Island. Just before we arrived there we met about two hundred Saux and Fox Indians, in their war paint, riding two and two. They neither turned nor looked to the right nor the left. What is now the city of Davenport had then just been laid out. There we saw Davenport, the interpreter, and Ke-o-kuk, the half-breed chief who had succeeded Black Hawk. He was partially dressed in citizen's clothes, and seemed to be a very mild kind of man. There were also a great number of Indians present, I think of various tribes, some in their war paint. Crossing the Mississippi there we came on eastward to where the city of Chicago now stands. After we came in sight we had to cross a big wet prairie a half-a-day's ride in width. The only dry place was around the mouth of the Chicago River, where there were something like a fort, a few Indians, a squad of troops, and perhaps three hundred white people. Now it is one of the leading cities of the world! From there we came home through northern Indiana to Ohio. But enough of episode.

After we returned home, I still pursued my legal studies at Lancaster, and was admitted to practice in the State and Federal Courts at Cincinnati in April, 1839. I traveled the circuit that year with the old lawyers—very much to my advantage—tried several cases, and, armed with my credentials, in October removed to Logansport, Indiana, where I have ever since resided. Col. Ewing was still a citizen of Logansport, with whom I became acquainted; but he soon removed —I think within a year—to Peru. Afterwards I saw him less frequently; but in a year or two from that time I became very closely and intimately acquainted with him. He was indicted, I think it was in the year 1843, in the Miami Circuit Court, for an assault committed on the Hon. Daniel R. Bearss, by shooting at him with two pistols—there were no revolvers then—with intent to commit murder. In person Ewing was a little over six feet in height, slim, and as straight as an Indian's arrow. His temperament was the nervous-sanguine, the nervous prevailing. A lively grey eye in his head, with one of the keenest, clearest, quickest minds that was ever given to brains. But his education was limited, and somewhat defective. His step was cat-like and elastic, and his manners princely. Bearss was a heavier man, more muscular, and known to be aggressive in personal conflicts—an over match for Ewing, and had threatened to whip him.

Their difficulty had grown out of some Indian affairs, not necessary to state. They were both Indian traders. Under these circumstances Ewing had armed himself with a pair of pistols, which he had frequently shown in public, declaring that he would kill Bearss if he ever attempted an attack upon him. They met. Bearss made some demonstrations, but no imminent attack. Ewing drew his pistols, fired them both at him. Neither took effect. Bystanders interfered; the affray was squelched. This was the case. Ewing came down from Peru to Logansport to employ me as his attorney and counsellor—arriving after 9 o'clock in the evening. He had a way of leaving and returning home without being missed by his neighbors. He remained closeted with me till after midnight. During his statement of his troubles, his keen mind, incisive words, and his flashing, basiliskal eye, several times led my mind away from the subject-matter, so that I had to ask him to repeat certain parts of his statement. But I got the matter well in hand before he left. In a few days afterwards I received a letter from him containing twelve sheets—I remember it well—of foolscap paper closely written. He had gone to the records of the court and obtained the names of the jurors for the term, who would necessarily have to try his case, and had given me a searching biography and character of each juror, which concluded with some prompt, vigorous words—such as : "This man is my peer, I am willing to be tried by him;" or, "this man is dull and ignorant; and do not want him;" or "this man is my enemy, we must get rid of him." It was a complete analysis of the character of each juror. He also gave me a similar account of each of the witnesses against him, as to which one was fair or prejudiced, intelligent or ignorant; and what points to press, or pass over tenderly, or to exclude if possible. Everything that could strengthen or weaken his defence was laid before me.

The trial came on. The Colonel sat by me, apparently indifferent, but his nerves were strung up to the highest pitch. I
had been so well posted that we had no occasion to consult
together during the trial, and we had no difficulty in acquit-
ting him. He was indeed not guilty of the *intent* charged
against him; and if he had been the question would have
arisen whether he was not justifiable. The professional
friendship he had for me became personal, and he was always
confidential with me afterwards. He died at Fort Wayne, in
the year 1866, in the 63d year of his age.

I heard but little of Frances Slocum for several years after
I settled in Logansport. Her case was the subject of conversation occasionally as very wonderful. Col. Ewing had written a letter to Pennsylvania, to what address I do not know,
giving an account of the discovery of Frances; but to this letter there never was any response that I know of; at least I
never heard anything additional about Frances until her
friends came to the West in search of her. The subject was
then very much talked about, and I remember distinctly what
was related as one of her remarks. When her friends urged
her to return with them to Pennsylvania she answered: ''No;
I have been a long time with the Indians; they have been good
to me; I have children. It is very easy to make an Indian
out of a white man, but you cannot make a white man out
of an Indian,''—which latter remark is profoundly true. I
recollect very well when Mr. Winter painted the portrait of
Frances Slocum; I think that it was at the request of Benson J. Lossing,* the author and publisher of many valuable
books on American subjects. It was after this when Mr.
Winter went to paint the portrait of Chief Godfroy that the

* It was painted at the request of her brother, Hon. Joseph Slocum.—Author.

Indians fell down on their faces, and hid them in various ways to prevent him from taking theirs also. This anecdote I believe I related to Mr. Meginness verbally. Mr. Winter was an English artist who came to Logansport at a very early date. About 1850 he removed to La Fayette, Indiana; visited California and the Pacific coast about a year; returned home to La Fayette, where he died suddenly in February, 1876.

Chief Godfroy was the war chief of the braves; Chief Richardville—pronounced *Roosheville*—was the civil chief of the tribe. He was a Frenchman, older than Chief Godfroy, and more astute in diplomacy. This anecdote is told of him as occurring at the treaty of 1826, held at Wabashtown. After the articles of the treaty were all agreed upon, and the chiefs were about to "touch the quill," which means signing the treaty, Richardville addressed General Lewis Cass, who was one of the Commissioners on the part of the United States: "General, you forgot one little ting." "What is that, Chief?" said the General. "Eighteen tousand dollar for de Chief, Roosheville." He would not "touch the quill" till that article was inserted in the treaty. And in the treaty it was perforce inserted.

Another anecdote of Chief Richardville: William G. Ewing—a brother of Col. George W. Ewing—had some difficulty with Mr. Berthelette, a Frenchman, another Indian trader, who was an intimate friend of Chief Richardville. Berthelette became very much incensed, and went to see the chief about his difficulty with William G. Ewing. His first salutation was: "Chief, I want your pistols." "Oui oui, si; what for you want my pistol, Mr. Bar-te-lette." "I want to kill Bill Ewing." Ah, oui, you shall have my pistol,

Mr. Bar-te-lette; but come in and eat some dinner with me."
The chief's hospitality to his friends was famous. Mr. Berthelette dined with the chief. After dinner was over Berthelette became very restless. The chief said nothing more
about the pistols. Berthelette addressed him: "Chief, now
for the pistols." "Ah, oui; I get you dem pistol." The
chief retired a few minutes, and came back with two bottles
of wine. "Here, Mr. Bar-te-lette, my pistol"—handing him
the two bottles of wine—"but take care, now, you shoot
yoursef." So the blood was turned to wine, instead of the
wine to blood.

The following anecdote was told of Chief Godfroy: When
the time arrived for the removal of the Indians west, according to the terms of the treaty, the Government sent Captain
Judson, of the regular army, with a single company of troops,
to conduct the removal of about eight hundred Indians. Captain Judson was a guest of the "Bearss Hotel," the principal
public house at that time in Peru. The chief met the Captain there frequently, and they became very friendly. But
after some time the chief became very cool towards the Captain. It was rumored that the traders had put up the chief
to be ugly, and oppose the removal. Finally the chief addressed the Captain: "Captain Judson, me not go; Indians
fight." The Captain touched the hilt of his sword at his
side: "Chief, that is my profession; that is what I came for."
There were no more objections to the removal. The removal was made; but it was pitiful. The great majority of
the Indians knew nothing of the treaty understandingly, and
were reluctant to leave their homes—the many more so because the few were excepted in the treaty, and allowed to
remain on their lands—among them Frances Slocum and
her family. And their dogs could not "bear them com-

pany." They left them in hundreds, tied, to howl to the wilderness and starve. And this was the last of the Miamis as a tribe.

JEAN BAPTISTE RICHARDVILLE.

Remarkable, indeed, was this French-Indian. He was the last *great* civil ruler and lawgiver of the Miamis, and so distinguished for bravery and executive ability as to deserve more than an ordinary notice in this connection.

His Indian name was Pe-che-wa (Wild Cat), but he was more generally known as John B. Richardville, (pronounced Roosheville) and so signed the treaty of 1838. According to the best authority he was the son of Joseph Drouet de Richardville,* who was of noble lineage, and was probably engaged as an officer in the French service in Canada, before being lured into the western wilds by the prospect of amassing wealth in the fur trade. He appears to have been a trader at Ke-ki-ong-a (Fort Wayne) before the ill-timed expedition of La Balm, in 1780, to capture that place. The mother of young Richardville was Taw-cum-wah, a daughter of Aquenock-que,† principal chief of the Miamis, and a sister of Little Turtle. He was born, as tradition has it, and as he himself often stated, near the "Old Apple Tree," in the midst of the Miami village at the junction of the St. Joseph's with the Maumee, about the year 1761. A brother of his father was a trader at "Post St. Vincents," or Vincennes, and descendants of his still reside at that place, who possess valuable French documents brought into the wilderness by the adventurous

---

* See Hist. Upper Maumee Valley, p. 33.

† He signed the first treaty with the Miamis at Lancaster, Pa., July 23, 1748.

sons of France nearly 170 years ago, which trace their ancestry back to 1162.

Helm, in his History of Wabash County, says that the associations clustering around the old apple tree where the chief
was born, and where he spent his childhood days, ever afterward gave him a profound regard, approaching almost to
reverence, for its continued renewal of the joyous scenes so
intimately blended with the recollections of his early life;
hence he was instrumental in its preservation as one of the
early relics of the past. This old tree was regarded with
such favor that an illustration of it was given in Brice's History of Fort Wayne. But like the famous chief who was
born under its boughs in the days of barbarism, it has long
since disappeared.

Lieutenant Governor Robertson, in the History of the Valley of the Upper Maumee, states that among the many thrilling and interesting incidents and narrations, as frequently
recited by the chief to Allen Hamilton, he gave an account
of his ascent to the chieftainship of his tribe. The occasion
was not only thrilling and heroic, but, on the part of his
famous mother and himself, will ever stand in history as one
of the noblest and most humane acts known to any people,
and would serve as a theme, both grand and eloquent, for the
most gifted poet or dramatist of any land.

It was in a wild and barbarous age. Ke-ki-ong-a still occasionally echoed with the shrieks and groans of captive men;
and the young warriors of the region still rejoiced in the barbaric custom of burning prisoners at the stake. A white man
had been captured and brought in by the warriors. A council had been convened, in which the question of his fate arose
in debate and was soon settled. He was to be burned at the
stake, and the braves and villagers generally were soon gath-

ered about the scene of torture, making the air resound with
their triumphant shouts of pleasure at the prospect of soon
enjoying another hour of fiendish merriment at the expense
of a miserable victim of torture. Already the man was lashed
to the stake, and the torch that was to ignite the combusti-
ble material placed about the same was in the hands of the
brave appointed. But rescue was at hand. The man was
destined to be saved from the terrible fate that surrounded
him. Young Richardville had for some time been singled
out as the future chief of the tribe, and his heroic mother
saw in this a propitious and glorious moment for the assertion
of his chieftainship, by an act of great daring and bravery—
the rescue of the prisoner at the stake. Young Richardville
and his mother were at some distance, but sufficiently near
to see the movements of the actors in the tragedy about to
be enacted, and could plainly hear the coarse ejaculations and
shouts of triumph of the crowd. At that moment, just as
the torch was about to be applied to the bark, as if touched
by some angelic impulse of love and pity for the poor captive, the mother of young Richardville placed a knife in her
son's hands, and bade him assert his chieftainship by the
rescue of the prisoner. The magnetic force of the mother
seemed instantly to have inspired the young warrior, and he
quickly bounded to the scene, broke through the wild crowd,
cut the cords that bound the man, and bid him be free ! All
was astonishment and surprise; and though by no means
pleased at the loss of their prize, yet the young man, their
favorite, for his daring conduct, was at once esteemed as a
god by the crowd, and then became a chief of the first distinction and honor in the tribe. The mother of Richardville
now took the man in charge, and soon quietly placing him
in a canoe and covering him with hides, in charge of some

friendly Indians he was soon gliding down the placid current of the Maumee, beyond the reach of the turbulent warriors.

At a later period in the life of the chief, being on his way to Washington, he came to a town in Ohio, where, stopping for a little while, a man came up to him, and suddenly recognized in the stranger the countenance of his benefactor and deliverer of years before, threw his arms about the chief's neck, and embraced him with all the warmth of filial affection. He was indeed the rescued prisoner; and the meeting between the two was one of mingled pleasure and surprise, and was the occasion of many joyous recurrences to the singular meeting and equally singular recognition.

Pe-che-wah was present and participated in the defeat of Harmar, in October, 1790, but was not characteristically warlike, being more disposed to exert his executive ability in other directions, better calculated to result in the improvement of his opportunities in after life.

At the treaty of St. Mary's on the 6th of October, 1818, he was there in behalf of his people as the leading chief and representative of his tribe, and as such signed the treaty for the cession of certain territory to the United States. Twenty-three years prior to that time, however, he appeared also as the representative of his tribe and signed the treaty of Greenville, concluded on the 3d of August 1795. The same act he performed, on the part of his people, at the treaty of Fort Wayne, in June, 1803, and at Vincennes in 1805.

"About the year 1827," says Mr. Dawson in his notes, "$500 were appropriated by Congress to each chief to build a residence. Richardville appropriated more, and built a substantial house five miles from Fort Wayne, on the south bank of the St. Mary's, on one of his reservations."

For many years he kept an extensive trading house in Fort Wayne, and in person lived there most of the time; but about 1836 he moved his store to Wabash and continued business there for many years—his wife and younger members of his family at all times remaining, till her death, at the home on the St. Mary's. His housekeeper at the forks of the Wabash was Madame Margaret La Folio, a French woman, in person graceful and prepossessing.

In stature Richardville was about five feet ten inches, with broad shoulders, and weighed about 180 pounds. His personal appearance was attractive, and he was graceful in carriage and manner. Exempt from any expression of levity—he is said to have "preserved his dignity under all circumstances." His nose was Roman, his eyes were of a lightish blue, and slightly protruding, "his upper lip firmly pressed upon his teeth, and the under one slightly projecting." That he was an Indian half-breed, there can be no doubt. His own statements and unvarying traditions conclusively prove that he inherited his position through his mother, by the laws of Indian descent, and contradict the theory that he was a Frenchman who obtained the chieftainship by trickery or purchase. In appearance he was remarkable in this—he was neither red nor white, but combined both colors in his skin, which was mottled or spotted red and white. His mother was a most remarkable Indian woman. Chief Richardville was an only son, and much beloved by her. Her reign continued for a period of some thirty years prior to the war of 1812, during which time, according to the traditions of the Indians, "she ruled the tribe with a sway, power, and success as woman never ruled before." After her reign, "she retired and passed the mace of power to her son."

Richardville was taciturn, and was dignified in manner, a habit almost assuming the form of extreme indifference; yet

such was far from his nature, for he ever exercised the warm-
est and most attentive regard for all of his people and mankind in general; and "they never called in vain; his kind and
charitable hand was never withheld from the distressed of his
own people or from the stranger." So wisely did he manage
the affairs of his tribe, with such wisdom and moderation did
he adjust and settle all matters relating to his people, that he
was not only held in the highest estimation by the Indians
generally throughout the Northwest, but honored and trusted
as their lawgiver with the most unsuspecting confidence and
implicit obedience, always adjusting affairs between his own
people as well as all inter-tribal relations, without resort to
bloodshed. A patient and attentive listener, prudent and
deliberate in his action, when once his conclusions were
formed he rarely had occasion to change them. Averse to
bloodshed, except against armed resistance, he was ever the
strong and consistent friend of peace and good will.

He died at his family residence on the St. Mary's August
13, 1841, aged about 81 years. He was buried on the following day, after services by Rev. Mr. Clark, Irish Catholic
priest, of Peru, held at the Church of St. Augustine, at Fort
Wayne. His body was first interred on the site of the Cathe-
dral in that city, subsequently erected. Afterward, however,
when it became necessary to make room for the building, the
remains were removed, and now rest in the Catholic burying
ground south of the city. A fine marble monument marks
the spot, which was erected by his three daughters, La Blonde,
Sarah and Catharine, on which is the following inscription:

East side—"Here rest the remains of Chief Richardville,
principal chief of the Miami tribe of Indians. He was born
at Fort Wayne, about the year 1760. Died August, A. D.
1841."

West side—"This monument has been erected by La Blonde, Sarah and Catharine, daughters of the deceased."

Comparatively little is known of the three faithful daughters. La Blonde was the mother of a daughter named Mont-o-so-qua. She married James Godfroy, a son of the celebrated chief, Francis Godfroy, who served as war chief under Richardville. They had twelve children. She was born near Fort Wayne, in 1835, and died in March, 1885. Mr. Godfroy, who was born in 1810, still survives. His family has dwindled to three members. George L. Godfroy, the youngest son, who was born October 2, 1850, received a good education, and resides on the reservation. He is engaged in farming, and is a citizen of good standing. He is said to be one of the very few Indians in Indiana, or the country, who are members of secret societies, and is the highest in Masonry of any Indian in Indiana and the world.

Catharine, whose Indian name was Po-con-go-qua, married Francis La Fontaine (To-pe-ah), who succeeded her father as civil chief. Of Sarah we know nothing.

The only son, Joseph, (Wah-pe-mun-waw), was a quarrelsome, fighting fellow. He was educated at Detroit, and had the accomplishment of violin and flute playing. But notwithstanding his education, he was a drunken and worthless character, and his reputation was in bad odor. In view of "Joe's" degeneracy, his father ever after opposed the education of the Indian as of no value.

Allen Hamilton, of Fort Wayne, the well known Indian agent and intimate acquaintance of Richardville, relates this anecdote: One day Mr. Hamilton was riding a very spirited horse through the streets of Fort Wayne, and on passing the chief's trading house the latter noticed him. In accordance with quite a prevalent custom among the Indians of the time, when they saw anything that pleased them very much, and taking a fancy to the animal, he cried out: "I strike on that horse, Mr. Hamilton." Seeing the chief had the advantage of him in the "strike," Mr. Hamilton at once alighted and handed the horse over to the future care and keeping of the chief, who, according to the custom, at once became the bona fide owner of the horse. The next "strike" necessarily fell to Mr. Hamilton, and he was not long indifferent to the right now in his possession. So, some time subsequent to this "strike" of the chief, he and Mr. Hamilton were riding together along the Wabash, where the chief had several very fine reserves of land, one of which, particularly, drew the attention of Mr. Hamilton, and he at once exclaimed to Richardville: "Chief, I strike on this section." "Well," said the chief, "I make you a deed for it, but we'll not strike any more!" Mr. Hamilton got the land; and though the chief had the *first* "strike," yet the former certainly had the largest. But the matter ended in the greatest good feeling.

Richardville, who had been granted nine sections of land by the government—nearly six thousand acres—became the richest Indian, so far as known, in this country. He was a shrewd trader and accumulated largely in this line of business. It is said of him that at the time of his death he was possessed of about $200,000 in money. And in order to keep it secure from thieves he used to bury it in boxes. After his death it was found that much of his silver had been buried so long that the boxes had commenced to decay, and the silver was very much discolored by being in the ground so long.

The life and character of this Indian statesman has afforded a theme for many writers, and poets, too, have invoked the aid of the muse to portray in glowing verse his shining qualities. Less than a year ago Mr. Frank C. Riehl, of Alton,

Illinois, paid this handsome poetic tribute to the old chief, which was published in the *Sentinel-Democrat*, of that city, August 28, 1890:

> "Beside St. Mary's silver stream,
> Whose laughing waters, all agleam,
> Flow past the city of Fort Wayne,
> Through Indiana's fertile plain,
> There stands within a churchyard gray—
> Long since surrendered to decay—
> A weather-beaten shaft of stone,
> With moss and lichens overgrown,
> Upon whose surface may be traced
> These words, by time almost effaced:

> "'Here rest the bones of Richardville,
> Great chief of the Miami tribe,
> An Indian statesman of great skill,
>   Who never gave or took a bribe.'

> "The story of this warrrior's name,
> Although, perchance, unknown to fame,
> Is still remembered and revered
> Upon the plains where he was reared,
> And honored as among the few
> Red men who were upright and true.
> Though now his race has passed away,
> And scarcely, in this latter day,
> Do we take trouble to recall
> The hated people from whose fall
> We date our own prosperity;
> Yet in this chieftain's life we see
> Enough of nobleness to prove
> That he, at least, could feel and love.

> "A hundred years ago or more,
> While yet on Miami's wooded shore
> The swarthy Indian proudly stood
> Supreme as monarch of the wood;
> When first the white man dared to brave
> The wilds beyond Ohio's wave,
> And many a hero lost his life

Upon the stake or by the knife,
Beside the peaceful river's wave
The tribe was met in council grave:
Some, boasting, showed their battle scars,
While others plotted future wars.
But this was not the business yet
For which the tribe that day was met;
'T was matter of a darker feather
That brought these forest seers together.

" From wigwams swaying in the breeze
Blue smoke curled upward through the trees;
Within the dusky squaws were bent,
Each at some toilsome task intent,
While on the stream, to instinct true,
The urchin plied his fleet canoe,
Or launched into a tree the dart
That should have pierced a foeman's heart;
Thus grouped the savage host, serene,
Encamped upon the peaceful scene.

" But slightly from the throng away
There stood a squaw, with locks of gray,
And at her side a slender youth,
Whose eye betrayed a heart of truth,
A soul with wild ambition fired,
A mind with lofty thoughts inspired.
His every look and move confessed
A nobler lineage than the rest
Gathered within the camp that day
To while the loitering hours away.
The woman was the widowed dame
Of him, now gone, whose peerless name
Honored by all the tribe had stood,
Supreme, the monarch of the wood.
Her fondest wish and single prayer
    Was that she might outlive the hour
To see the lad beside her there
    Invested with his father's power.

" But valor was the only rod
By which these warriors would be ruled;

In danger's front had they been schooled,
And they would brook no other god.
Thus, though they owned the prince's blood,
Those heroes of a hundred wars,—
Deep seamed with honored battle scars,—
Would never bow beneath his will
Until, by some brave act of skill,
Or master deed, he should evince
The prowess of an Indian prince.
Hence was the tribe together come,
To choose from out their number one
To lead their wars and councils sage,
'Till their young prince should be of age.

" But hark! above the lazy breeze
That whispers soft among the trees
Is heard the sound of many feet,
As through the forest's still retreat
A party comes with hurried tramp,
Dragging a prisoner to camp.
With hands and feet securely bound,
The captive sank upon the ground—
A son of that despised race!
Reflected on his handsome face
The resignation of despair;
For well he knew no friends were there
To save him from his awful fate
The savage zeal to satiate.
Past was the time of lethargy;
All danced about in savage glee,
Anticipating soon to see
Their victim writhing at the stake,
Which awful rite alone could slake
The vengeance of the savage heart.
Shortly the chiefs communed apart,
Not long, for in each heart, fore-doomed,
The verdict was: "To be consumed
By torture at the burning stake."
So spake they all; none there to take
The pale-face part. The dread decree,
Announced, was hailed with wildest glee.

"Some hastened to prepare the tree,
While others for the fagots went
In frenzied zeal; each soul was bent
On hastening the fearful rite.
The prisoner, lying pale and white,
Heroically endured the taunts,
The cruel blows and savage vaunts
Cast upon him from every side.
At last he stood, securely tied;
All was prepared; the lighted brand
Blazed in the iron warrior's hand.

"'Now go, my son, and do thy part,'
Cried she who all the while apart
Beside the youth in silence stood;
'Now go, and prove thy sire's blood
Runs not for nothing in thy veins!
Quick! or too late will be thy pains!'
Then, suddenly, the flames leaped out,
As round the pile, with savage shout,
The awful dance of death began,
When lo! athwart the circle ran,—
Resistless as a thunder storm,—
With lightning speed, a slender form;
Scattered like reeds the burning brands,
Released the prisoner's feet and hands,
And placing in his grasp the knife,
Bade him begone and fly for life,
Then turning to the astonished band,
He shouted, with uplifted hand:

"'If you must kill, then murder me,
But let this luckless man go free!
My father's blood is in these veins,
And well ye know his soul disdained
Thus cowardly to take the life
Of one with whom he had no strife!'

"Half stupefied, the warriors gazed
Upon the youth, and saw, amazed,
Him who had dared this brave relief—
The son of their departed chief.

The flash of anger in their eyes
Gave place to looks of deep surprise.
Then admiration for his deed
Secured for him the highest meed
Which a brave warrior could receive.
Thus, what began an awful rite,
Ended a feast of proud delight:
Each warrior in that savage band
Advanced to kiss the stripling's hand,
And owned him ruler of the land.

" Long lived the youth, a warrior brave,
Beside St. Mary's peaceful wave;
He drew his bow in many a fight,
But ever in the cause of right,
And through his life, until the end,
He still remained the white man's friend;
In battle brave, in council skilled,
He won the name of Richardville,
And over Indiana's plains,
Where erst this noble savage reigned,
That name is known and honored still.

In after years, when wars had ceased,
While signing documents of peace,
He met the man whose life was saved
When first his people's wrath he braved;
'T is said the men became fast friends,
And so remained until the end.
The debt of life was well repaid;
And when the warrior's bones were laid
To rest beside their native stream,
The friend, in token of esteem,
Raised o'er his dust this shaft of stone,
And carved the lines you see thereon:
' Pilgrim, when idly passing here,
    Tread lightly o'er this sacred mound,
And moist it with a passing tear,
    For know, you tread on sainted ground.' "

In his death the Miamis lost the greatest chief who ever
ruled over them, and since that time their decline has been

marked and rapid. It is fitting, therefore, that his name and fame should be perpetuated by a marble shaft reared near the place of his birth by the hands of those who loved him best in life.

———

CHIEF FRANCIS GODFROY.

Pa-lonz-wa, or Francis Godfroy, the last war chief of the Miamis, and whose name is closely associated with the history of Frances Slocum, because he succeeded her husband, She-pan-can-ah, when he retired from the chieftainship, was the son of Jacques, or James Godfroy, a French trader among the Indians, and was born in March, 1788, near Fort Wayne. He and his brother Louis were distinguished men among the Miamis from early manhood, and took part in the battle of Fort Wayne, as well as several other engagements. When the Miamis settled on the Wabash, Francis, following the inclinations of his father, established a trading post about four miles above Peru, which became a noted point. Being a representative man in his tribe, he naturally wielded great influence and commanded much respect. His mother was a Miami woman, but the French largely predominated in his character.

His trading post, which was named Mount Pleasant, became a place of much resort and was visited by many eminent men of the period. His business was heavy and profitable, as he supplied the Indians with large quantities of goods. He was a large and handsome man, standing about six feet in height and weighing over 300 pounds. He was genial, generous and dignified; sincere in his friendship, paternal in his rule and princely in his hospitality.

About 1822 he brought a carpenter from Fort Wayne, who

built him a house of hewn logs. It was regarded as a wonderful improvement at that time, and was a great attraction among the Indians.

The first wife of Francis Godfroy, and her sister, the wife of White Wolf, were daughters of a white man named Cole, who, when a child, was captured by the Indians in Kentucky, and grew up with them. He then married a Miami woman and raised several children. Godfroy's wife was named Sac-a-qua-tah, and she died February 28, 1869, aged 74 years, and is buried by his side. Her sister, Elizabeth, who married White Wolf, died December 7, 1871, aged 85 years. Gabriel Godfroy, one of the sons of Sac-a-qua-tah, has tried to trace the ancestry of his mother's father, but without success. It is a singular circumstance that his maternal grandfather was a white man, and that he (Godfroy) should marry a granddaughter of Frances Slocum, a white woman. Here is another singular instance of the peculiar blending of American French-Indian blood.

The eldest son, James R. Godfroy, lives near Fort Wayne, and is a farmer. He married Mon-to-so-qua, daughter of La-Blonde, the daughter of John Baptiste Richardville, (Pe-che-wah,) the famous civil chief of the Miamis, who was the leader at the treaty of 1838. She was born near Fort Wayne in 1835, and died in March, 1885, leaving twelve children.

Francis Godfroy, by virtue of his standing and influence among the Miamis, was granted some six sections of land at the treaty of 1838, and he acquired one or two more by purchase. This princely estate was sufficient to have made all his heirs very wealthy, if it had been fairly administered. One section is embraced in the southern part of the city of Peru, and is composed of the rich alluvial soil found along the Wabash. "Out of that fine tract of land," said one of his sons to the writer, "my mother and her children only realized one thousand dollars!" It is worth more than half a million to-day.

There were five sons and four daughters in the family of Francis Godfroy, viz: James R., William, George Washington, Thomas, Gabriel, Louisa, Sarah, Frances and Clemence. He died May, 1840, in the 53d year of his age, and was buried in the cemetery situated on the hillside a few hundred yards in front of his residence. His death was greatly deplored by his numerous relatives and friends, and there was much sorrow and mourning over his loss. His funeral was one of the notable events of the day, and was attended by hundreds of Indians and whites, who came to testify their respect for the deceased. The principal address was delivered by Wa-pa-pin-sha, a noted Indian orator of that tribe. Translated, it is as follows:

"Brothers, the Great Spirit has taken to Himself another of our once powerful and happy, but now declining, nation. The time has been when these forests were densely populated by the red men, but the same hand whose blighting touch withered the majestic frame before us, and caused the noble spirit by which it was animated to seek another home, has dealt in a like manner with his and our fathers; in like manner will he deal with us. Death, of late, has been common among us. So much so that a recurrence of it scarcely elicits our notice. But when the brave, the generous and patriotic are blasted by it, then it is the tears of sorrow freely flow. Such is now the case.

"Our brother, who has just left us, was brave, generous and patriotic, and as a tribute to his merit and reward for his goodness the tears, not only of his own people, but of many white men, who are here assembled to witness his funeral rites, freely flow. At this scene the poor of his people weep because at his table they were wont to feast and rejoice. The weak mourn his death because his authority was ever directed to their protection. But he has left the earth—the place of vexation and contention—and is now participating with Pocahontas and Logan in those joys prepared by the Great Spirit for such as well and faithfully discharge their duties here. Brothers, let us emulate his example and practice his virtues.''

In after years his sons erected a handsome marble monument as a testimonial of respect for their father, and it looms up conspicuously on the hillside to-day. On one of the panels appears this inscription:

CHIEF FRANCIS GODFROY,
Natus, March, 1788.
Obit, May 1, 1840.

On the other side is the following, deeply chiseled in the white marble:

''Late Principal Chief of the Miami Nation of Indians. Distinguished for courage, humanity, benevolence and honor, he lived in his native forests an illustration of the nobleness of his race, enjoying the confidence of his tribe and beloved by his American neighbors. He died as he lived—without fear or reproach.''

Chief Godfroy, inasmuch as he had acquired a large amount of personal property, and was the owner of several thousands of acres of land, was thoughtful enough to make a will for its distribution among his heirs, and as it is a curious document, as well as appropriate to the pages of this history, it is given herewith in full:

'' I, Francis Godfroy, a Miami Indian, of the County of Miami, Indiana, being desirous to settle and dispose of my worldly affairs, while in a sound mind, memory and understanding, do publish and declare this as my last will and testament:

"First: I desire my body to be decently interred at the discretion of my executors hereinafter named.

"Secondly: It is my will and I hereby bequeath to my beloved son James R. Godfroy, one section of land, to include my mill on the creek below Peru, commonly called Little Pipe Creek.

"Thirdly: I will and bequeath to my beloved son William Godfroy, one section of land lying on the Mississinewa River, being the section of land granted to O-san-di-ah, at the treaty between the United States and the Miami Indians of 1838, which I purchased of the said O-san-di-ah.

"Fourthly: I give and bequeath to my beloved son George Washington, the section of land lying opposite the town of Peru on the Wabash, being the same on which Peter Gibanet now lives.

"Fifthly: I will and bequeath to my dearly beloved sons Thomas Godfroy and Gabriel Godfroy, as tenants in common, three-fourths of the section lying above and adjoining the town of Peru, which three-fourths of a section so bequeathed as aforesaid, is a part of the section granted to me adjoining the town of Peru, at the treaty between the United States and the Miami Indians, of October of 1834.

"Sixthly: For purposes of educating my son Gabriel, I hereby will and bequeath to him in addition to my former bequest, the one-quarter section of land lying opposite my house, being the same purchased of John B. Richardville.

"Seventhly: I will and bequeath unto my two wives, or the mothers of my children, Sack-a-che-qua and Sac-kah-qua-tah, and my beloved children, my eldest unmarried daughter Louisa, to my daughter Sally, to my daughter Frances, to my daughter Clemence, the four sections of land and improvements where I now live, during the lifetime of my said wives, to be decided in case of dispute by my executors, during the lives of my wives, then two of the four sections of land, aforesaid, to include the houses and improvements, I will and bequeath to my said daughters, Louisa, Sally, Frances and Clemence, as tenants in common, and to their heirs forever.

"The remaining two of the four sections aforesaid I will and bequeath to all my children and their heirs or assigns, as well as those who are devisees to this will, as also, Poqua, and the wife of Gudboo, to be equally divided among them all.

"Eighthly: It is my will, that after the personal property which I may be possessed of at the time of my death, should be exhausted, that my executors or the survivor of them, or the person who may administer on my estate, shall sell so much of my real estate as he or they may deem necessary for the payment of my debts, the same to be sold for prices as he or they may deem reasonable, such real estate to be sold, to be such as is not devised individually to any member of my family.

"Ninthly: I will and bequeath such property as I may die possessed of, both real and personal, not heretofore disposed of, after my debts are paid, to be equally divided among all my children, share and share alike.

"Tenthly: All the property devised to all the devisees in this my last will is hereby bequeathed to them, their heirs and assigns forever.

"Lastly: I hereby constitute and appoint Allen Hamilton and John B. Richardville, of the County of Allen, to be the sole executors of this my last will and testament. In case of the death of either of them, the other to be sole executor, or in case one fails to serve, then the other to be the executor. In testimony whereof, I have hereunto set my hand and seal, the twenty-sixth day of February, eighteen hundred and forty.

"FRANCIS (his X mark) GODFROY. [Seal.]

"Signed, sealed, published, declared, by the testator, as and for his last will and testament, executed in the presence of the undersigned, who signed the same as witnesses, in the presence of each other, and in the presence of the testator, subscribed their names as such witnesses at the request of said testator, 26th February, 1840.

"EDWARD A. GODFROY.
"PETER (his X mark) ANDRE.
"B. H. SCOTT.
"F. S. CORNWALL.

Codicil to This My last Will and Testament.—It is my further will and desire and I hereby order and direct, that in the event of the titles being contested to the several tracts of land purchased by me of Wa-pa-pin-cheau, Squirrel and O-san-de-ah, or either of them, that the executors acting under my will, or my administrator, employ James Raridon, Esq., to advocate my claims thereto, and that for his services, if successful in establishing said claims, that my executors or administrators allow him for such services one-half section of the said lands, to be surveyed from either of said sections which the said Raridon may designate. It is my further will and desire, and I hereby order and direct, that my executors or administrators do immediately after my decease, give to my wife Sack-kah-qua-te, the sum of one thousand dollars in specie, the remainder in her possession to be expended under her direction for the maintenance and support of my infant children. I do further will and direct that my executor or administrator lay off within three months after my decease, on the quarter section of land immediately joining the town of Peru, town lots and streets in continuation and corresponding in size and width with the lots and streets in Peru, excepting only that portion of said quarter section near the sand hill, suitable for tannery sites, for which purpose I desire that it should be laid off in lots of two acres each; that every fourth of the town lots and tannery sites be reserved and titles for the same forthwith executed to my son James Godfroy, and the remaining three-fourths of each description of said lots to be sold at public auction, to the highest bidder, on the following conditions, to wit: One-third of the purchase money to be paid at the expiration of six months from the day of sale, the remainder in two equal payments, at the expiration of twelve and eighteen months from the day of sale; and I hereby authorize and empower my said executor or administrator, when full payment is made by the purchasers, to make, seal and deliver deeds for the conveyance of said lots to the purchasers, their heirs or assigns, hereby vesting him with full power and authority to act in the premises as fully to every intent and purpose as I myself could do if living. The proceeds of the sales of the aforesaid lots I hereby direct my said executor or administrator to apply to the discharge of my just debts, and in the event of there being thereafter a surplus, that the same be by my said executors invested in bank stock, and the annual interest thereon be applied to the discharge of the taxes on my estate.   FRANCIS (his X mark) GODFROY.

" It is my further will and desire and I hereby give and bequeath to my son James R. Godfroy, my two yoke of work cattle and wagon; the remainder of my horses and cattle of every description, I desire should be divided equally among my several children under the direction of my executor.

" It is my further will and desire and I hereby order and direct, that my executor or administrator continue my cousin, Edward A. Godfroy, in his employ to aid in settling my estate, and to collect the debts due to my trading establishment, near the present residence of my family on the Wabash River. That he be permitted to dispose of my stock of merchandise at private sale, on terms most favorable to the interest of my heirs, and to furnish from time to time to my family, from said stock, such articles as their necessities may require, rendering an account thereof to my executor, to be allowed him on the final settlement of my estate; and it is my will and desire and I hereby order and direct, that my executor, or administrator, pay to said Edward A. Godfroy, at the rate of eight hundred dollars per annum for his services, payable quarterly from the date of his first employment in my service, to wit: from the sixth day of September, one thousand eight hundred and thirty-nine.

"I further desire and direct that my executors, or administrators, do at the next treaty, use all proper influence to obtain for my family from the government of the United States, one section of land for each of my children; and the same privileges in regard to the payment of their annuities, and those of my wife, as are now granted to Chief Richardville.

"In testimony whereof, I have hereunto set my hand and seal to this codicil, to wit: my hand to the bottom of the first side of this sheet, and my hand and seal to this the last side of this sheet, this first day of May, in the year of our Lord, one thousand eight hundred and forty.

"FRANCIS (his X mark) GODFROY. [Seal.]

"Signed, sealed, published and declared by the testator, Francis Godfroy, as a codicil to his last will and testament, in the presence of us, who have subscribed our names as witnesses in the presence of the said testator, and in the presence of each other.

"EDWARD A. GODFROY.
"BENJAMIN H. SCOTT.
"DANIEL TAGGART.

"I, Benjamin H. Scott, Clerk of the Probate Court of the County of Miami, in the State of Indiana, do certify the annexed to be a true copy of the last will and testament of Francis Godfroy, late of the said County, deceased, and that Allen Hamilton, one of the executors therein named, has duly proved the same according to law, and is duly authorized to take upon himself the administration of the estate of the said testator according to the said will.

"Witness my hand and the adopted seal of the said court, the sixteenth day of May, in the year of our Lord, one thousand eight hundred and forty.

"[Seal.]   B. H. SCOTT, Clerk.

"Transcript of will, recorded April 8th, 1854, in Deed Record 'G,' on pages 687, 688, etc.

"Probate Court, Miami County, Indiana, May 18th, 1844. Probate Order Book 'A,' page 43."

Many anecdotes are related of Francis Godfroy, one in particular of which is worth recording, as it shows the liberality of the man. He was reckless and careless of money, and having more land than he knew what to do with, he scattered his favors with a prodigal hand. It is told of him that being on one occasion at La Fayette when a steamboat arrived there from the Ohio, he offered the captain a half section of land if he would convey him and his party to their homes, some three miles above where Peru now stands. The offer was accepted and the trip made, but the steamer was lost on its return to La Fayette. Godfroy made a deed of the promised half section of land, and sent it to the captain of the boat. It was difficult to navigate the Wabash so far up, and it was only the smallest class of boats that could ascend that distance at the highest stage of water. And the loss of the steamer on its return shows the peril of making such a voyage.

Butler was the name of the township in which Chief Godfroy lived and died. His trading post was a famous place in early times and it is one of the landmarks of the township to-day. One of the log buildings is still standing and is now occupied as a dwelling by one of the sons of Gabriel Godfroy, who is the owner. The Chief lived in the style of a baron of feudal times, and kept a large retinue of his people constantly around him.

A very pretty legend showing how he came to be selected as war chief is still preserved. There was a very bad Indian in the tribe known as Ma-jen-i-ca. He was a drinking, quarrelsome man, and frequently killed those who displeased him. Being the chief of a village he was greatly feared. Once upon a time, as the story runs, he was in a boisterous condition at a council, which was being held on the hill just above where the Godfroy cemetery is now located. Francis Godfroy, then a young man, was present. From some remark he incurred the displeasure of Ma-jen-i-ca, who commanded him to sit down, telling him that he was no man. Young Godfroy resented the insult and told him *he* was no man—that he was a coward—that he should desist from stabbing and killing his own people for trivial causes. These remarks greatly excited Ma-jen-i-ca, and drawing his knife he rushed on Godfroy. The latter being brave and powerful, quickly seized his assailant by the wrist and held his arm firmly. Then he drew his own knife and told him the braver way would be to fight him a duel. Still holding him by the arm he commanded him to look upon yonder sun for the last time if he proposed to fight. If not intending to fight, and if he was a brave man, he would drop his knife. Godfroy stood firm and ready to fight, and being a giant in strength, caused his assailant, through his determined look, to quail. Finally the big chief dropped his knife and yielded to the superior will power of Godfroy. This act of bravery resulted in the latter being made war chief when She-pan-can-ah, the husband of Frances Slocum, resigned his position.

William, one of the sons of Francis, lives on a farm which he inherited from his father. George Washington, when only fourteen years of age, was killed by lightning in May, 1841, while sitting on his horse, with several others, in the road in front of the trading post. There was scarcely a cloud in the sky when the bolt descended. His death caused a profound sensation at the time, and was regarded with superstitious awe by the Miamis. A large boulder, now lying on the roadside, is pointed out to show near where he sat when death came so suddenly from the sky.

Gabriel Godfroy, now in his 57th year, resides on a splendid farm containing 220 acres, lying in the forks of the Wabash and Mississinewa Rivers. It is looked upon as one of the best farms in the State, on account of its beautiful location and richness of the soil. There is really not a foot of land in the whole 220 acres which is not tillable. Mr. Godfroy's residence, a modern two story brick house, with a fine lawn, faces the Mississinewa. His barns and outbuildings are ample, and he carries on farming on a large scale, as he owns other lands not embraced in this tract. Mr. Godfroy has been married three times. His present wife, whose name was Martha Jane Logan, claims a distant relationship with the late General Logan, of civil war fame. Gabriel Godfroy is very popular among his acquaintances, and is noted for his liberal and princely hospitality. He is widely known, and is visited by many strangers, on account of being the son of the last war chief of the Miamis, and the husband of a granddaughter of Frances Slocum. As shown in Chapter XI., he owns many relics which once belonged to Frances Slocum, the "white woman," and his distinguished father. Among the latter are a coat and war bonnet, a fine ceremonial tomahawk, with a pipe in the poll, and the handle ornamented with inlaid silver bands and designs, and a number of silver medals. One of the medals is oval shaped, measuring six inches by five. On one side are the words "George Washington, President, 1793," and a medallion representing an Indian holding the pipe of peace to a colonist, while a tomahawk is carelessly thrown aside. In the background is seen a pioneer at the plow. On the reverse is seen the coat of arms of the United States. This medal was presented to the Wyandotte tribe by Washington, and afterwards by the Wyandotte chieftain to William Pe-cong-a, a Miami. An offer of $500 has been refused for this rare medal.

There are three other silver medals in the collection, circular in form, and two and one-half inches in diameter. On the obverse side they bear a pipe and tomahawk crossed; on the reverse, two hands clasped, with the motto: "Peace and Friendship. A. Jackson, President, 1829." These medals were given Francis Godfroy and two minor chiefs by President Jackson in 1829, and one of them bears the portrait of "Old Hickory" in relief. They are rare and valued relics, and Mr. Godfroy sets great store by them.

The vast landed estate left by Chief Godfroy has dwindled away until comparatively little of it remains. Many of the heirs having long since disposed of their shares, the lands are now in the hands of strangers.

REV. PETER BONDY.

Rev. Peter Bondy, who was the last husband of O-zah-wah-shing-qua, still survives. He spends a portion of the time with his children on the old homestead, and the balance with relatives in Grant County. He remained single several years after the death of O-zah-wah-shing-qua, when he took for his second wife a sister of Gabriel Godfroy. There has been no issue by this marriage.

Mr. Bondy is of French-Indian origin. His father, Antoine Bondie, was a French trader, holding forth near Fort Wayne. He had lived among the Indians since he was twelve years of age, and was recognized by the Miamis as one of their

tribe. He is said to have been an extraordinary character.
At one time he would appear to be brave and generous, at
another meanly selfish. About the time the siege of Fort
Wayne was contemplated by the Indians and British, Bondie,* who was at his trading post, was secretly informed of
what was proposed, and advised to leave. He straightway
communicated his information to the commanding officer,
but the latter discredited him. He moved into the fort with
his family, when the siege was soon after commenced, but
ultimately failed.

Peter Bondy was born on Eel River, a few miles north of
Fort Wayne, July, 1817. His mother, he says, was a Mohican woman. He grew to manhood among the Indians of
that section, and about 1840 was adopted by the Miamis.
According to the custom of the tribe, upon the death or loss
of children, another was adopted to supply the place made
vacant by what means soever. The circumstances giving
rise to the ceremony about to be described, says Helm in his
history of Wabash County, were in substance as follows:
"Al-lo-lah, the Black Raccoon, without a child or children
of his own, married a squaw, who was the mother of a son,
the issue of a former marriage. According to the usage of
the tribe, a man marrying an Indian woman with a child or
children, accepted and recognized the latter as his own, and
they became members of his family, entitled to all the rights
and privileges of his own offspring. In the course of time
this son and heir came to his death by violence, leaving him
childless. A proper time having elapsed after the happen-
ing of that event, a selection was made for a substitute, who,
when he had passed through the prescribed formula, should
supply the place of the dead one. Peter Bondie, or as he

* See Valley of the Upper Maumee, Vol. 1, p. 134.

BONDY'S ADOPTION DANCE.

was known and called by the Indians, Gradeway Bundy, was the person so selected and upon whom the mantle of sonship was to fall, as the custom authorized and prescribed.

"When it had been determined by the chief to consummate the selection, he gave notice of his purpose to the head men of the tribe in the vicinity, declaring the time when the ceremony would take place. Having done so, preparations began to be made on an extensive scale. A beef from the woods was killed, weighing 1,800 pounds. After being dressed, the meat was cut into large pieces, then put into great kettles and thoroughly boiled. Afterward, the meat was cut into small pieces and piled on blankets spread upon the ground for the purpose, preparatory to the coming feast.

"At the appointed hour, a distant rumbling noise was heard in every direction, as of many horses in rapid flight, and not unlike the mutterings of far off thunder. The sounds grew nearer and nearer, becoming momentarily more distinct. Finally about the hour of 10 o'clock at night a fierce yell resounded from every point of the compass, when, as if they had come by previous concert, Indians on horseback dashed in, meeting at a designated spot.

"Soon after these arrivals were announced, a suitable plateau was selected and the festival inaugurated by the commencement of a grand dance, at a late hour in the evening. First two young squaws entered the ring caparisoned for the dance. Then came two young braves who at once joined in the movement, when two other squaws came forward, dancing after their style. The dance was continued, the number of participants increasing from time to time, by two squaws joining in followed by two braves, as in the beginning, during the night. Meanwhile, a council of the head men of the tribe was in progress in the wigwam of the chief, Al-lo-lah, and at short intervals messengers were sent to inform the dancers of the progress made in the proceedings. These announcements were usually accompanied by an eloquent speech from the bearer of the tidings, greeted by acclamations of satisfaction and approval. At length, the final announcement was made, declaring as the decision of the council, upon mature deliberation, that the proposed adoption had been satisfactorily consummated. This announcement, especially, was made with a solemn flourish, and received with extraordinary demonstrations of joyous satisfaction by two of the festive throng. While these things were in progress, and whenever the demands of appetite made it necessary, the enhungered ones repaired to the commissariat where the bounteous supply of pieces of beef had been piled away on the blankets, and partook to their satisfaction of the luscious viands.

"The adoption ceremonies being completed, the company filed off and departed for their several homes, well satisfied with what had taken place. And ever afterwards Peter Bondy was acknowledged as the son and heir of the chief Al-lo-lah."

This strange Indian ceremony is said to have taken place in 1840, and a prominent white settler named Jacob D. Cassatt, first sheriff of the county, and afterwards a member of the Legislature, weighed the beef when it was killed.

Under the pious ministrations of Rev. George R. Slocum Mr. Bondy became a convert to the doctrines of the Baptist Church, and for many years he has been a consistent and active member. He informed the writer that for twenty-six years he had labored as a missionary among his people, and, notwithstanding there was much evil to combat, he felt that his labors had not been in vain. His name appears as a trustee of the Antioch Missionary Baptist Church, of Waltz

Township, Wabash County. He is pious and devout, and in his intercourse with his people, sets them a good example. He speaks broken English with a strong French accent, and upon important topics he prefers to converse through an interpreter. At table, before partaking, he asks a blessing in the Miami tongue, which, judging from the softness and beauty of the language, and the intonation of the words, is eloquent and impressive.

In personal appearance, Mr. Bondy is dignified and commanding. He stands nearly six feet in height, and weighs 240 pounds. His countenance is indicative of mildness and benignity; his intellectual powers are good, and he is a pleasant companion. In his actions and conversation it is evident that the Indian character predominates, notwithstanding his long association with the whites. Like his brother-in-law, Gabriel Godfroy, he can neither read nor write.

FRANCIS La FONTAINE.

It is learned from the history of Wabash County that Francis La Fontaine, whose Indian name was To-pe-ah, was the immediate successor of Richardville as the principal chief of the Miamis. He was a lineal descendant of the family of this name who figured so conspicuously in the political affairs of Canada in the latter part of the eighteenth century. His father was of French extraction, and was at one time a resident of Detroit, and his mother was a Miami woman. He was born near Fort Wayne in 1820, and spent the greater part of his life in the immediate vicinity. In his younger days he was noted for his great strength and activity, and was considered the most fleet of foot of any man in his tribe.

At the age of about twenty-one Francis La Fontaine married Catharine, (Pa-con-go-quah) the second daughter of Richardville. For some time after his marriage his residence was on the prairie, between Huntington and Fort Wayne, on lands granted to him at the treaty of 1838. Manifesting great interest in the welfare of his tribe, he became very popular, and, after the death of Chief Richardville, he was selected principal chief of the Miamis.

When the Miamis moved west in 1846 he accompanied them to their new reservation and spent the first winter with them. The following spring he started homeward. At that time the route of travel was from Kansas Landing (now Kansas City) down the Missouri and Mississippi to the mouth of the Ohio, then up the latter to the mouth of the Wabash, and thence up that river to La Fayette—all the way by steamboat. At St. Louis he was taken sick, and his disease had made such progress that upon his arrival at La Fayette he was unable to proceed further, and died there on the 13th of April, 1847, at the age of thirty-seven years.

He was embalmed at La Fayette, and his remains were brought to Huntington, where he was buried in the grounds now occupied by the Catholic Church. His body was subsequently removed to the new cemetery.

Francis La Fontaine is described as a tall, robust and corpulent man, weighing usually 350 pounds, and generally dressed in Indian costume. There are two oil paintings of him in existence. He left seven children. Less than two years after his death his widow married F. D. Lasselle, of Fort Wayne, but lived only a short time.

John La Fontaine, the last son of this historic family, and a grandson of the chief, died at Huntington in December, 1889. His mother died when he was about five years old, and he was placed in the care of Col. I. N. Milligan, but being deeply imbued with the traditions of his race, a roving disposition seized him, and he joined the remnant of his tribe in Kansas. He soon tired of their romantic life and returned to Huntington. His ancestors at one time owned all the land in that section, but he died a poor man. So ends the name of La Fontaine.

GEORGE WINTER, THE ARTIST.

As the name of George Winter frequently occurs in this work in connection with Indian paintings, a short sketch of his life is not out of place. Hon. Horace P. Biddle, of Logansport, who knew him well, writes:

"George Winter was born on the island of Portsea, in the town of Portsea, in the county of Hants, in England, in the year 1810. He was sent to school when quite a child, and received a general course of English education under English teachers. It does not appear that he was ever a graduate of any university or college. He early exhibited a taste for the fine arts; was encouraged and instructed by local artists; went to London where he was entered a student in the Royal Academy, and where he remained during four years. He also had the entry to the National Gallery and other public institutions. In 1830 he came to America. In New York he became a student in the Academy of Design, where he remained several years. From there he went to Cincinnati, where he sojourned but a short time. In the year 1837 he came to Logansport, Indiana, where he resided until 1850, when he removed to La Fayette, Indiana. In 1873 and 1874, Mr. Winter visited California and the Pacific Slope, where he executed many valuable paintings. He returned to La Fayette, which place remained his home until he died, February 1, 1876.

"Mr. Winter was an English gentleman of a higher type than those who merely repose on the virtues of their ancestors. As a man, he possessed a nice sense of honor and integrity, and made these principles practical throughout his life. Socially he stood very high with all who knew him. He was a gentleman under all circumstances, with a ready and agreeable wit, a genial and engaging humor, and an equable and chastened temper. As an artist Mr. Winter ranked high—particularly in landscape and Indian pieces. In water color sketches and miniature he also excelled. His portrait of Chief Godfroy seemed to be Godfroy himself; and that of the young Chief Aub-e-naw-be was an admirable specimen of art in portraiture. He also painted, besides the excellent portrait of Frances Slocum, several young Indian maidens who were very beautiful. Indeed, he painted before he left England a battle piece which became very celebrated. In America, particularly in the great Northwest, Mr. Winter became widely known as an artist of high repute. Many of his paintings were engraved for the magazines of the time.

"In 1840 Mr. Winter married Mary Squiers, the daughter of Timothy Squiers, the proprietor of a line of coaches from Dayton, Ohio, westward. They were blessed with an only son and an only daughter, both of whom, with the mother, survive the husband and father. The son—George Winter, resides in California; the daughter—Mrs. Nettie W. Ball, and the mother, still have their homes in La Fayette, where they enjoy the respect of a large circle of friends."

As Judge Biddle has referred to the success of Mr. Winter in painting Indian portraits, and a battle piece in England, it may not be out of place to speak of his views of the battle

ground of Tippecanoe, and for this purpose his own words
are used. In an autograph letter* to Mr. E. Campbell, editor
of *The Spirit of the Times*, Cincinnati, under date of Logansport, January 1, 1841, Mr. Winter says:

"The paintings that I have nearly completed are six in
number. Two of them measure 152 square feet each, and
the other four comprehend an equal surface. I chose such
views that would best convey an idea of the ground and surrounding romantic country. One view is taken from the La-
Fayette road, which represents the point near Barnet's Creek
where the subtle savage tomahawked the sentinel. I then
followed the road (which passes through the whole of the
ground upon which the remarkable battle was fought) and
took my station about 60 feet from the fence, or southwestern
gateway of the enclosure, and known as Spencer's line.
From this point you get nearly in perspective with the whole
surface upon which the gallant army encamped.

"You now stand upon an elevation of seventeen feet from
the surface of the prairie on either side. The prairie to the
right is called the marsh—it extends before you as far nearly
as the eye can see; it is skirted by oak openings, and at a
point projecting, as it were, upon the prairie the wily Prophet
sat during the conflict of battle chanting and propitiating the
power of the Great Spirit.

"Another view I took from the Log Cabin which was
erected at the convention in May [1840] last. This compre-
hends a view of the interior of the enclosure, (about forty

---

* Through the courtesy of Dr. Lyman C. Draper, of the Wisconsin Historical Society, the author was placed in possession of this letter, as well
as another bearing date, "Logansport, Ind., September 21, 1838." Both are
written in a neat, compact, plain hand, and each one covers four pages of
foolscap, barely leaving room enough for the address, when folded, as no
envelopes were in use in those days. The latter is principally devoted to
literary topics and is of no interest to the public.

acres.) It assumes a park-like appearance—the timber not
being crowded. The sun now and then throws in his bright
rays, which give a cheerful and pleasing effect, and the mind
being enraptured with so lovely a spot, is robbed almost of
the belief that it is associated with human blood.

"I have not space to enter into a detail now of the scenes
I have spoken of; and the others I can merely say are views
of the graves of those who slumber on the field of Tippecanoe, and some trees from which Davis was trying to dislodge
some Indians when he fell. I have a view, too, of Prophet's
Town.

"Although I have been defeated in getting these views
before the public eye at the time when political excitement
ran high, yet I have often indulged in the consoling hopes
that Harrison would be elected, and that an interest would
still be felt for a peep at the ground on which such conflict-
ing opinions have been expressed. I think if I could get
these pictures to Cincinnati some time before the General sets
out for the White House, that the feelings of 'fellow citizens' will be warmed up again, and it would be a favorable
time to exhibit them. I have also thought that it would be
a propitious time, too, either at the inauguration, or during
the spring, to exhibit them at Washington."

It is not known whether Mr. Winter succeeded in his
plans, or what disposition was finally made of these paintings.

AN INDIAN BURIAL GROUND.

George Winter, the artist, devoted much attention to literature as a pastime, and he contributed many sketches of
the country, and Indian character, to the press while he lived
at Logansport. It is understood that he left voluminous un-

published notes, which are supposed to be in the hands of his widow at La Fayette. In a description of an Indian burial ground near Logansport, he says:

"No doubt but what this depository of the aboriginal dead was mostly confined to the Indians who died at the village of Ke-na-pa-cum-qua, which stood on the north bank of Eel River, some six miles above the confluence with the Wabash. 'Charley's Reserve' is known as being in the vicinity of this old village. Many of the older citizens are familiar with the beautiful view that could be seen from Reed's old log cabin on the northern bank, near the Peru road. The scene that thus presented itself to the eye included the old site of the village of Ke-na-pa-cum-qua. The Miami burial ground near Logansport, contained the remains of the renowned chief and warrior, No-ka-me-nah, or as he was more familiarly called, Captain Flowers. The graves were generally covered with bark. The chief's loomed up above all others of lesser consequence. It was rudely constructed of logs, within which was placed a pine box, or che-pe-em-kak, protecting the remains. The chief's rifle, tin cup, powder horn, and other relics were deposited so that the spirit might carry along with it in its flight the chosen earthly objects to the beautiful world of the future hunting grounds. There are no signs now to indicate the burial ground. I remember well when the same spot yielded to the ploughshare. It proved a rich soil, but it seemed strange to see the beautiful tassel of the corn thrown out where, but a few years ago, there was a breathing of sanctity upon the lowly graves. When the ploughshare ran deep into the graves the—

"Brown skulls, in spite of ugly death,
    On the grasss grinned merrily.
You could hear men's rotting and crumbling bones
    Rattle together with unctuous glee,

For they mocked the sighs and scoffed at the moans
Of silly and frail humanity.''

" It was a painful fact, of which no doubt existed, that the body of No-ka-me-nah did not rest long after burial, in peaceful repose. It was a good rifle they consigned to the grave with the chief, but the enterprising Christian man had soon possession of it, and many a deer has fallen since at its sharp crack, and the venison sold for fifty cents per saddle, proving satisfactorily that the violations of a red man's grave was a pecuniary gain!

" But why should we underrate moral acts? Stealing from an Indian grave is, after all, but a white man's 'smart trick' of trade!''

ERRATA.

Page 100, first line in Chapter heading, for "oldest" daughter read eldest.

Page 159, last line of text, for "four" years read five.

Page 162, eighteenth line, for "niece" read granddaughter.

Page 162, foot note, for "Memorial" read Manual.

Page 164, eleventh line, for "newphew" read nephew.

BIBLIOGRAPHY.

Following is a list of the authorities consulted in the preparation of the Biography of Frances Slocum:

Loudon's Indian Narratives.
> Two Volumes. By Archibald Loudon. Carlisle, from the Press of A. Loudon, 1808.

A Sketch of the History of Wyoming.
> To which is added an Appendix containing a Statistical Account of the Valley and Adjacent Country, by a Gentleman of Wilkes-Barre. By Isaac A. Chapman. Wilkes-Barre, Sharp D. Lewis, 1830.

The Poetry and History of Wyoming,
> Containing Campbell's Gertrude, with a Biographical Sketch of the Author by Washington Irving, and the History of Wyoming by Wm. L. Stone. New York and London, Wiley & Putnam, 1841.

The Lost Sister of Wyoming.
> An Authentic Narrative. By Rev. John Todd. Northampton, Pa., J. H. Butler, 1842.

History of Wyoming,
> In a series of letters from Charles Miner, to His Son, William Penn Miner, Esq. Philadelphia, published by J. Crissy, 1845.

The Pictorial Field Book of the Revolution.
> Two Volumes. By Benson J. Lossing, LL. D. New York, Harper & Brothers, 1859.

Annals of Luzerne.
> A Record of Events, Traditions and Anecdotes, from the First Settlement of Wyoming to 1860. By Stewart Pearce. Philadelphia, J. B. Lippincott & Company, 1860.

Wyoming :
> Its History, Stirring Incidents and Romantic Adventures. By George Peck, D. D. New York, Harper & Brothers, 1860.

The Valley of Wyoming ;
> The Romance of its History and its Poetry. By a native of the Valley. New York, Robert H. Johnston & Co., 1866.

History of the Lackawanna Valley.
> By H. Hollister, M. D., Scranton. Philadelphia, J. B. Lippincott & Company, 1855.

The Wyoming Valley, Upper Waters of the Susquehanna, and the Lackawanna Coal Region.
By J. A. Clark, Scranton, Pa., published by the author, 1875.

Wyoming Memorial.
A Record of the One Hundredth Year Commemorative Observance of the Battle and Massacre. Edited by Wesley Johnson, Esq., Secretary of the Association. Wilkes-Barre, Pa., Beardslee & Co., 1882.

Frances Slocum, the Lost Sister.
A Poem. By Caleb Earl Wright. Robert Baur & Son, Wilkes-Barre, Pa., 1889.

Historical Sketches of Plymouth, Luzerne County, Pa.
By Hendrick B. Wright. Philadelphia, T. B. Peterson & Brother, 1873.

Brief of a Title in Seventeen Townships in the County of Luzerne.
A Syllabus of the Controversy Between Connecticut and Pennsylvania. Read before the Historical Society of Pennsylvania. By Gov. Henry M. Hoyt. Harrisburg, Lane S. Hart, 1879.

Historical Collections of the State of Pennsylvania.
Its History and Antiquities. By Sherman Day. Philadelphia, George W. Gorton, 1843.

Early Times on the Susquehanna.
By Mrs. George A. Perkins. Binghamton, Malette & Reed, 1870.

An Illustrated History of Pennsylvania.
Civil, Political and Military, including Historical Descriptions of each County in the State. By William H. Egle, M. D., State Librarian. Harrisburg, De Witt C. Goodrich & Co., 1876.

The Aboriginal Races of North America.
Origin, Antiquities, Manners and Customs. By Samuel G. Drake. New York, Hurst & Co., 1880.

Magazine of American History.
New York. Edited by Mrs. Martha J. Lamb, July, 1890.

Harpers' Monthly Magazine.
New York, Harper & Brothers, August, 1858.

History of Cass County, Indiana.
By Thomas B. Helm. Chicago, Kingman Brothers, 1878.

History of Fort Wayne,
From the Earliest Known Accounts. By Wallace A. Brice. Fort Wayne, Indiana, D. W. Jones & Son, 1868.

History of Wabash County, Indiana.
By Thomas B. Helm. Chicago, John Morris, 1884.

Valley of the Upper Maumee River,
With Historical Accounts of Allen County and the City of Fort Wayne, Indiana. The Story of its Progress from Savagery to Civilization. Two Volumes. Madison, Wis., Brant & Fuller, 1889.

History of Miami County, Indiana.
Its Early Settlement and Progress. Chicago, 1888.

History of Lancaster County, Pennsylvania,
With Biographical Sketches of Many of its Pioneers and Prominent Men. By Ellis & Evans. Philadelphia, Everts & Peck, 1883.

A History of Indiana,
From its Earliest Exploration by Europeans to 1856. By John B. Dillon. Indianapolis, Bingham & Dougherty, 1859.

Pennsylvania Magazine of History and Biography.
No. 1, Vol. III. Edited by John W. Jordan. Philadelphia, 1879.

History of the Slocums, Slocumbs and Slocombs of America.
Genealogical and Biographical. By Charles Elihu Slocum, M.D., Ph. D., Defiance, Ohio. Published by the author, 1882.

Wyalusing.
Its History from the First Settlement until 1779. By Rev. David Craft. Towanda, 1870.

History of Bradford County, Pennsylvania.
By Rev. David Craft. L. H. Everts & Co., Philadelphia, 1878.

General Sullivan's Expedition Against the Six Nations oj Indians in 1779.
By Frederick Cook, Secretary of State, N. Y. Auburn, Knap, Peck & Thompson, 1887.

Frances Slocum, the Indian Captive.
Pamphlet by James Slocum. Brownsville, Pa., 1878.

History of the Girtys,
Thomas, Simon, James and George. By Consul Willshire Butterfield. Cincinnati, Robert Clarke & Co., 1890.

Historical Record.
A Monthly Publication Devoted Principally to the Early History of Wyoming and Contiguous Territory. Edited by F. C. Johnson, M. D. Three Volumes. Wilkes-Barre Record, 1886 to 1889.

Journal of Captain William Trent,
From Logstown to Pickawillany, A. D. 1752, with an Historical Sketch of the Miami Confederacy. Edited by Alfred T. Goodman. Cincinnati, Robert Clarke & Company, 1871.

Beautiful Wyoming.

A Poem for the Celebration of the Hundredth Anniversary of the Battle, Massacre and Flight, 1778, July 3, 1878. By Henry Coppee. Philadelphia, Claxton, Remsen & Haffelfinger, 1878.

Annals of the West.

A Concise Account of Principal Events which have Occurred in the Western States and Territories to the year 1856. By James R. Albach. Pittsburgh, W. S. Haven, 1857.

History of Luzerne, Lackawanna and Wyoming Counties, Pennsylvania.

With Illustrations and Biographical Sketches. New York, W. W. Munsell & Co., 1880.

Families of the Wyoming Valley.

Biographical, Genealogical and Historical. Sketches of the Bench and Bar of Luzerne County, Pa. By George B. Kulp. In three Volumes. Wilkes-Barre, 1885—'89—'90.

A Manual of Gold and Silver Coins of All Nations,

Struck Within the past Century. By Jacob R. Eckfeldt & William E. DuBois. Philadelphia, 1851.

INDEX.

SUPPLEMENTAL.

In some respects there has been almost as much difficulty encountered in gathering information relating to the history of Frances Slocum as was experienced by her brothers who sought to find her after her capture, with the difference, however, that their search was continued through many long and weary years. This seems to be a part of the mystery which has always surrounded her case. In collecting data for this work it was believed that if Mrs. Eliza O. Slocum, the widow of George R., could be found, she would be able to furnish valuable information, on account of her association with the old lady and her daughters. After a long search she was located at Sioux City, Iowa, where she was living with a daughter, Mrs. Eliza J. Ford, and a series of questions were prepared by Dr. Charles E. Slocum, of Defiance, Ohio, and forwarded to her. Not hearing from her for a long time, the matter was finally dropped, the book closed, the printing completed and the sheets sent to the binder. But, fortunately, before fifty copies were bound, she was heard from. She had been severely ill for some time, but realizing the importance of the interrogations, she dictated the following information to her daughter, which is deemed of sufficient importance to be printed in supplemental form and added to those copies which have not been bound:

CAPTURE OF FRANCES AS TOLD BY HERSELF.

"My father was at the fort. [Wilkes-Barre]. I heard a gun go off and I ran and hid under the stairs. Three big Indians came to the door and took up my brother Ebenezer. His foot was lame; a cart had run over it. My mother went to the door to tell them he was lame; took up both his feet and showed them. I was afraid my mother was going away, so I came out and ran to my mother. The Indians saw me, and pushing my brother toward mother, took me. My hair

Q

fell over my face. I took my hand and brushed it away, and saw my mother for the last time. They took me down a deep ravine a long way, when we came to a cave and went in. I saw my father through a little hole hunting me. I was going to scream, when an Indian held a big knife over me and looking cross, said, 'me kill, me kill.' That was the last time I saw my father.

"At night the Indians waded in the water down the creek a long distance, when they came to their horses. We rode all night and came to an Indian camp. A little boy and I were given to two Indians, and we started one way—the rest of the Indians went another way. They had nine captives with them. We went north and crossed under the big water. [Niagara Falls]. The big water went boom, boom. After a while we came to an Indian camp. I don't know anything about the boy—don't know what became of him. They took me to an old man and his wife, and they always took care of me. One day, when I was twenty-one years old, there was a big stir in camp; the old man and his wife took me and got in a boat in a great hurry, and we went a long way, when we came to another camp. The old man then gave me to the chief, and then I took care of my own wigwam."

"When Frances gave this account of her capture," says Mrs. Slocum, "her daughters were present and interpreted for her."

MARRIAGES OF FRANCES.

"At one time I was at their house, when O-zah-wah-shing-qua, or Mrs. Bondy, as we called her, and we were alone, I asked her to tell me of her mother's marriages, as I had heard she was married twice. She said: 'The first time she was married she was not happy.' I asked her how they got married. She replied: 'Frances' father said to him, [first husband], 'You love him squaw?' He said, 'Yes.' The father replied, 'Well, take him, and no 'buse him.' Mrs. Bondy continued, 'After a while he 'buse him, and he [she] came home, but her husband came and made good promises to treat her well. She tried again, but he was abusive. She left him again, came back, and they drove him away, and she never saw him again.'

"'The second marriage,' said Mrs. Bondy, 'came about as follows: Frances, her father and mother, started down the river. Before they reached Fort Wayne they passed an Indian battle ground. The dead were lying on every side. They heard groans, when they stopped, and in the brush they found a chief of the Miamis wounded. They took him in their boat and went about twelve miles below Fort Wayne. It was late in the fall. They nursed him until he recovered from his wound, but he was lame. At one time they were out of food, when the young chief walked to Fort Wayne to obtain something. He was gone four days, when they saw him afar off returning. Frances went out and met him. He was much wearied and quite sick. Through gratitude for what he had done for them, Frances' Indian father gave her to him in the early spring. They then went down the Wabash River and joined his tribe at the Osage village. This was She-pah-can-a, or the Deaf Man.'

"Mrs. Bondy once dressed me in Frances' best dress, with beaded moccasins and leggins, a fine felt blanket wrapped around me as a shirt, which was so completely covered with scarlet and green silk ribbon an inch wide, and sewed together so closely you could see no felt on the right side; a short gown of navy blue, with extra cape covered all over with silver bangles, a sash of scarlet four yards long with white tasssels at the ends. My head was crowned with a wreath of black ostrich feathers with silver broaches on the front. The back feathers were very long.

"Mrs. E. O. SLOCUM."

VALUABLE INFORMATION.

Following are the answers of Mrs. E. O. Slocum to questions submitted to her by Dr. Charles E. Slocum:

"What was the duration of Frances' last sickness?"

"Less than a week."

"What doctor did she have, and would she take his medicine?"

"She died forty-two years ago the 6th* of next March. [1891.] There was no white doctor on the Reserve at that time. The Indians used their system or treatment. She would not have taken white folks' medicine if there had been a doctor."

"What was her sickness, and the cause of her death?"

"Pneumonia. The Indians had been having a thankoffering. They cooked a deer whole for the Great Spirit and put it on a table. They sat around it and sang, but did not eat. They sang all night and she caught cold."

"What minister preached her funeral sermon?"

"Joseph Davis, an exhorter. There was no minister within reach at the time. It was not the custom for the Indians to bury their dead in a coffin at that time; but they were given to understand that she was a white woman and should be buried according to the custom of white people. A coffin was then obtained, but it was found to be one foot too long. They then put a little brass kettle, a cream pitcher and other things in the vacant space at her feet."

"Did you see her every day?"

"Yes; we lived near."

"Did you spend much time in visiting her?"

"Yes; either myself or husband were there most of the time."

"Were you very intimate with her?"

"Yes; she thought a great deal of us. Of course, we spoke different languages."

"Did she retain any of her mother's teachings? If so, give examples."

"I think so. She kept her house very much better than the native Indians. And her lessons of cleanliness to her girls were something to wonder at. Both she and her daughters were very neat with their needles. In neatness and order she and family were far above the native Indians."

---

* All other accounts agree in fixing the date of her death on March 9th.

" Did she use any English words ? If so, to what extent ?''

" Yes; she and I were sitting alone one evening, and I became anxious about Mr. Slocum's return from payment [annuity] when she said: ' Pretty soon George come; moon shine.'' These are the only words I ever heard her say; but I think she could understand.''

" Did she show much interest in her white relatives?''

" Yes; for those whom she knew she seemed to think a great deal of.''

" Did she at any time show any of the Indian's distrust of the white man in her intercourse with her white relatives? If so, give examples.''

" No; she had her interpreter write two letters to her brother Isaac to come out on business. He came, when she said her business with him was to ask him to give his son George to her to care for her property, and be her son. She said she would make him an equal heir with her two girls.

" Isaac said, ' George is my youngest son, the one I have picked out to live with me and care for my interest in my old age.' Frances replied, ' You know I was taken away when I was little, and had no care from my people, while you had a father and mother's care, and all the property. And you have other sons to care for you, and I have no sons and a large property to look after. Now, give me George to be my son and I will make him equal heir with my two girls.'

" Isaac said, ' George is married and has a family, and I don't know whether he will be willing to come; but if he is willing I will give my consent.'

" When Isaac started home she gave him a very nice pony, saddle and bridle, a pair of new moccasins nicely beaded, and a lot of dried venison. That was in June. When he reached home he did not tell George, but advised him to go in the fall to attend the land sales.

" Frances told him of the adoption and had him stay till after the annuities were paid, when she divided the money equally between her girls and George. When he started for home she gave him some kind of presents as she gave his father, which made the adoption legal according to the tribal laws—she knew no other law.

"George finally decided to come and look after her affairs. He bought eighty acres of land in January, and moved his family out in November following. He gathered her ponies together—about 100 head—and disposed of them for her, and attended the payment to receive her annuity. Frances died the 6th of March, 1847. George staid on his farm, two miles away, and cared for their interest until his death [January, 1860,] without any further recompense."

"Did she show much interest in your children? If so, in what manner?"

"Yes; she used to love to hold the baby, [now Mrs. L. G. Murphy of Xenia, Indiana,] and wished it given her Indian and white name—Frances—Ma-con-a-qua. But she was already named Mary Cordelia. Frances' daughter [O-zah-wah-shing-qua] always called her mother, and the grandchildren call her grandmother to this day."

"Did she have the Indian's love for bright colors?"

"No; I never saw anything bright or gay, either in her clothing or house."

"Was she at times very talkative and sociable?"

"Yes; she at one time told me about her captivity, but she was not unusually sociable."

"Was she easily offended?"

"No."

"Did she hold offense long, or was she quick to forgive and make up friends?"

"I never saw an exhibition of temper. She was always pleasant."

"Was she revengeful? If so, give examples."

"No."

"Was she ever violent in her temper?"

"No."

"Was she ever sulky and morose? If so, did these moods last long?"

"No."

"Did she use tobacco? If so, in what way?"

" No, no, no!''

" Did she use whiskey? If so, to what extent and regularity ?"

" No, indeed; never!''

" Did she ever show any desire to follow the ways of white women? If so, give examples.''

" I was the only white woman there at that time. Frances used to come to my house and watch me work. Her daughter and she used to admire my quilts and other things about the house.''

" Did she get any idea of the teachings of Christianity? If so, to what extent?''

"George used to read the Bible to her and talk with her. She paid strict attention to all he said. I cannot tell how much she understood his teachings. She did not live long after we moved there.''

" Did she show much lasting interest in the efforts of her white friends to improve her mental and moral condition? If so, give examples.''

" Yes; it seemed so, at least to all appearance.''

" Was your husband a Missionary, appointed by the Baptist church ?''

" No; he was only a good, honest minded Christian man; a member of the Missionary Baptist Church—a deacon.''

" Did he teach them to read and write?''

" Yes.''

" Did he learn their language?''

" Yes.''

" Did he speak to them in their language, or through an interpreter?''

"First through an interpreter; soon in their own language.''

" Did Frances attend his meetings?''

" He went to their house to teach them; Frances was there.''

" Did your husband receive his support from the church ?''

" No, never.''

"Did Frances make a will before her death at any time?"

"Yes; I was there at the time her eldest daughter was sick. Frances was talking to the younger one, [O-zah-wah-shing-qua]. I understood the names—'a saddle,' 'horses,' 'hogs,' 'land,' &c. She was talking of them, and she mentioned George's name—my husband. I went home and told George that he had better go and see what his aunt wished to tell him. He went, but she seemed too tired to talk. He asked O-zah-wah-shing-qua if he should not get an interpreter. She answered, 'No, she has told me all, and I will tell you.' That was 4 o'clock p. m., and she died at 11 o'clock that night. O-zah-wah-shing-qua proved treacherous to her mother's trust, and never told what was imparted to her, thereby showing her Indian nature; consequently none of us ever received any recompense for our years of labor and self-sacrifice in their behalf."

"Did she express any feelings about death, or have any theory concerning it?"

"No; none at all; her mind seemed calm, which showed that she was prepared for the change."

E. O. S.

Sioux City, Iowa, Dec. 1, 1890.

NOTE.

The careful reader will note on page 11 that the time of her death is given as occurring in 1849, instead of 1847. This was caused by confounding the proper date with that given by Mrs. Eliza O. Slocum. In two or three other places her age is inadvertently given at the time of capture as four years and seven months, when it should be *five* years and seven months. She was born in Rhode Island, March, 1773, and carried into captivity Nov. 2, 1778, and died March 9, 1847.

Dr. Slocum, the genealogist, truly says that her case is "the most remarkable and interesting of individual captivities. Her considerate treatment through a long life is one of the brightest and most creditable paragraphs in the story of the North American Indians."

Women in America

FROM COLONIAL TIMES TO THE 20TH CENTURY

An Arno Press Collection

Andrews, John B. and W. D. P. Bliss. **History of Women in Trade Unions** (*Report on Conditions of Woman and Child Wage-Earners in the United States,* Vol. X; 61st Congress, 2nd Session, Senate Document No. 645). 1911

Anthony, Susan B. **An Account of the Proceedings on the Trial of Susan B. Anthony, on the Charge of Illegal Voting at the Presidential Election in November, 1872,** and on the Trial of Beverly W. Jones, Edwin T. Marsh and William B. Hall, the Inspectors of Election by Whom her Vote was Received. 1874

The Autobiography of a Happy Woman. 1915

Ayer, Harriet Hubbard. **Harriet Hubbard Ayer's Book:** A Complete and Authentic Treatise on the Laws of Health and Beauty. 1902

Barrett, Kate Waller. **Some Practical Suggestions on the Conduct of a Rescue Home.** *Including* **Life of Dr. Kate Waller Barrett** (Reprinted from *Fifty Years' Work With Girls* by Otto Wilson). [1903]

Bates, Mrs. D. B. **Incidents on Land and Water;** Or, Four Years on the Pacific Coast. 1858

Blumenthal, Walter Hart. **Women Camp Followers of the American Revolution.** 1952

Boothe, Viva B., editor. **Women in the Modern World** (*The Annals of the American Academy of Political and Social Science,* Vol. CXLIII, May 1929). 1929

Bowne, Eliza Southgate. **A Girl's Life Eighty Years Ago:** Selections from the Letters of Eliza Southgate Bowne. 1888

Brooks, Geraldine. **Dames and Daughters of Colonial Days.** 1900

Carola Woerishoffer: Her Life and Work. 1912

Clement, J[esse], editor. **Noble Deeds of American Women;** With Biographical Sketches of Some of the More Prominent. 1851

Crow, Martha Foote. **The American Country Girl.** 1915

De Leon, T[homas] C. **Belles, Beaux and Brains of the 60's.** 1909

de Wolfe, Elsie (Lady Mendl). **After All.** 1935

Dix, Dorothy (Elizabeth Meriwether Gilmer). **How to Win and Hold a Husband.** 1939

Donovan, Frances R. **The Saleslady.** 1929

Donovan, Frances R. **The Schoolma'am.** 1938

Donovan, Frances R. **The Woman Who Waits.** 1920

Eagle, Mary Kavanaugh Oldham, editor. **The Congress of Women,** Held in the Woman's Building, World's Columbian Exposition, Chicago, U.S.A., 1893. 1894

Ellet, Elizabeth F. **The Eminent and Heroic Women of America.** 1873

Ellis, Anne. **The Life of an Ordinary Woman.** 1929

[Farrar, Eliza W. R.] **The Young Lady's Friend.** By a Lady. 1836

Filene, Catherine, editor. **Careers for Women.** 1920

Finley, Ruth E. **The Lady of Godey's:** Sarah Josepha Hale. 1931 **Fragments of Autobiography.** 1974

Frost, John. **Pioneer Mothers of the West;** Or, Daring and Heroic Deeds of American Women. 1869

[Gilman], Charlotte Perkins Stetson. **In This Our World.** 1899

Goldberg, Jacob A. and Rosamond W. Goldberg. **Girls on the City Streets:** A Study of 1400 Cases of Rape. 1935

Grace H. Dodge: Her Life and Work. 1974

Greenbie, Marjorie Barstow. **My Dear Lady:** The Story of Anna Ella Carroll, the "Great Unrecognized Member of Lincoln's Cabinet." 1940

Hourwich, Andria Taylor and Gladys L. Palmer, editors. **I Am a Woman Worker:** A Scrapbook of Autobiographies. 1936

Howe, M[ark] A. De Wolfe. **Memories of a Hostess:** A Chronicle of Friendships Drawn Chiefly from the Diaries of Mrs. James T. Fields. 1922

Irwin, Inez Haynes. **Angels and Amazons:** A Hundred Years of American Women. 1934

Laughlin, Clara E. **The Work-a-Day Girl:** A Study of Some Present-Day Conditions. 1913

Lewis, Dio. **Our Girls.** 1871

Liberating the Home. 1974

Livermore, Mary A. **The Story of My Life;** Or, The Sunshine and Shadow of Seventy Years . . . To Which is Added Six of Her Most Popular Lectures. 1899

Lives to Remember. 1974

Lobsenz, Johanna. **The Older Woman in Industry.** 1929

MacLean, Annie Marion. **Wage-Earning Women.** 1910

Meginness, John F. **Biography of Frances Slocum, the Lost Sister of Wyoming:** A Complete Narrative of her Captivity of Wanderings Among the Indians. 1891

Nathan, Maud. **Once Upon a Time and Today.** 1933

[Packard, Elizabeth Parsons Ware]. **Great Disclosure of Spiritual Wickedness!!** In High Places. With an Appeal to the Government to Protect the Inalienable Rights of Married Women. 1865

Parsons, Alice Beal. **Woman's Dilemma.** 1926

Parton, James, et al. **Eminent Women of the Age:** Being Narratives of the Lives and Deeds of the Most Prominent Women of the Present Generation. 1869

Paton, Lucy Allen. **Elizabeth Cary Agassiz:** A Biography. 1919

Rayne, M[artha] L[ouise]. **What Can a Woman Do;** Or, Her Position in the Business and Literary World. 1893

Richmond, Mary E. and Fred S. Hall. **A Study of Nine Hundred and Eighty-Five Widows Known to Certain Charity Organization Societies in 1910.** 1913

Ross, Ishbel. **Ladies of the Press:** The Story of Women in Journalism by an Insider. 1936

Sex and Equality. 1974

Snyder, Charles McCool. **Dr. Mary Walker:** The Little Lady in Pants. 1962

Stow, Mrs. J. W. **Probate Confiscation:** Unjust Laws Which Govern Woman. 1878

Sumner, Helen L. **History of Women in Industry in the United**

States (*Report on Conditions of Woman and Child Wage-Earners in the United States,* Vol. IX; 61st Congress, 2nd Session, Senate Document No. 645). 1910

[Vorse, Mary H.] **Autobiography of an Elderly Woman.** 1911

Washburn, Charles. **Come into My Parlor:** A Biography of the Aristocratic Everleigh Sisters of Chicago. 1936

Women of Lowell. 1974

Woolson, Abba Gould. **Dress-Reform:** A Series of Lectures Delivered in Boston on Dress as it Affects the Health of Women. 1874

Working Girls of Cincinnati. 1974